Third Edition

Critical Infrastructure

Homeland Security and Emergency Preparedness

Third Edition

Critical
Infrastructure

Homeland Security and
Emergency Preparedness

Robert Radvanovsky
Allan McDougall

CRC Press
Taylor & Francis Group
Boca Raton London New York

CRC Press is an imprint of the
Taylor & Francis Group, an **informa** business

CRC Press
Taylor & Francis Group
6000 Broken Sound Parkway NW, Suite 300
Boca Raton, FL 33487-2742

© 2013 by Taylor & Francis Group, LLC
CRC Press is an imprint of Taylor & Francis Group, an Informa business

No claim to original U.S. Government works

Printed on acid-free paper
Version Date: 20130220

International Standard Book Number-13: 978-1-4665-0345-8 (Hardback)

Library of Congress Cataloging-in-Publication Data

Radvanovsky, Robert.
    Critical infrastructure : homeland security and emergency preparedness / Robert S. Radvanovsky, Allan McDougall. -- 3rd ed.
       p. cm.
    Includes bibliographical references and index.
    ISBN 978-1-4665-0345-8 (hbk. : alk. paper)
    1. Infrastructure (Economics)--Security measures--United States. 2. Civil defense--United States. 3. War damage, Industrial--United States. 4. Emergency management--United States. I. McDougall, Allan. II. Title.

HC110.C3R33 2013
363.34′70973--dc23   2013004138

Visit the Taylor & Francis Web site at
http://www.taylorandfrancis.com

and the CRC Press Web site at
http://www.crcpress.com

Dedication

From Bob

This book is dedicated to my loving wife, Tammy, who has always supported and been patient with me, especially while this book was being written.

From Allan

This work is dedicated to my wife, Angela, and those who make great efforts to continuously improve the overall critical infrastructure protection domain. My particular thanks to Wayne, Ian, Richard, and Shawn for their moral support as we grappled with some of the interesting challenges that presented themselves.

Contents

Preface

By failing to prepare, you are preparing to fail.

—Benjamin Franklin

This book represents a culmination of research activity that has gone on over the past several years. The intent of presenting the materials in this book is to represent the significant strides made in understanding the fundamentals behind securing, protecting, and safekeeping the operations of our world's infrastructures—their relevant industries, their landmarks, as well as their national assets—that are considered critically vital to the continued economic success and operation of our society.

From the time that the first edition of this book was conceived to present day, the importance of identifying what is critical to our society—worldwide—has evolved into new perspectives to many countries throughout the world. As nations explore their response to the critical infrastructure protection challenge, we have seen a shift from the hard postures of robustness and force protection to more fluid postures associated with resiliency and the establishment of redundant infrastructure. The fact is that many nations have learned, often through bitter experience in the current economic clime, that the traditional approaches of simply applying more and more preventative controls to protect infrastructure can have disastrous consequences economically and socially. What is becoming more apparent is that if certain nations want to retain their competitive advantage or position in the world's international hierarchy, they need to become far more resilient and creative in their thinking so that they can identify new opportunities for efficiency. Otherwise, their current efforts to protect their infrastructure will have the unintended consequence of stifling their industries and economic engines, causing the nation to ultimately fail in its overall goal to protect its international position, citizens, economies, and sovereignty. Many interesting developments have been conceived over the past several years. From those developments, new and useful protocols, procedures, and guidelines have been formulated and are either now in use or will be implemented shortly. These procedures and guidelines provide a base, a foundation, on which our world's infrastructures depend. Those who implement their operation, maintain their integrity and functional status, and safeguard them against deliberate, accidental, or natural threat depend on those procedures and guidelines and must demonstrate their fundamental understanding and comprehension. Key factors, terms, and guidelines must be conveyed to everyone in a manner that is generally understood and, more importantly, accepted. Without acceptance and the fundamental understanding of that knowledge being conveyed, those countries that have come to understand the importance of securing their infrastructures may not prosper.

Since the initial inception of this book, there have been significant strides in efforts of safeguarding the operations of our world's infrastructures. This edition represents further developments since the second edition of this book appeared.

AUTHORS' NOTES

This publication offers an aid in maintaining professional competence, with the understanding that the authors, editor, and publisher are not rendering any legal, financial, or any other professional advice.

Due to the rapidly changing nature of the infrastructure security industry, the information contained within this publication will become outdated, and therefore the reader should consider researching alternative or other professional or more current sources of authoritative information. The significant portion of this publication was based on research conducted over several years from a plethora of government and public domain resources, publications, and Internet-accessible Web sites, some of which may no longer be publicly available or may have been restricted due to laws enacted by a particular country's government.

The views and positions taken in this book represent the considered judgment of the authors and editor. They acknowledge with gratitude any input provided and resources offered that contributed to this book. To those who have contributed to the book's strengths and characteristics, we thank you for your contributions and efforts. For any inconsistencies that may be found, we alone share and accept the responsibility for them and will gladly make corrections as needed.

One additional note concerns the evolutionary process that we are witnessing within this industry. We are seeing a shift from the force-protection doctrine that concentrates on the protection of vital nodes and infrastructure to a doctrine that relies more heavily on the assurance of critical services and establishing and then maintaining resilient networks. Realistically, private citizens, corporations, and governments alike all see the flow of services and goods, such as electricity, drinkable water, etc., as a service; we turn on a light switch or a faucet, and it just works, and we do not concern ourselves much with the route that the service or product takes to get to its final destination. This paradigm shift is being driven by the continuously evolving threats and the realization of increasing costs associated with the force-protection doctrine's relatively reactive approach to risk management.

In an effort to keep the references available for the readers, we have provided a set of "snapshot of the Web site" links for all government and public domain Web site references. As these Web site references change, become deleted, etc., it is important that readers know what the references were at the time of the writing of this book. This will ensure that those references are "frozen in time," and will not be changed or altered in any fashion whatsoever. We consider this a value-added feature to this book, and invite you to review those Web site references now in case they become unavailable over time. You may access this information via a dedicated Web site at http://cipbook.infracritical.com.

SYNOPSIS

This book is divided into eight categories that represent years of research. These emphasize those factors comprising functions used within and throughout critical infrastructures. These factors are categorically subdivided into unique and prioritized levels, beginning with Chapter 1 as the foremost chapter of the book, Chapter 2 slightly less important than Chapter 1, and so on. Each subsequent chapter emphasizes a different meaning that is being conveyed such that it can be structured and remembered in an easy, cognitive fashion. A brief summary of each chapter and its function is provided here.

CHAPTER 1: INTRODUCTION TO CRITICAL INFRASTRUCTURE ASSURANCE AND PROTECTION

This chapter provides the base for the entire book and what is described in some of the historical backgrounds of critical infrastructure, and why it is important to society. There are some terms and definitions covering a brief synopsis of the intent of this book and what is to be expected from critical infrastructure assurance and protection specialists and professionals.

CHAPTER 2: DEMAND, CAPACITY, FRAGILITY, AND THE EMERGENCE OF NETWORKS

This chapter is more theoretical than most in that it identifies an emerging trend in thinking rather than describing some of the changes in the strategic infrastructure that have taken place since the first edition appeared. At the time of the first edition, much of the focus on critical infrastructure protection efforts was at the very local level—how to protect key facilities. Recent infrastructure issues have highlighted the fact that this infrastructure is subject to impacts that can flow along interdependencies and also disruptions within its networked environment. This chapter reflects that current trend.

CHAPTER 3: BEYOND NATIONAL FRAMEWORKS

In March 2008, the Department of Homeland Security (DHS) created the National Response Framework (NRF), which is a guide to conduct all-hazards responses—from the smallest incident to the largest catastrophe. This key document establishes a comprehensive national, all-hazards approach to domestic incident response. The framework identifies the key response principles, roles, and structures that organize national response. This chapter revises the current U.S.-based framework and expands into a more globalized context.

CHAPTER 4: PUBLIC-PRIVATE PARTNERSHIPS

This chapter discusses the relationships between governments (public sector) and corporate entities (private sector). The reader should understand that the divide between the public and private sectors is becoming more grey and flexible through the concept of public-private partnerships.

CHAPTER 5: THE REINVENTION OF INFORMATION SHARING AND INTELLIGENCE

This chapter outlines the shift from the concept of the need to know to the concept of the need to share, and how it affects the movement of information between organizations and the nature of the controls that need to be in place in order to share information. By comparing regimes that are based upon restrictive principles (need to know), and the challenges that have arisen in that approach, to the concept of the ability to have information flowing freely within trusted clouds, it will become clear that the current approach toward information security needs to evolve.

CHAPTER 6: EMERGENCY PREPAREDNESS AND READINESS

This chapter deals with how organizations need to adopt resilient planning, implementation, and decision-making processes in order to be able to respond to changes within the threat environment. While the concept of contingency planning (in anticipation of certain kinds of threats) continues to have significance, this chapter looks at the requirement for organizations to possess adequate levels of expertise and structure so that they can observe, orient, decide, and act effectively in a new, and often obscured, threat environment.

CHAPTER 7: SECURITY VULNERABILITY ASSESSMENT

This chapter is the meat of the book and provides the backbone for reasons of what, where, why, and how risk assessments are to be performed; why they are needed; and what causes them to be needed. This chapter is representative of a set of guidelines that both military and government agencies are currently using or improving.

CHAPTER 8: REGULATIONS

This chapter examines the strengths, weaknesses, opportunities, and threats associated with no regulation, individually applied self-regulation, industry regulation, government regulation, and law enforcement. Each of these is looked at in terms of the opportunity that they afford for organizations to be creative and explore new options on how to maintain critical services while also maintaining the necessary level of public accountability.

CHAPTER 9: INFORMATION SHARING AND ANALYSIS CENTERS

This chapter outlines and summarizes all relevant Information Sharing and Analysis Centers (ISACs), which are information dissemination and distribution points for critical information that may pertain to a particular sector. Not all sectors listed within Homeland Security Presidential Decision Directive (HSPD)-7/HSPD-8 outline all ISAC organizations; however, an effort was made to provide as much information as possible, and how it is relevant and pertains to critical infrastructure environments.

CHAPTER 10: SUPERVISORY CONTROL AND DATA ACQUISITION

This chapter discusses control systems used within and throughout just about every sector. Control systems consist of two subset topics: distributed control systems, which are the distribution mechanisms of a large geographical area, and supervisory control and data acquisition (SCADA) systems, which are devices that interface with noncomputing functions that are critical to that sector (value control, switch control, flow metering, etc.). This chapter also discusses some of the current challenges faced with SCADA and control systems security-related issues, and how to possibly address them.

CHAPTER 11: CRITICAL INFRASTRUCTURE INFORMATION

Critical infrastructure is largely owned by the private sector, yet the administrative checks and balances are tailored toward government and public institutions. This chapter looks at the current challenges associated with establishing a trusted network across various sectors and how the current approach to oversight constitutes a significant vulnerability to the concept of critical infrastructure assurance. It will also look at models of how information can be categorized and communicated within trusted communities to better assure the public-private relationship. This chapter outlines and attempts to summarize all classifications of information that would apply to critical infrastructures. Additionally, any legal ramifications and enforcement capabilities, along with the definition of the term *critical infrastructure information*, are outlined.

Acknowledgments

Some materials used in this book were taken in part or in their entirety from several very reliable and useful sources. Any information that may appear to be repetitive in its content from those sources was taken to provide a more introspective perception of what defines critical infrastructure assurance.

The authors, editor, and publisher thank the following organizations for their contributions of references and materials

U.S. Department of Homeland Security (www.dhs.gov)

Federal Emergency Management Agency (FEMA), which is part of the U.S. Department of Homeland Security's Emergency Preparedness and Response Directorate (www.fema.gov)

U.S. Department of Homeland Security's National Cyber Security Division's Control Systems Security Program (www.us-cert.gov/control_systems)

Public Safety Canada (www.publicsafety.gc.ca)

About the Authors

Bob Radvanovsky is an active professional in the United States with knowledge in security, risk management, business continuity, disaster recovery planning, and remediation. He obtained his master's degree in computer science from DePaul University in Chicago. He has significantly contributed toward establishing several certification programs, specifically on the topics of critical infrastructure protection and critical infrastructure assurance.

Bob has special interests and knowledge in matters of critical infrastructure, and has published a number of articles and white papers regarding this topic. Although he has been significantly involved in establishing security training and awareness programs through his company, Infracritical, his extracurricular activities include working with several professional accreditation and educational institutions, specifically on the topics of homeland security and critical infrastructure protection and assurance. This includes maintaining and moderating the SCADASEC mailing list for SCADA and control systems security discussion forums and working as an active participant with the U.S. Department of Homeland Security Transportation Security Administration's Transportation Systems Sector Cyber Working Group, as well as the U.S. Department of Homeland Security Control Systems Security Program's Industrial Control Systems' Joint Working Group; both working groups are part of the Obama administration's Cyber Security Initiative.

Bob has written five books, all published by Taylor & Francis, Boca Raton, FL. His first book, *Critical Infrastructure: Homeland Security and Emergency Preparedness* (2006), is a reference work dealing with emergency management and preparedness and defines (in greater detail) what critical infrastructure protection is. *Transportation Systems Security* (2008), was designed for educating mid-level management (or higher) about aspects of holistic security analysis and management of the transportation sector. *Critical Infrastructure: Homeland Security and Emergency Preparedness,* Second Edition (2009), further evolves and incorporates critical infrastructure assurance as part of the critical infrastructure protection model. *Handbook of SCADA/Control Systems Security* (2013), provides fundamental security management techniques and principles that can be applied to industrial and automation control systems environments that are utilized in just about every critical infrastructure sector. *Critical Infrastructure: Homeland Security and Emergency Preparedness,* Third Edition (2013), takes on a more globalized approach to the critical infrastructure protection model, applying strategies, tactics, and techniques now found on a global scale.

Both Bob and Allan McDougall have established a private research enterprise investigating concepts surrounding critical infrastructures, how they are impacted, and how they may be preserved.

Allan McDougall has worked on various projects (with a strong element of research) in the public and private sectors. Following his military service, he continued public service as a security advisor to a number of federal agencies. Within this context, he became recognized as a technical expert in the corporate security management domain and was asked to participate in a number of emerging endeavors, including the Strategic Leadership in Government Security and other courses. Within the private sector, his desire to look toward sound and innovative solutions soon had him participating in a number of efforts toward the professionalization of critical infrastructure protection, including the development of certification level training.

These efforts have resulted in his certification as a Professional in Critical Infrastructure Protection, Certified Master Antiterrorism Specialist, and Certified Information Systems Security Professional. Allan's primary focus is on the transportation sector, where he works within a number of communities. He serves as the vice chair of the Supply Chain and Transportation Security Council for ASIS International, president of the International Association of Maritime Security Professionals (IAMSP), and chair of the Transportation Security Committee for the Antiterrorism Accreditation Board (ATAB). He is a recognized training provider of ship security (International Ship and Port Facilities Security Code) and has been invited to speak to local and federal professional associations, including at the Information Resources Management College at National Defense University, Washington, D.C.

Allan is the founder and owner of Evolutionary Security Management and lives with his wife in Arnprior, Canada.

1 Introduction to Critical Infrastructure Assurance and Protection

1.1 INTRODUCTION

Critical infrastructure protection (CIP) is a topic that is now beginning to span generations. Some will remember the year 2000 (Y2K) issue as an emerging crisis. For others, the issue began shortly after the attacks on September 11, 2001. And the list is not going to end anytime soon. What this book addresses is a fundamental shift in how we look at CIP—changing the approach from one that can be described as a series of connected, consecutive mad dashes to one that better approximates a marathon.

The mad dashes began with Y2K when the situation became dire enough that airline executives had to board aircraft to fly across 0 hour in order to demonstrate that their planes were still safe. While Y2K caused concerns at a technical level, the events of 9/11 led to urgent calls for the protection of critical infrastructures—calls that were likely well founded when considering bombings in London and Spain and various other threats. Populations have become less confident that critical services can be protected and delivered at all times.

For example, one analytical method for prevention is to perform penetration tests (formerly referred to as *tiger teams*,[1] now referred to as *red teams*[2]). *Tiger teams*[3] is a former U.S. military term[4] defining government- or industry-sponsored teams of experts and professionals who attempt to break down (or through) any defenses or perimeters in an effort to uncover, and eventually patch, any security holes.[5] This concept is useful for short-lived projects or tasks that involve designating individuals within a given organization to think, act, and behave in a manner that supports the way criminals or terrorists would think, attack, and study their approach to set targets and priorities.

In U.S. military history, these teams were made up of paid professionals who performed hacker-type tricks; for example, leaving cardboard signs displaying the word *bomb* within critical defense installations or leaving handwritten notes stating "Your codebooks have been stolen" (even though they usually were not) inside safes or locked, secured areas. In some instances, after a successful penetration mission, when an official security review was conducted the next morning, officials would find signs, notes, etc., placed by the security team(s) of the previous day or week, which sometimes resulted in the "early retirement" of base commanders or their security officers. It is generally assumed that, with CIP initiative, the bad guys are determined adversaries—flexible, creative, resourceful—and able to learn how to target vulnerable areas while avoiding those that are more protected and predictable. In many situations, modern, sophisticated, or technologically advanced societies are perfect targets for terrorists; businesses that are not flexible enough also make perfect targets.[6]

1.2   WHAT IS CRITICAL INFRASTRUCTURE?

The term *critical infrastructure* refers to assets of physical and logical systems that are essential to the minimum operations of the economy and government. They include, but are not limited to, telecommunications, energy, banking and finance, transportation, water systems, and emergency services, both governmental and private. As these systems become further interconnected, we see two major trends becoming apparent. The first trend involves the pace at which technology evolves. This is not a constant around the world, and as time progresses, we are likely to see societies either fall behind, struggle to keep up, struggle to maintain control over the pace of evolution, or even make revolutionary leaps forward. The second trend involves understanding that what is critical infrastructure for one community may well not be critical infrastructure for another. Consider the sources of energy used to heat homes. These are essential in colder climates, but are relatively benign in climates that are considered tropical. As a result, CIP practitioners need to understand the contexts (economic, environmental, cultural, and political) within which critical infrastructures can be found. Thus, due to advances in information technology and efforts to improve efficiencies in these systems, infrastructures have become increasingly automated and interlinked. These improvements have created new vulnerabilities relating to equipment failure, human error, weather and other natural causes, as well as physical and computer-related attacks.

Over the past decade, various levels of government have been held responsible for the protection of their own infrastructure. As the world moves inexorably toward a global-centric network, we are seeing levels of government, along with the private sector, and even individual citizens, having responsibilities take a more global approach. It is not unusual for individuals to call service centers halfway around the world to assist them with their networking difficulties. At the same time, global supply chains require that private entities become much more aware of events around the world that can affect the resilience of their supply chains. What this means is that local efforts that were seen as manageable, if somewhat uncomfortable, have grown exponentially into international "monsters." As a result, the previous process associated with critical infrastructure assurance has grown in scope from consistent testing and evaluation of local infrastructures to one that is at its beginning of understanding the vast influences that operate at a much more global level. This has changed the playing field—significantly—from one where the edicts coming from national capitals are now the second step in a much grander process that involves balancing of international interests and priorities with national responsibilities.

1.3 WHAT IS THE PRIVATE SECTOR?

The private sector of a nation's economy consists of those entities not controlled by the state, such as private firms and companies, corporations, private banks, nongovernmental organizations (NGOs), etc.[7] Many nations have entities that are established to deal with the private sector. Often these are linked to applying requirements or to the contracting arrangements that can be made between the government and the private sector. What needs to be understood here is how controls differ between the two. The private sector entity may influence laws or government policy, but does not have the authority to set that policy. Even in arrangements where the government delegates work, it is always done under the oversight of some legal mechanism. The private sector may also have to respond to authorities that are outside of the nation—such as those imposed on it by parent companies, partners, or even financial institutions. This can lead to a level of complexity when attempting to determine what the requirements being placed on the private sector actually are.

The second aspect to remember about the private sector is the nature of its finances. Regardless of good intentions and public messaging, the private sector entity seeks to generate wealth. In return for some consideration, companies that operate for-profit business models tend to seek to increase that wealth, while those that operate not-for-profit business models attempt to balance their cash flows with their operations. In short, decisions are made with a very clear understanding that there are financial risks involved.

This financial risk is also different than that of the government. The government operates on a fiscal year that allows for budgets to be reset to a starting point and also has a significant ability to determine its level of debt. The private sector does not have this. Budgets are linear in that if money out is greater than money in, then eventually the company will first go into debt, then insolvency, and then finally cease to exist. This has a profound effect on how organizations look at their budgets and new requirements—the government may see issues in terms of "costs of doing business," while the private sector may interpret those new measures as another step on the road toward "going out of business."

With increases in globalization, differences in the competitive playing field can either exacerbate this challenge or mitigate it. In the context of critical infrastructure assurance (making sure it's there), we need to take a whole-picture approach to this issue. If competition is based on lowest dollar value or even best dollar value approaches, entities operating within those states with lower costs of production are able to market their goods or services globally at a lower cost. This is a major issue associated with issues such as outsourcing or offshore production that, while reducing financial issues and fostering a competitive position on the surface, may actually result in a condition where various sectors begin to lose control over their supply chains.

What is important to understand here is that the management of the company makes these decisions in the private sector unless they are constrained through regulation or law or by being aware of issues that could arise, such as damage to brand (stock value).

1.4   WHAT IS THE PUBLIC SECTOR?

The public sector consists of government-owned or government-controlled corporations, as well as government monetary institutions.[8] This includes offices, departments, ministries, and agencies of these organizations or entities that receive monies or appropriations from public interest groups, public funding committees, and tax revenue centers.

Public sector entities may be involved in two major functions. The first function is regulating the behavior of those persons or entities that fall within their jurisdiction. This is accomplished through legal tools that may include laws, regulations, rules, measures, or simple direction. Compliance with any of these is considered mandatory in the eyes of the state, and breaches of compliance may result in penalties ranging from financial to significantly more severe.

The concept of jurisdiction is reasonably important, particularly when looking at issues that involve international operations—such as shipping. In these cases, the mechanism by which the state generates its requirements often involves participation in groups of various sizes and whose decision-making processes are guided by consensus that is taken back to the various national governments. Depending on the nature of the international group within which the nation-state is participating, the laws and regulations that it passes may be constrained in terms of operating within the constraints of the consensus of the international group or body.

This leads to the second function, which is the protection of people, property, and operations under its care. Generally, public safety will look more toward people and property, with operations being included as part of the suite of business risks. The nation-state will operate bodies that are designed to protect those persons that are abiding by its requirements in most legitimate forms of government, and against significant events such as natural disasters, fire, etc.

This level of constraint may also have an involuntary aspect. Over the past decade, the world has seen an increase in international bodies becoming involved in settling national disputes. Organizations such as the United Nations, Gulf Cooperation Council, and other similar bodies have taken on an increasing role in determining what constitutes acceptable national behavior. We see this in international bodies sanctioning actions that range from trade restrictions to enforcement through military intervention. As we move toward more international operations, these international bodies are taking on increasing roles in overseeing the decisions of their individual members. This has been particularly evident in situations associated with the financial sector in Europe, where the EU essentially dictated what financial controls the Greek government was to put in place in order to receive bailout funds. While this dynamic is still evolving with respect to critical infrastructure assurance and protection doctrine, the fact that international bodies appear to be becoming more active should at least be in the back of the researcher's mind when looking at potentially evolving challenges.

1.5   WHAT IS CIP?

The term *CIP* pertains to activities for protecting critical infrastructures. This includes people, physical assets, and communication (cyber) systems that are indispensable for national, state, and urban security, economic stability, and public safety. CIP methods and resources deter or mitigate attacks against critical infrastructures caused by people (terrorists, other criminals, hackers, etc.), natural calamities (hurricanes, tornadoes, earthquakes, floods, etc.), and hazardous materials accidents involving nuclear, radiological, biological, or chemical substances. Essentially, CIP is about protecting those assets considered invaluable to society and that promote social well-being.[9] CIP is often considered a reactionary response to threats, risks, vulnerabilities, or hazardous conditions. It does entail some preventative measures and countermeasures but usually is reactive by nature.

CIP has two goals. The first goal can be related back to an alternative way of thinking. By definition, a critical infrastructure involves physical and logical systems necessary to support the safety, security, and economic well-being of communities (to paraphrase the growing list of definitions). The second goal should be more concerned with the protection of the infrastructure (in its physical and constructional contexts), and whether it is capable of delivering its anticipated services to the community.

1.6   WHAT IS CIA?

Most asset protection programs and their efforts often begin with determining why something needs to be protected. The first part of this is generally defined in terms such as *identification of assets* or *mission analysis*. Various inputs are identified and assigned value based on their contribution to the given system and its desired outputs or results. The second part focuses on threats and assets (things) that can or might disrupt processes. These steps become the foundation for such statements as risk being a "possibility of loss or injury" of "a factor of asset value, threat, and vulnerability."

The value associated with a critical infrastructure can be divided into several parts. The first part involves circumstances in which the critical infrastructure provides a unique service within and to a community. This is often the case where infrastructure costs are relatively (or even prohibitively) high, such that the community can only afford one of the installation types. An example that supports this premise might be that it is unlikely that you will see a town of 7,500 inhabitants with a water purification plant able to handle a population of 15,000 suddenly decide that it is time to put in place a second similar installation. In this example, the concept of physical security or force protection[10] becomes vital, given any potential impacts associated with the interruption, loss, or destruction of that particular infrastructure—in this case, the loss of fresh drinking water to the local community.

In a networked environment, an additional layer of protection is possible when leaving the local level as one begins to look at state/provincial, regional, or even national levels. Depending on the nature of the service being provided, the networked environment allows for an application of robustness, resilience, and redundancy to be designed. When one infrastructure suffers a negative impact, the loss of its performance in one area is offset by the remaining elements within the network by either increasing or reallocating their own contributions so as to either reach the desired level of overall performance or, in more extreme cases, reduce the amount of impact associated with the disruption.

The question becomes whether to protect an individual infrastructure or the ability of the networked environment to perform at a level that meets the demands. The truth is that both are needed. Individual nodes and conduits associated with an infrastructure network are intrinsic to that network's ability to function. Simultaneously, individual nodes operating in isolation must be looked at closely in terms of residual risks allowed into a system that is essentially a single point of failure. Another harsh reality of the critical infrastructure domain is that there are people (i.e., families) who rely on those operating in that field ensuring that services are there when needed.

A range of events illustrates this reality. During the 1998 ice storm in Canada and the August 2003 blackout that affected much of the northeastern portion of the United States, the challenge was that electrical power was not available to maintain either heating and sumps (ice storm) or refrigeration and heating, ventilation, and air-conditioning systems (2003 blackout). This lack of availability prompted the declared states of emergency, and resulted in organizations putting their business continuity plans in motion and practicing other extraordinary measures. The use of Canadian National Railway locomotives and generators to supply electricity (in response to the ice storm) tends to point toward a lack of electricity being the problem and not simply a specific electrical transmission line being disrupted.

Consider another example involving the U.S. postal system. Does it really matter what street the mail comes from before it gets to your home? The answer would be "of course not." What does matter is that your mail arrives at your home on time and in unbroken condition. The concern sets in when we wonder whether the mail or post is actually being delivered at all—something that affects our paying of bills, receipt of ordered goods, and other forms of communication.

Finally, consider the U.S. water supply systems. Again, we are less concerned with whether the water is coming through a central pipe or some peripheral parts of the system. We tend to become significantly concerned if the water supply fails to provide water to our homes.

Other examples will tend to follow the same suit, because it is the lack of critical services that poses the risk to society. Some might argue that the population is only concerned about protecting critical infrastructure insofar as that protection ensures the availability of the service to the public.

This leads to the concept and definition of CIA. The definition of CIP focuses on protecting the nodes and conduits of any given infrastructure that delivers services to its community through force protection. Although CIP tends to focus on an all-hazards approach, it tends to operate at a very basic or local level—say, one facility, one road, etc.

CIA, on the other hand, tends to focus on a layer higher than CIP, which includes the necessary arrangements to shift production around within the network or surrounding networks so that demand is met, even if a local node or conduit is disrupted.

If we were to take our two power-based examples, we would see the difference in the approach. CIP would tend to focus on a very granular level—power production facilities would be protected against various types of physical attacks or hazards. CIA looks at the entire power grid, ensuring that the system can detect disruption, shift capacity to meet demand, and ensure that services are being met—often transparently to the consumer. In this context, it might be argued that CIA is the holistic view that is actually sought by most CIP professionals.

1.7   WHAT ARE PUBLIC-PRIVATE PARTNERSHIPS?

The divide between the public and private sectors is becoming more grey and flexible through the concept of public-private partnerships. A public-private partnership is an agreement between a public agency and a private sector entity that combines skills and resources to develop a technology, product, or service that improves the quality of life for the general public. The private sector has been called upon numerous times to use its resources, skills, and expertise to perform specific tasks for the public sector.[11] Historically, the public sector has frequently taken an active role in spurring technological advances by directly funding the private sector to fulfill a specialized need that cannot be completed by the public sector. What this arrangement seeks to accomplish is a stable relationship between the two that allows a more efficient and effective delivery of services. This is discussed in detail in Chapter 2.

1.8   CRITICAL INFRASTRUCTURE FUNCTIONS

Defining, using, and maintaining critical infrastructure is a combination of processes. When looking at what should be defined as a critical infrastructure, we need to move beyond the convenient definition and shopping lists promulgated by governments and associations and ask three fundamental questions:

- Is the infrastructure necessary for the preservation of life or the continuation of a society?
- Is the infrastructure operating in a very limited context or across a much broader context? Meaning, is that infrastructure only specific to a local community, or does it interconnect with other communities to make a much larger, more fragile community? This may influence whether the infrastructure is considered to be a critical infrastructure in the national context or a vital asset at the local level.
- Is the infrastructure operating as a singly or uniquely organized entity, or is it a community of coordinated efforts put forth by several parties? This is important to understand because the infrastructure, and its capacity, needs to be understood in terms of assurance to its operations.

The answers to each of these three questions will have a profound impact on the methods needed to protect the infrastructure and ensure delivery of its services. This in turn will have an impact on the various methodologies and measures that are available to those seeking to accomplish the same. It should not be looked upon as a purely administrative process guided by checklists and prescriptive formulas.

1.9 EVOLUTION OF CRITICAL INFRASTRUCTURE

What many policy makers consider critical infrastructure has been evolving and is often ambiguous. Twenty years ago, the word *infrastructure* was defined primarily with respect to the adequacy of the community's public works. In the mid-1990s, however, the growing threat of international terrorism led policy makers to reconsider the definition of *infrastructure* in the context of security at national levels. Successive government policies and laws have become refined and more understood based on the expanded number of infrastructure sectors and the types of assets considered critical for purposes of an economy's security.[12]

This definition was adopted, by reference, in the Homeland Security Act of 2002 (P.L. 107-296, Sec. 2.4),[13] and it established the U.S. Department of Homeland Security (DHS). The national strategy adopted the definition of *critical infrastructure* in P.L. 107-56, providing the following list of specific infrastructure sectors and its assets falling under that definition.

Sectors include:

- Agriculture and food production
- Banking and finance
- Chemical production
- Critical manufacturing
- Communications
- Emergency services
- Energy
- Government facilities
- Information technology
- Nuclear energy and facilities
- Postal shipping - *Transportation*
- Public health and healthcare
- Transportation and logistics services
- Water and wastewater treatment

Key resources include:

- Defense industrial base
- Commercial facilities
- Dams
- National monuments and icons - *Government facilities*

The critical infrastructure sectors within the national strategy contain many physical assets, but only a fraction of these could be viewed as critical according to the DHS definition. For example, out of 33,000 individual assets cataloged in the DHS national asset database, the agency considers only 1,700, or 5%, to be nationally critical.[14] Of the 33,000 assets listed in the DHS database, only a small subset is defined as critical infrastructure sectors.[15] Because federal, state, and local governments, as well as the private sector, often have different views of what constitutes criticality, compiling a consensus list of nationally critical assets has been an ongoing challenge for the DHS.

NOTES

1. www.tsl.state.tx.us/ld/pubs/compsecurity/glossary.html (alt URL: http://cipbook.infracritical.com/book5/chapter1/ch1ref2.pdf).
2. http://www.idart.sandia.gov/ (alt URL: http://cipbook.infracritical.com/book5/chapter1/ch1ref3.pdf).
3. Ibid.
4. www.comedia.com/hot/jargon-4.2.3/html/entry/tiger-team.html.
5. Def: "Tiger team: (n.)—1. Originally, a team (of sneakers) whose purpose is to penetrate security, and thus test security measures. These are paid professionals who do hacker-type tricks; for example, leave cardboard signs saying 'bomb' in critical defense installations, hand-lettered notes saying 'Your codebooks have been stolen' (they usually have not been) inside safes, etc. After a successful penetration, some high-ranking security type shows up the next morning for a 'security review' and finds the sign, note, etc., and all hell breaks loose. Serious successes of tiger teams sometimes lead to 'early retirement' for base commanders and security officers (see the *patch* entry for an example). 2. Recently, and more generally, any official inspection team or special *firefighting* group called in to look at a problem.

   A subset of tiger teams are professional *crackers*, testing the security of military computer installations by attempting remote attacks via networks or supposedly 'secure' communication channels. Some of their escapades, if declassified, would probably rank among the greatest hacks of all times. The term has been adopted in commercial computer-security circles in this more specific sense" (http://catb.org/~esr/jargon/html/T/tiger-team.html).
6. http://faculty.ncwc.edu/toconnor/431/431lect06.htm.
7. FEMA Emergency Management Institute, U.S. Department of Homeland Security Federal Emergency Management Agency, *Principles of Emergency Management Supplement*, p. 5, released September 11, 2007; http://training.fema.gov/EMIWeb/edu/08conf/Emergency%20Management%20Principles%20Monograph%20Final.doc (alt URL: http://cipbook.infracritical.com/book5/chapter1/ch1ref10.doc).
8. National Archives (United Kingdom), Cabinet Papers 1915–1978, the International Monetary Fund and Bretton Woods Conference; http://www.nationalarchives.gov.uk/cabinetpapers/themes/bretton-woods-conference.htm (alt URL: http://cipbook.infracritical.com/book5/chapter1/ch1ref4.pdf).
9. www.usfa.fema.gov/subjects/emr-isac/what_is.shtm (alt URL: http://cipbook.infracritical.com/book5/chapter1/ch1ref1.pdf).
10. A term used by the military establishment of the United States and other countries to define the following: "preventative measures taken to mitigate hostile actions against Department of Defense personnel (to include family members), resources, facilities, and critical information. Force protection does not include actions to defeat the enemy or protect against accidents, weather, or disease" (Joint Publication 1-02, *Department of Defense Dictionary of Military and Associated Terms*, April 12, 2001 (as amended through August 26, 2008), pp. 213–214).
11. http://www.dhs.gov/xlibrary/assets/st_innovative_public_private_partnerships_0710_version_2.pdf (alt URL: http://cipbook.infracritical.com/book5/chapter1/ch1ref12.pdf).
12. Library of Congress, CRS Report for Congress, *Guarding America: Security Guards and U.S. Critical Infrastructure Protection*, CRS-RL32670, November 2004; http://www.italy.usembassy.gov/pdf/other/RL32670.pdf (alt URL: http://cipbook.infracritical.com/book5/chapter1/ch1ref5.pdf).

13. http://frwebgate.access.gpo.gov/cgi-bin/getdoc.cgi?dbname = 107_cong_public_ laws&docid = f:publ296.107.pdf (alt URL: http://cipbook.infracritical.com/book5/ chapter1/ch1ref9.pdf).
14. Liscouski, Robert, Asst. Sec. Infrastructure Protection, Department of Homeland Security, testimony before the House Select Committee on Homeland Security, Infrastructure and Border Security Subcommittee, April 21, 2004. Note that DHS's list of 1,700 critical assets may not include the 430 U.S. commercial airports with passenger screeners, whose security is primarily administered by the Transportation Security Administration; http://www.italy.usembassy.gov/pdf/other/RL32670.pdf (alt URL:http://cipbook.infracritical.com/book5/chapter1/ch1ref5.pdf).
15. For example, in the chemicals sector, DHS has identified 4,000 facilities as potentially critical out of 66,000 total U.S. chemical sites. See Liscouski, Robert, Asst. Sec. Infrastructure Protection, Department of Homeland Security, testimony before the House Committee on Government Reform, Subcommittee on National Security, Emerging Threats and International Relations, *Combating Terrorism: Chemical Plant Security*, serial no. 108-156, February 23, 2004, p. 13; www.access.gpo.gov/congress/ house/house07ch108.html or http://bulk.resource.org/gpo.gov/hearings/i08h/94257. pdf (alt URL: http://cipbook.infracritical.com/book5/chapter1/ch!ref6.pdf and http:// cipbook.infracritical.com/book5/chapter1/ch1ref6a.pdf).

2 Demand, Capacity, Fragility, and the Emergence of Networks

2.1 INTRODUCTION

This chapter is more theoretical than most in that it identifies an emerging trend in thinking rather than describing some of the changes in the strategic infrastructure that have taken place since the first edition. At the time of the first edition, much of the focus on critical infrastructure protection (CIP) efforts was directed at the very local level—how to protect key facilities, etc.

This has evolved over time. Recent infrastructure issues have highlighted the fact that this infrastructure is subject to impacts that can flow along interdependencies and also disruptions within its networked environment.

2.2 WHAT ARE WE TRYING TO PROTECT? THE CONCEPT OF CAPACITY

If critical infrastructure is really about the infrastructure necessary to preserve the safety, security, and economic well-being of citizens, then shouldn't the focus necessarily be on protecting infrastructure or assuring that a given service continues to be delivered as required? Although the former is certainly important, the latter aligns much more closely with the stated goals of CIP.

The fact is that a given infrastructure at the local level is there to provide some level of contribution into the system. The sum of these contributions, the ability to coordinate how those services are delivered, and the means of delivering them to their intended recipients may be best described as the capacity of the system.

These three elements (safety, security, and economic well-being) are important because they operate similarly to the fire triad (heat, oxygen, and chemical reaction). If the infrastructure can generate a significant amount of the service but cannot identify where it is useful or deliver it to those points, then the system has essentially failed. At the same time, a well-coordinated and well-maintained grid that does not have anything sent through it is still failing to meet the final goal. The ability of the system to produce, distribute, and deliver can be described as the system's capacity.

2.3   DEMAND: THE REASON FOR CAPACITY

Demand and capacity exist in a constant balancing act. This is not to say that they are always in equilibrium—they rarely are. It simply means that where there is a demand, capacity will attempt to fill that demand. Where there is surplus capacity, there is likely going to be a demand attempting to exploit that capacity. Those with a background in a supply-and-demand economics will find this concept very familiar.

2.3.1   THE CONCEPT OF PERFORMANCE

The concept of performance basically describes whether the system works with sufficient capacity to meet its demand. For example, if there is a demand for 500 units of something, then the system would be considered in balance when it delivers those 500 units, and otherwise out of balance.

Because of the nature of critical infrastructure, it can be reasonably argued that three imbalances have to be considered. The most serious of these involves a situation where the capacity does not meet the demand. This may be represented by a situation in which some portion of the population does not receive an expected level of the critical service—such as occurs during a power failure. The second most serious condition occurs when the capacity exceeds the demand, but leads to a response where the capacity is reduced, leaving the system vulnerable to a spike in demand. This might be exhibited in situations where the private sector is primarily involved in the delivery of the service, but due to a surplus of supply, businesses leave the market because they become intolerably unprofitable. The final imbalance is a sustained surplus of capacity.

2.3.2   LOCAL IMPACT AND THE INFLUENCE ON CAPACITY

When infrastructure is disrupted at the local level, that disruption loses its ability to provide the expected level of capacity into the overall system. At the local level, the clearest understanding regarding the loss of capacity will flow from activities less associated with physical security, but rather with business continuity planning (BCP). Within BCP, thresholds are communicated that are used to determine the severity of impacts or losses of key resources, etc. Although BCP generally ends at the edge of the organization's responsibility or mandate, the concept of CIP urges this approach to be carried on throughout the organization and into progressively larger systems.

Some care has to be taken here to ensure that the quality of service is maintained at a manageable level. What if the final product (e.g., a fuel) fails to reach that level of quality for it to be usable in the system? This aspect of integrity is somewhat different than the traditional "nothing added, nothing deleted, and only authorized changes made through well-formed or defined processes" and more closely in line with the traditional views of quality assurance and quality management.

2.3.3 RESULTS OF A LOCAL IMPACT IN THE IMMEDIATE SENSE

When something is disrupted, we return to the concept that the availability of the critical service has been reduced. This leads to three important events that are worthy of study. The first event involves what the loss or reduction of that service means to the overall system. This revolves around the concept of what consequences arise should the organization fail to meet its goals—again, a power failure, loss of transportation, etc. The second event involves what the loss or reduction of that service means to the internal use or management of inputs that would normally be used to maintain that level of service delivery. How do the unused inputs survive the impact? Are they perishable or must they be used within a certain time frame before they are no longer of value? Are they persistent in that they can be stored nearly indefinitely without a loss of value? These factors should generally be included in the basic impact analysis—often in consultation with operations or material management personnel. The third event involves how the organization manages the fact that it is no longer consuming those inputs at the same rate. Does this mean that it will stop purchases of future inputs or that it will simply delay the delivery of some? These upstream impacts are also important factors to be considered both in the local impact analysis and later in the understanding of the impact on the overall system. For those seeking parallels, concepts defined in supply chain management and logistics provide some input.

Generally, at the local level, four classes of impacts are observed. The first are delaying impacts that essentially slow the inward flow of something into the system. This concept is seen when warehouses are filled—at some point, the warehouse is full but we still need to store the material. The second involves the concept of lag. This category of disruption describes the condition where something else is slowed down because the necessary amount of inputs is not being received. Finally, at the other end of the spectrum, the system will attempt to balance itself through either the third class, push (seeking to find new demand), or the fourth class, pull (seeking to find surplus capacity that can be aligned against unmet demand).

2.3.4 RELEVANCE TO CIP

The concepts of push, pull, lag, and delay are becoming increasingly understood at the local level. This was initially established through bodies of knowledge associated with supply chains and logistics; it then moved into the realm of BCP, and has now become more understood in the realm of CIP. Where the divide currently resides is between the local and regional (small system) levels when you look at the CIP services that have stemmed from such concepts as force protection, infrastructure protection, etc. For the reader, having an awareness that this bridge is likely to be built in the near future has a significant impact on how organizations can prepare and integrate their corporate security, information security (including information technology (IT) security and network security), BCP, incident response (in both the physical and informatics senses), business resumption planning, and disaster recovery planning programs.

2.3.5 Push, Pull, Lag, and Delay in the Network Environment

The concept of push, pull, lag, and delay is not unique to the transportation system—but is rather characteristic of any system that involves exchanges. The concept is familiar within the energy sector in pipelines and across transmission lines. These topics are also familiar in water systems and networks, and although they illustrate applications in physical networks, the concept is similar to various other concepts, such as bandwidth, throughput, and buffering within the logical realm.

For the CIP professional, an understanding of how these four elements operate is of vital importance. Fortunately, these sectors have already carried out significant research with respect to each of these elements as they work on understanding and refining their understanding of their own risks.

2.4 AT THE REGIONAL (SMALL SYSTEM) LEVEL

Returning to the first principle, we find that the core values associated with critical infrastructure services can be prioritized in order of availability, integrity, and confidentiality, as we migrate to a smaller system, usually at a regional level. Understanding what the concept of push, pull, lag, and delay means within that small system plays a vital role in the ability to assure delivery of critical services—now being thought of in some limited circles as critical infrastructure assurance.

2.4.1 Influence at the Small System Level

When attempting to assure these services, it is most important to understand how these concepts operate at the small system (regional) level. Consider that each node (or intersection) and each channel (or conduit) can only handle a certain capacity. If there is no release to the surplus demand (e.g., through a release of pressure), then the system simply operates as it is best able to. Beyond that, however, the system begins to clog as the surplus demand that cannot be handled attempts to find other options and, if this is not possible, remains in place.

This concept can be seen in most metropolitan automotive traffic congestion conditions quite clearly. A route can handle a certain number of cars in a certain amount of time. When that level is exceeded, the route begins to fill. When the space between intersections is full, cars cannot pass through the intersection or will block the intersection, thus compounding the problem, and the system begins to fill.

What becomes important at this point is the ability to identify that a disruption has taken place, find alternatives that can release the pressure, and then route or reroute the demand onto those alternatives. The release of pressure, if balanced correctly, allows the system to break the cycle of cascading and expanding failure, and regain that delicate operating balance between capacity and demand.

There are two factors that have a serious influence on this. First, what if there is no surplus capacity available in the system? In this instance, the system fills. It is also important to note that where the system is full, it, too, denies further movement through the system. The second factor may be whether surplus capacity within the system can actually be reached from the disruption. The routes between nodes fill as a result of the surplus demand; here again we have a situation where the impact is cascading and expanding.

2.4.2 Current Efforts and Research

As the reader will soon see, the legislation, regulation, and other forms of oversight regarding the local layer associated with critical infrastructure have evolved somewhat since the first edition of this book.

The first significant line of research has focused on the concept of interdependencies. Interdependency is where the level of one system's product is reduced, and this reduction causes an impact in another system. For example, a loss of fuel production impacts the transportation sector or a loss of electrical power affects telecommunications. For those involved in BCP, the concept of interdependency may appear to be complicated from an operational viewpoint, but is relatively simple to accept at a theoretical level.

The challenge here is that the concept of interdependencies is approaching a situation much like cancer research. Most of us understand that the term *cancer* actually represents a significant number of different diseases. As a result, one might fund "cancer research" (and we would certainly not discourage you from doing so) but not have a clear sense as to what form of cancer is being researched. The same might be argued for interdependencies (see the example reports within the footnotes, especially the one from Idaho National Laboratories[1]).

The second challenge is associated with the concept of network fragmentation and dissolution. Since the first edition, significant work has been carried out in the transportation and energy sectors to try to understand how the disruption in one part of the system impacts the rest of the system. For some, it is simply akin to the butterfly effect—an assumption that may hold true for nearly inconsequential parts of the system, such as a terminal or isolated node. On the other hand, disruptions at major infrastructure points may be apparent rather quickly, as the impacts flow throughout the various connections and begin to influence the capacity at other locations. Documentation has been published through the U.S. Department of Homeland Security's Transportation Security Administration fairly early on, and recently, entire works have been dedicated to the concept of using technology such as intelligent transportation systems as a safeguard against this type of issue.

2.4.3 The Interdependency Hydra

We have alluded to the concept that the term *interdependency* is becoming used to describe a number of states within and between networks and their interrelation between other systems. A number of projects have recently attempted to quantify and qualify the relationship between sectors. In Canada, these studies have resulted in Defence Research and Development Canada putting forward a call for proposals and papers as late as November 2008.[2] Similar projects have existed within the United States for a number of years.

Several centers have been involved in this type of research over the past few years. In 2006, the Idaho National Laboratory conducted a survey to identify the major works associated with "critical infrastructure and interdependency modeling."[3] Private researchers have also published since the publication of the first work (including the authors), often through Web portals and university publication portals.

When considering interdependencies, one might argue that there needs to be a basic understanding of how the impact flows between or across sectors. These might include, as a basic system of categorization, the following:

Interdependencies flowing out of one system (host) and impacting an independent system in that the impact does not cycle back onto itself (the host)—henceforth, this would be more of a dependency rather than an interdependency.

Interdependencies flowing out of one system (host) and impacting a system that provides a direct good or service back into the host system, leading to an elevated rate of deterioration attributable to the initial disruption.

Interdependencies flowing out of one system (host) and impacting a system that then provides a service to another sector that then has an influence on the host.

There is still a significant amount of work to be done with respect to the proper categorization and definition of these types of events. The questions that persist across a number of blogs and discussions where researchers tend to communicate continue to center on a general acceptance that some of the underpinning principles appear to be common, but are still difficult to quantify.

2.4.4   Network Fragmentation and Dissolution

The concept of interdependencies and cascading impacts has also worked in parallel and even contributed to a growing amount of research into the fragmentation and dissolution of networks. Much of this still focuses on the concept of mathematical models and translations of informatics systems into physical infrastructure. Again, there is merit to this research: Where such concepts translate gracefully into the physical domain, they are worth keeping. Where a concept is discounted, the results of the research still have value in that they can narrow the focus of other research based not on pet theories or whimsical intuition, but rather on sound scientific bases.

For those entering the arena of critical infrastructure assurance, the concept of network fragmentation and dissolution is relatively simple to explain—if one does not get bogged down in the complexity. Consider capacity and demand. Where there is a surplus of demand, it will seek out spare capacity (or where there is an ability to meet the demand, surplus capacity will be sought). This goes back to what was discussed in terms of how impacts affect the small system level.

What has become increasingly important to researchers is the ability to predict how that system will collapse and break apart. This is important for two reasons. First, a predictive model enables effective preventative measures (focusing on the robustness of the system) and also pre-position mitigation and response strategies (focusing on the recovery aspects) to be established. To return to the traffic congestion example, this is somewhat akin to being able to identify where the traffic jam is most likely to appear next.

It is perhaps fortuitous that this research has coincided with difficult economic times. This is because both U.S. and Canadian administrations appear to have committed to working on significant infrastructure upgrades as part of their economic recovery packages. Prudent planning would involve a forward-looking approach that identifies what capacity will be needed, rather than simply restoring overburdened infrastructure to its original design.

2.5 CYBERTERRORISM

In addition to the physical and operational safeguards, the concept of cyberterrorism has approached the forefront of many critical infrastructure issues. Outside of Hollywood's extrapolation of potential events, the world has seen clear examples of the results of coordinated cyberattacks in Estonia and Georgia as part of political and military campaigns. We have also seen the specter of groups of cybercriminals operating out of Asia with potential ties to state actors. These issues are of significant concern.

The Gilmore Commission[4] noted that the "cyberattacks incident" to conflicts in the Middle East "emphasized the potentially disastrous effects that such concentrated attacks can have on information and other critical government and private sector electronic systems."[5] The commission concluded that although not "mass destructive," attacks on critical infrastructure would certainly be "mass disruptive." It also concluded that likely perpetrators of cyberattacks on critical infrastructures are terrorists and criminal groups rather than nation-states. As a result, the commission predicted that detection of these attacks would fall primarily to the private sector and to local law enforcement authorities.[6]

This statement, however, has taken on additional importance. There is now increased recognition within industry and government that if key resources (this term is chosen specifically to align with BCP approaches) are connected through Internet-enabled technology, cyberthreats to those key resources need to be recognized and addressed.

2.5.1 THE PENDULUM OF CONVERGENCE

Convergence, simply put, is the gradual integration of physical and logical infrastructure. For those without degrees in architecture (logical or physical), it may be described as the gradual march onto the network-enabled system.

Convergence is really being driven by two interrelated variables. The first variable involves the need for increased efficiency and situational awareness. This is a direct result from the need to be increasingly competitive on a global stage. Where North American markets used to be serviced by North American companies, one might argue that the past 25 years have essentially destroyed that concept, particularly when considering issues associated with supply chains and offshore production. As a result, there is an increasing intolerance for isolated or stand-alone systems that cannot be expanded as operationally required or as per the will of management. The second variable involves changes in technology. The current generation of engineers and developers is not particularly enamored of the concept of working with single-purpose, analog systems. The generation that did have to work with that technology is gradually moving on into its retirement years—something that some consider a crisis and others a blessing. The end result, however, is the deployment of key resources using a type of technology that may, if not treated carefully, be subject to the same types of attacks that were present within the context of cyberterrorism. These two factors, the increasing pressure toward network-enabled systems and the decreasing supply of those able to work in past logical environments, will likely change the face of physical security and enterprise security.

The concept of convergence does not simply mean a change in the application of technology; it also requires a change in organizational culture and personal approaches to the issue of security. Some of the basic concepts will, of course, be consistent. As we look at how issues are identified, problems and issues are scoped, challenges are met, and solutions are applied, however, the traditionally diverging IT and physical and personnel security communities will be forced back to the same tables. Although the security industry is in for some interesting years as the various elements in these communities go through the normal processes associated with storming and finally norming, the end result for industry may well be worth the effort if both sides remember the primacy of operations.

2.5.2 CONVERGENCE AND THE UNDERSTANDING OF THREAT

Convergence is also going to impact on how threats are considered within an organization. The all-hazards approach has been front and center in the past—but its application has largely looked at the surface layers of threat. For example, keeping a cybercriminal at bay was a matter of installing a firewall, whereas keeping a prowler out was a matter of locking the door. Today's criminal, however, has access to both tools, and with the change of technology, it may be that the prowler is unknowingly working for the cybercriminal and has access to complex tools specifically conceptualized, designed, and used for defeating security infrastructure through logical means.

Perhaps this example can be described by providing three divergent threat scenarios—each of which intersects with the critical infrastructure and key resources domain. First, consider the Federal Bureau of Investigation (FBI) report on December 3, 2008, that identified another threat to U.S. infrastructure—the theft of copper that is being fed by an increasing demand for the metal, including in overseas markets.[7] Although it may be argued that all network infrastructure runs on fiber optics (it does not), it should be noted that this is not the type of traditional threat that might appear on a technical vulnerability analysis. The second threat involves personnel. Again, the FBI published (December 16, 2008) a report describing how certain elements of organized crime were able to infiltrate, through financial means, seaports along the East Coast.[8] In this case, the threat vector was not asset based, but rather personnel based as the gradual trapping of individuals who had been given access. Finally, in a similar report in *CSO* magazine, a network administrator was able to establish himself as the key source of control over much of the city's network infrastructure.[9] These three events show how a potential adversary or attacker could gain access over key resources using indirect methods.

Of significant concern today is the concept of the hybrid attack. As noted earlier, changes in technology and the availability of more and more processing power (an ongoing challenge) are leading to situations where adversaries have a wider array of tools at their disposal. Thus organizations that tend to focus their security activities in such a way that any one of the personnel, information, or physical safeguards are often left more exposed may be at risk of an attacker identifying, examining, and finally exploiting that vulnerability.

Consider, for example, a meeting room in a public area. On one hand, the fact that it is intended for public access and resides outside of the more sensitive work areas is good; on the other hand, one has to examine whether the IT infrastructure installed in that boardroom is sufficiently hardened. This should be done so that an attacker does not simply bypass the physical security infrastructure by using the network connectivity to pass through the barrier in a way similar to crawling over a dropped ceiling or defeating a weak lock. Although hard connections are reasonably simple to address, the propensity of several organizations to work toward wireless access points or capabilities means that the physical security expert will have to look not only at the physical design, but also at how to establish the necessary levels of shielding and standoff—particularly if the adversary can simply sit in public areas where it is difficult to control his or her activities.

2.5.3 SETTING THE STAGE FOR FRAGILITY

Given a basic understanding of some of the pressures within the system and some of the upcoming challenges associated with understanding how the infrastructure is protected, we can begin to look at a concept called fragility. Fragility, although reasonably new in this context, is not mystical—it has been inferred in such fields as *reliability engineering* for some time.

Fragility can be described in terms of the propensity of something to fail. At the local level, this aligns reasonably closely with the concept of the risk of loss associated with availability and, as a secondary factor, integrity. In reality, this can be divided into three major categories.

The first of these categories refers to the design of objects. When an engineer designs something, he or she indicates some level of assurance with respect to the design actually performing as intended. This is largely tied to the amount of effort spent in design, implementation, and other aspects of quality assurance. Aircraft manufacturers and other entities are subject to strict safety regimes; for example, they may have remarkably low tolerances for failure. Other industries, where the impacts are not so grave, may have considerably lower thresholds. Thus, given that an engineer may ensure that an aircraft design will work 99.5% of the time, whereas another engineer may only have to ensure that his product will work 75% of the time, we have our first significant difference in fragility.

This fragility, however, is often based on averages, norms, or set ranges of conditions. These norms or averages are used to provide that final calculated value that gives us that assurance regarding the design. We know, however, that as conditions change, they may have an impact. Personnel may be less able to perform tasks in extreme heat or cold, assets may be susceptible to certain conditions (e.g., low humidity leading to static electricity near computers), facilities may require that certain environments be maintained, information may require certain systems for handling in order for it to be considered trusted, etc. As we look at the item being examined (similar to a target), we may find that certain inputs into the system do not perform as well under certain conditions—for example, workers in high-heat areas may not be able to exert themselves the same way. This leads to the second type of fragility, *natural* fragility, so named because it is based on how the target would perform within the immediate environment.

As has been noted by scientists and poets alike, change is a constant within our environment. Cyclical fragility brings together the major elements discussed earlier—the concept of systems being sustained by the efforts of various inputs (persons, objects, facilities, information, and activities), the concept of capacity and demand attempting to maintain a level of equilibrium, and finally the fragility that is intrinsic at each point of time within the system.

For personnel, there are a number of cycles that one must remain aware of. In the longer-term view, we have the current issues associated with an aging population and the impact this will have on corporate knowledge. At the same time, there is the time involved in developing bodies of knowledge and communicating it to people, such as what we are seeing with the convergence issue. Within the medium term, the life cycle associated with business and with labor contracts provides another example. At the very short and immediate end, one might even argue that the various cycles are associated with fatigue and attention spans. As one will quickly realize, many of these do not impact the security realm—but have a significant bearing on the concept of critical infrastructure assurance when looking at potential sources of disruption.

Assets face similar challenges. When engineers design things, they generally include a life cycle based on adherence to a specific maintenance cycle and without certain constraints. We see this with our cars. They are anticipated to last a certain period—but only when you do not abuse them and keep the necessary maintenance up to date. Perhaps the most advanced bodies of knowledge in this regard involve life cycle management and safety programs. These programs track the use, maintenance, and age of assets as part of a means of reducing the risk of failures that can lead to either loss or accidents. Again, however, this type of approach has a significant bearing on critical infrastructure.

Facilities provide a nexus between two types of cycles. The first cycle, the age and usefulness of the facility, can be linked back to the same issues associated with assets. Materials deteriorate and require replacement. Structures become outdated in terms of the infrastructure they can provide. Another variable, weather, plays a significant role. Again, in the longer term, seasonal changes can affect the ability of persons, assets, or activities to perform as intended. Although some of these may be reasonably innocuous (e.g., a slight change in temperature), others may be profound, such as periodic flooding or dry spells. In the short term, the simple change between day and night may lead to different levels of risk.

Information and data, however, are somewhat different. In this context, the cycles are not attached so much to natural conditions, but rather to operations and what the information describes. Consider, for example, a table associated with the movement of a container—the value associated with the movement of the container shifts as one moves across the planning stage, through coordination and monitoring, and finally into audit and review. The cycles associated with information, one might argue, are inexorably linked to the timeliness and relevance of the data and what they represent.

Finally, consider the concept of activities. Cycles play a factor here. Looking at activities, we cannot ignore the effects of fatigue associated with persons and their assets. Thus we cannot ignore that various activities are more relevant at some points than others. These are generally associated with operations and coordination—points that permeate various systems and processes.

So how do these factors impact critical infrastructure? The answer lies in the need to ensure that the critical services are, in fact, available on demand and can be relied on from a quality assurance perspective. Although this approach argues that these five categories (persons, objects, facilities, information, and activities) cover significant aspects of a process, it is still incumbent on those conducting assessments to examine each process thoroughly. The challenges associated with convergence and new ways of thinking play a significant role given that those deficiencies in current and forecasted ways of doing things lead to gaps in understanding and knowledge with respect to the risk to critical infrastructure.

2.5.4 Fragility and Destabilization of Systems

At the regional or small system level, all the factors cited above have an influence on the capacity of the system. These influences can skew the balance between demand and capacity, shifting it in ways that lead to situations involving push, pull, lag, and delay. Where these influences stem from single infrastructure points, the effect manifests itself first in that local area. Depending on the nature of the effect, it will then influence those areas around it until the system is able to naturally restore balance.

The immediately impacted area will often depend on the level of capacity delivered by the infrastructure into the overall system. A relatively inconsequential or insignificant piece of infrastructure may cause some destabilization within an area that can be corrected reasonably quickly. On the other hand, where a key piece of infrastructure is disrupted, the immediately impacted area may be much larger and the system more destabilized; for example, the removal of a central hub within a transportation system or a key power production facility. How these disruptions cascade through the system will again depend on the system resiliency and redundancy.

The second consideration is where the full small system is impacted. The factors involved in this case are those that span the full system—in any of the categories of personnel, assets, facilities, information, or activities. We see this illustrated in terms of weather, labor disruptions, certain types of cyberattacks, and similar types of threat vectors. Where these are involved, the capacity in the overall system becomes diminished, again leading to disruption of the equilibrium between demand and capacity.

2.5.5 Fragmentation and Dissolution of Networks

Fragmentation and, catastrophically, dissolution of systems occurs when elements of the system are no longer able to communicate and coordinate their activities, essentially becoming individual entities encapsulated within the system. Although the local level looks at this in terms of a disruption, the same can be said at the small system or regional level.

Following a disruption at an infrastructure point (e.g., a facility), the next phase involves fragmentation. Although the concepts of push, pull, lag, and delay provide a mechanical description of the system-level impact, one can also divide the impacts into two broad categories.

The first category concerns disruptions involving the loss of infrastructure. This category involves situations where the infrastructure essentially fails, resulting in the contribution of capacity being lost to the system. We have seen these types of events in a range of bridge collapses, failures in the surface system, manufacturing sectors, and so on. When that infrastructure is lost, the capacity is lost, and the loss of capacity skews the equilibrium between demand and capacity in such a way that the system suffers disruption until it can rearrange itself by determining new options on how to meet the demands placed on it.

Fragmentation occurs under two conditions. First, the disruption may be at a key point that severs two parts of the system, essentially creating a number of smaller systems until it can be reestablished. In this context, the concept of fragmentation comes from the loss of what could be considered a key resource. It may be characterized by a single event, and because of its localized nature, there may be a significant focus on building up the robustness in terms of its ability to withstand impacts.

The second category involves conditions where the system essentially fills due to a surplus of demand combined with a reduction in capacity. If the capacity of the system involves a rate, then that rate becomes a very important factor, particularly where the system is working at near capacity. A reduction in the rate of being able to handle demand is essentially a reduction in capacity—and when demand is approaching the limit of capacity, then the system will begin to fill. Once the system is filled, and if the demand continues to try to exploit the capacity, it will not be able to do so. As a result, the system will gradually slow down and, if the reduction in capacity is serious enough, the operations will abruptly halt. This essentially fragments the affected area from the system, although recovery can be attained once the rate at which demand is handled allows for the system to clear itself.

Dissolution of the network involves fragmentation at a catastrophic level. In this case, the impacts are adequately severe so that the various components within the system can no longer communicate with each other. The end result is that the network becomes a community of individualities, unable to coordinate its activities.

Dissolution of the network becomes a real risk where the network relies on a single service, a single type of service, or is subject to a sector-wide vulnerability. Again, we have to return to the concept of persons, objects, facilities, information, and activities at this point. As with BCP, the concept of having single points of failure at the network's strategic level should be anathema.

2.6   DISSOLUTION AND CONVERGENCE: AN EMERGING RISK

Where all aspects of an infrastructure share common characteristics or where systems rely on a common point of service, the overall infrastructure or system becomes vulnerable. Given the trend toward convergence and network-enabled infrastructure, it would be worthwhile to include some brief and introductory comments regarding the risk of dissolution and the concept of convergence.

2.6.1   CONVERGENCE, NETWORK EXPANSION, OPEN ARCHITECTURE, AND COMMON CRITERIA

The increasing reliance on networks illustrates one potential avenue that could become a sector- or systemwide vulnerability if not handled diligently. First, convergence describes a condition by which the physical and asset protection infrastructure is becoming increasingly network enabled. Similarly, operational networks are expanding with new partnerships being formed to streamline delivery of services.

The concepts of open architecture and common criteria pose a significant challenge at this point. By publishing the open architecture and common criteria, a determined attack planner can identify certain characteristics that are common across the system and can attempt to reverse-engineer those characteristics or criteria in an attempt to determine a weakness. Given that both of these concepts communicate on a global scale, one can only assume that this potential threat vector is likely to occur.

However, the same concepts, in their development, also allow for a wide community challenge to the architecture and criteria, thereby reducing a number of the vulnerabilities in the system. The key here is in allowing for that broad and diligent consultative period before moving the overall structures into the public domain.

This concept has been a challenge for cryptographers and cryptoanalysts for quite some time. The result is reasonably simple. The encryption process uses a similar process in the development of new methods of protecting data against unauthorized disclosure or modification. For the critical infrastructure sectors, the principle may be similar. On one hand, the common criteria and open architecture may be globally available, but the specific and detailed information necessary to exploit something at the local level remains hidden from view. Again, however, the concept hinges on an approach that was rigorously challenged at the front and then monitored in terms of its effectiveness.

2.7   MARKING THE JOURNEY

Up to this point, we have looked at a theoretical situation that describes critical infrastructure assurance as an overarching, system-based, mission-focused view of how critical infrastructure sectors function. One might ask why this appears at the relative start of the work. The answer lies in three important steps.

First, we understand the nature of the changes that occurred as a result of 9/11. Many of us do not realize that the changes at that time were a fusion of the changes that followed the Y2K concerns of 1999.

Second, by providing two benchmarks based on the first and second editions of this work, we can define some of the changes to date. The first edition marks a point where one might argue that Western society was in a significant mitigation phase with respect to the 9/11 attacks—the term *mitigation* being used in its emergency preparedness context of those immediate steps used to contain damage. The second edition came at what might arguably be at the end of that phase.

Third, we understand that the business of CIP, homeland security, and similar programs is likely to undergo a significant change. We have looked briefly at convergence and the challenges of an evolving hybrid (physical and cyber) threat. There is also a new pressure to address economic and social issues—it may be argued that the old way of doing business (massive contributions and spending) is about to dry up as we look at renewed fiscal responsibility and restraint. Finally, the people involved are changing—from the retirement of many of the Cold War era security specialists through the process and systems engineers who defined what we now call critical infrastructure.

Thus this final step is about looking back into the past, and then looking at what is in place today and understanding and questioning the changes that have taken place. Finally, it is about extrapolating that information into the future to best estimate what is likely to be.

2.7.1 Overview

The period following September 2001 was a period of treaties, legislation, and regulation—much of it done quickly to respond to perceived needs. The marine industry is the clearest example of this, where entirely new regimes were constructed from an amendment to a safety code (Safety of Life at Sea [SOLAS]) in response to the events.

2.7.2 Legislation: 107th Congress (2001–2002)[10]

As we look at the legislation that has been passed since the 107th Congress (2001–2002) and up to the 110th Congress (2007–2008), we see what may be described as the response to one block of activity. In the 107th Congress, one might argue that the focus was on immediate responses to events—particularly within the transportation sector (particularly aviation, seaports, and pipelines), border security, dams, and the beginning of the push into cybersecurity. One must also note the legislation that gave rise to the Department of Homeland Security.

2.7.3 Legislation: 108th Congress to 109th Congress

We see, from the 107th Congress through to the 109th Congress (inclusively), a shift from the very general legislation to issues that are more granular. For example, in the transportation sector, we see the initial marine security bills being general in nature, whereas in 2006, marine security was beginning to legislate the approach of layered defenses (HR4954) and increasing granularity up to 2008.

We also need to understand that legislation, where none exists, can be challenging in democracies. As a result, we also see, particularly in Canada and the United

States, a gradual shift from legislation to regulation through rule and measure making. There are challenges with this approach—the oversight mechanisms for each of these are fundamentally different. Although not fully examined, one might wonder if there is a research opportunity for someone to examine the nature of this shift with respect to the oversight mechanisms used to create it.

2.7.4 THE STATE TODAY: A RECAP

Today's situation puts the critical infrastructure protection and critical infrastructure assurance domains at a crossroads.

First, there are significant resource issues. The collapses within the financial and automobile sectors put a significant strain on the economy. Concurrently, the costs associated with foreign wars and activities have put strains onto existing economies in terms of debt. Finally, there is the challenge of the reducing tax base caused by an aging population that packs two punches—reduced income through management of fixed incomes (pensions, etc.) and lost earnings (in terms of income tax), as well as the costs to social security and social support programs. In essence, one might argue that although the cupboard is not bare, we have certainly seen the back of the cupboard and realized that things cannot carry on as they have.

Second, there are significant knowledge base issues. The aging population noted earlier also carries within it a significant portion of the corporate knowledge associated with the infrastructure involved. We are also finally beginning to make the shift from an asset protection mode (some would theorize this being a mitigation response to 9/11) back to an infrastructure assurance mode where a new level of understanding has to be overlaid on top of traditional security and protection approaches. The issues of convergence mean that traditionally separate communities will now be forced, through necessity (even if to survive in the economic sense), to interact and cross-pollinate, and as we address these issues within our own community, our adversaries and competitors are working on harnessing opportunities provided in the new structure and our readiness to accept it.

Finally, there is the concept of public-private partnerships. With significant portions of the infrastructure operating outside of federal, or even government, ownership, governments have had to adjust their thinking from a span of control approach (e.g., through the dictating of plans) to a span of influence approach (indicated by the shift toward frameworks).

2.7.5 RESEARCH AND UNDERSTANDING

For those involved in CIP, homeland security, and emergency preparedness, these are also exciting times in the research community. The concepts described here are those that are openly researched in the community—concepts that are driving new technologies and approaches to infrastructure management. These concepts also cause friction between communities, particularly those that are firmly attached to rigid doctrines and dogmas and are unwilling to expand the breadth and depth of those approaches into new areas.

2.8   AUTHORS' NOTES

Flexibility in thinking for the professional can be challenging—particularly when the profession demands that the professional remain compliant with a certain approach or in line with a certain body of knowledge. Today, the infrastructure and asset protection communities have a plethora of certifications that can be applied to certain aspects or sectors.

Within organizations, there is a certain inertia that resists change. Pride in the organization's culture, heritage, or traditions can be either an anchor in the storm or an anchor in the race to reach new destinations. The key is to see the anchor for what it is—a tool that needs to be applied correctly. Will organizational issues be a help or a hindrance—and can the conflicts and frictions that inevitably come with changes of culture be managed effectively, or will they pose greater vulnerability to the infrastructure in question?

Finally, where does the leadership in the critical infrastructure assurance question lie? Does it lie with society and its duly elected representatives, or does it lie in the private sector? If you have a specific answer to the question, what does this mean to the role of government and oversight? What if times change and new approaches are needed? Is our own organizational structure resilient enough to meet those challenges? These are some of the questions within this field—making it awesome in its scope and more than a little exciting in terms of its application.

NOTES

1. Idaho National Laboratory, *Critical Infrastructure Independency Modeling: A Survey of U.S. International Research*, ed. P. Pederson, S. Dudenhoeffer, S. Hartley, M. Permann, August 2006; http://www.inl.gov/technicalpublications/Documents/3489532.pdf (alt URL: http://cipbook.infracritical.com/book5/chapter2/ch2ref10.pdf).
2. The call for proposals can be found at www.css.drdc-rddc.gc.ca/program/index-eng.asp. Although the proposals technically closed in November 2008, this kind of research is often ongoing and will require significant studies in the future (alt URL: http://cipbook. infracritical.com/book5/chapter2/ch2ref1.pdf).
3. A clear reference for this work can be found at http://homelandsecurity.tamu.edu/framework/criticalinfra/general-issues-and-recommendations/critical-infrastructure-and-interdependency-modeling-a-survey-of-us-and-international-research.html/. (Document identified within the Web site, entitled "Critical Infrastructure and Interdependency Modeling: A Survey of US and International Research," Idaho National Laboratory, U.S. Department of Energy, 2006, may be found at http://cipbook.infracritical.com/book5/chapter2/ch2ref2.pdf and http://cipbook./infracritical.com/book5/chapter2/ch2ref2a.pdf).
4. The Gilmore Commission is an advisory panel that assesses the capabilities for responding to terrorist incidents in the United States involving weapons of mass destruction. Response capabilities at the federal, state, and local levels are examined, with a particular emphasis on the latter; the secretary of defense, in consultation with the attorney general, the secretary of energy, the secretary of health and human services, and the director of the Federal Emergency Management Agency, entered into a contract with the RAND National Defense Research Institute, a federally funded research and development center, to establish the advisory panel, which released its fifth and final report in December 2003.

5. 80-337PS/2003 Homeland Security: The Federal and New York Response, field hearing before the Committee on Science House of Representatives, One Hundred Seventh Congress, Second Session, June 24, 2002, serial no. 107–71; http://commdocs.house. gov/committees/science/hsy80337.000/hsy80337_0.htm (alt URL: http://cipbook.infracritical.com/book5/chapter2/ch2ref9.pdf).

6. Committee on Science, U.S. House of Representatives, Hearing Charter, Cyber Terrorism—A View from the Gilmore Commission, October 17, 2001; www.house.gov/ science/full/oct17/full_charter_101701.htm (alt URL: http://cipbook.infracritical.com/ book5/chapter2/ch2ref7.pdf).

7. www.fbi.gov/page2/dec08/coppertheft_120308.html (alt URL: http://cipbook.infracritical.com/book5/chapter2/ch2ref3.pdf and ch2ref3a.pdf).

8. www.fbi.gov/page2/dec08/unirac_121608.html (alt URL: http://cipbook.infracritical. com/book5/chapter2/ch2ref4.pdf and ch2ref4a.pdf).

9. www.csoonline.com/article/437873/IT_Admin_Locks_up_San_Francisco_s_Network.

10. http://thomas.loc.gov/cgi-bin/bdquery/z?d109:HR04954:@@@D&summ2 = m&fTOM:/ bss/d109query.html (alt URL: http://cipbook.infracritical.com/book5/chapter2/ch2ref5.pdf).

11. http://clinton4.nara.gov/OMB/legislative/sap/106-2/S1993-s.html (alt URL: http://cipbook.infracritical.com/book5/chapter2/ch2ref6.pdf).

12. http://clinton4.nara.gov/OMB/legislative/sap/106-2/S1993-s.html (alt URL: http://cipbook.infracritical.com/book5/chapter2/ch2ref6.pdf).

13. http://www.fcw.com/fcw/articles/2000/1016/web-gisa-10-16-00.asp.

14. http://csrc.nist.gov/drivers/documents/HR3394-final.pdf (alt URL: http://cipbook.infracritical.com/book5/chapter2/ch2ref8.pdf).

3 Beyond National Frameworks

3.1 INTRODUCTION

This chapter outlines the movement beyond national frameworks to international frameworks. This most closely reflects the international nature of delivering the services associated with critical infrastructure and moves somewhat away from the administratively driven protection of physical infrastructure. While still early, we can perhaps track these efforts based on strategic interests (such as in energy) and economic ties (supply chains, etc.).

3.2 MEETING THE DRAGONS ON THE MAP

Ancient maritime maps marked the edge of known territory with statements such as "here be dragons."[1] From an administration and policy perspective, we are now entering a phase in critical infrastructure protection that marks us beginning to navigate in the territory of these dragons. For years, government organizations have been able to work within their span of control—exercising the ability to dictate requirements based on legitimate authority. They were able to maintain the sovereign interests of their country and national priorities through the use of laws, regulations, and similar mechanisms.

They were also operating in areas where the priorities of government were largely known to the policy organizations. In the international arena, this is no longer necessarily the case—even friendly nations compete on certain issues and strive for some kind of advantage. Canada and the United States, for example, have had one of the most enviable relationships on the planet—unless, of course, you worked in the softwood lumber industry. In these international settings, public positions are known, sensitive information can be shared under certain conditions, but the ultimate priorities and secrets of the state are still kept from each other.

And this is why we can call this the territory of dragons. It is not because of potential threats. It is because these international frameworks operate at a level where their foundations are based upon the agreement of friendly competitors with secrets held between them and not necessarily a single interest.

For example, in addition to the National Response Framework (NRF) and National Response Plan (NRP), there is the *Canada-United States Action Plan for Critical Infrastructure*.[2-4] This document openly recognizes, in its objective, the "interconnected nature of critical infrastructure"[5] and the need for collaboration across the border.[6] One can also see this in *The European Programme for Critical Infrastructure Protection*,[7] which one may argue is slightly more mature, given its inception through communication from the commission of December 12, 2006.[8]

One might ask how Europe arrived at this condition before North America. The answer is relatively simple: necessity. The EU was operating on a common economic framework, had a common currency, and was operating largely as a single trading block. As a result, the protection of infrastructure had to follow the same approach.

For Canada and the United States, the infrastructures were connected and the economies were linked, but the approaches to common government administration and goal setting were still farther apart. While the EU could not have independent countries operating in isolation where the whole would be affected, no such comparable limitations existed with respect to North America. Canada and the United States were still able to set individual goals and priorities without affecting the North American level.

The key element here is recognizing the mechanics of how the critical infrastructure sectors deliver their services. While the August 2003 blackout in North America showed an ability of the two countries to cooperate, this cooperation was largely limited to matters of trade (exports controls, etc.) and defense (NORAD, etc.). Today, efforts to understand dependencies and supply chains have made people far more aware of the international nature of many of these sectors.

Does this mean that the national plans are no longer part of the map? Of course not.

These international agreements operate in a cycle. National priorities are brought into the discussions that form the agreement. The agreement then sets goals and objectives that are carried back into the national structures. In short, you still need to know about the NRF—but you also need to understand that the contents of these are now based on a broader context than sole national interest, if indirectly.

3.3 WHO OWNS THE TREASURE?

For many, the concept of international influence is an uncomfortable one and raises the issue of national sovereignty. What needs to be understood is that this discomfort is the result of circumstances where national or international priorities do not appear to be treated adequately at the other level.

National frameworks and their plans may be described in terms of *what we want to see happen* for certain sectors. They are linked to the priorities of government, which are in turn linked to the government responsibility to protect its overall population. This much has not changed—the government still has the authority to make its own decisions and decide how things are going to happen.

International agreements are best described in terms of *what can we live with.* If any lesson has been taught in the recent series of conflicts, it is that even through military might and conquest, one is not necessarily assured that the outcome will be exactly what one wants. In negotiations, which are less intense than war, the goal is to be able to project your own interests outwards while protecting your core values against undue or inappropriate influence. In short, the question of national sovereignty is answered by making nations ratify agreements or include the requirements of agreements in their own legal structures.

So we all own the treasure—but we own it in terms of a community of signatories and not as individual signatories. From a pure perspective, this does result in some erosion of national sovereignty because we cannot deviate from our agreements without also making the decision to go against our commitments that are part of our belonging to that community.

3.4 WHAT VALUE?

The treasure can be defined in how these international agreements respond to the challenges that arose when nations were operating in isolation. This is another reason for looking at the international agreements in terms of an evolution of previous efforts and not a catastrophic shift in philosophies. In short, we drifted onto the right part of the map.[9]

The core of these agreements focuses on the sharing of information. This information is used to develop awareness of the threats to infrastructure, how infrastructure operates, and how the various sectors (both public and private) would respond to incidents.

In order to effectively share this information, each partner in the agreement has to oversee its appropriate use and controls. In short, a layer of management must be built that allows these information sharing principles and agreements to operate in a risk-managed, if not trusted, environment.

Examples of this can again be found in the U.S.-Canada agreement. Section 3.2 focuses almost exclusively on the sharing of information, the improvement of information products, and coordination of the dissemination of those products. For the information security professional trained in the Cold War era, this violates a number of principles—the giving up of secrets and vulnerability information to persons who operate outside of a community of trust.

In order to reestablish this trust, we see the agreement from organizations like the Emergency Management Consultative Group (EMCG), various groups that focus on sector-specific collaboration, and groups associated with ensuring that information is kept within the new community.

We also see this in the tone of the agreement, particularly in Section 3.6 describing the way forward. In this case, national priorities are considered inputs from the international working group. The limit of this is more apparent in the second priority, which identifies the need for the development of compatible mechanisms and protocols. Compatibility does not mean same or equal, and it can be inferred from the statement that each nation has the ability to exercise its own power and authority when looking at the specifics. We also see this in goals that include terms like *collaboration* and *mechanisms*.

3.5 TARGET AUDIENCES

There is an old adage that you have to write for your audience. This situation is no different. While the international agreements will define how states interact with each other, the national structures and frameworks continue to be of utmost importance to commercial organizations.

This is because the process is now a three-step process, one of which is somewhat less visible to the general population. The first step, nearly invisible, involves the setting of the agreement that results in the creation of an international agreement. In these cases, the designated authority from each state will represent its own public and private interests at the table. The fruit of that agreement is more directly applicable to nations than it is to the private sector. The second step is determined by the nation-state making adjustments to its own requirements that it places on its people. The third and final step becomes the various entities that fall under the control of that state making the necessary adjustments or incorporating the necessary requirements into their own efforts.

At the grassroots level, the situation does not actually change all that much. The government entities responsible for overseeing certain activities make edicts and issue requirements, and the private sector looks at those requirements and integrates them into the working environment. It is for this reason that the NRF still remains very relevant. The framework itself may be adjusted to fit the new requirements, but it is still the cornerstone of the national program.

This structure works better in some industries than in others. This is generally the result of two kinds of bodies that are able to write their own "variations" on the theme. The first group of bodies is the international associations that have been granted some level of authority in overseeing the activities of their members. Consider, for example, the North American Electric Reliability Council (NERC), which is "certified by the Federal Energy Regulatory Commission to establish and enforce reliability standards for the bulk power systems."[10] In this context, the state does not develop its own standards; it relies upon the international body to develop and enforce hose reliability standards, assess the adequacy of them annually, and monitor the bulk power system.[11]

This is the first variation on the theme. Remember that the main cycle involves the regulatory body going to the international body and then integrating the international requirements. In this case, the national body has shortened the loop by essentially delegating the international body to act on its behalf. In this case, the national endorsement of the international body can be removed by the federal authority should it be determined that the international body is no longer acting in line with the national interest. The second part of the variation involves the international authorities being able to exercise a level of direct oversight on the various individual members. Again, this occurs under the delegated authority (in this case certification) of the national body.

This variation does incorporate some loss of national sovereignty in the sense that the international body interacts directly with the individual participants. The filter between the two groups is essentially removed. This is indicative of two situations—one where the overall body is clearly subject to impacts that can quickly affect the whole, and the second being where the issues are limited to technical issues. We see this in the evolution of the system following the August 2003 blackout that clearly demonstrated how far and fast impacts could spread through the energy grid.[12] In this context, the requirement to maintain the electrical grid trumped political considerations, particularly during the response and recovery phases of the situation.

While the issues surrounding the August 2003 blackout may illustrate a condition where the international body steps in more prominently to fill a technical role at the behest of the state, other conditions may still exist. These conditions do not involve the state delegating authority to some international body, but that the international body assumes authority because events are occurring in a vacuum. This can be seen in the international response to piracy off of the Horn of Africa. In that context, the International Maritime Organization (IMO) is charged with the "responsibility for the safety and security of shipping and the prevention of marine pollution by ships."[13] The variation on this theme involves the level of participation of the various individual actors—usually in the form of trade associations that are formed to represent certain interests. Instead of nation-states putting forward their requirement to the IMO and the IMO coordinating the overall response, one sees the IMO taking a front-seat role in the response, but the technical details of that response largely sidestepping the national priorities, many of which were not defined, and coming from the various private sector bodies without significant participation by the national bodies. This is particularly evident in the standardized contract put forward by BIMCO[14] that pushed certain of its own priorities into the international arena, using the IMO as a voice to give its position authority.[15]

These two variations on the standard theme reveal a critical vulnerability within efforts to protect critical infrastructure. That vulnerability can be linked directly to the observe-orient-decide-act (OODA) loop of the international body and its national participants. The OODA loop is a structure that is used to measure the speed and efficiency with which organizations can adapt to changes in their environment. While the NERC structure was able to identify the change in its environment and adapt to it reasonably quickly, the challenges associated with piracy and international shipping cannot make the same claim. The difference here lies in the level of control that is assumed by the international body. The NERC is very clear in that it is certified by national bodies to perform certain roles that interact directly with the individual members. On the other hand, the IMO is equally clear in its role as a coordination body that does not produce requirements, but rather issues guidance that is to be brought back to each individual nation. In short, the OODA loop involving NERC is relatively clear in that it is comprised of a single cycle that acts within a context set by the various certifying (i.e., national bodies) participants. The OODA loop for the IMO, however, can be described as being complicated in that, as a more participatory body, it can be vulnerable to situations where the individual participants fall prey to a slow or poorly defined OODA cycle.

3.6 APPLYING THE NRF TO NATIONAL RESPONSE EFFORTS

This raises an important question with respect to how the various requirements come into being, are communicated, are applied, and are finally maintained. Again, one needs to understand that these requirements are intended to focus on specific outcomes—such as keeping an electrical grid delivering power (in terms of availability and quality). Where this system is challenged is when the actual problem becomes less clear. In the case of the IMO, the system was challenged in that it needed to define the context of its challenge—more appropriately defined as a series of inter-connected and interrelated issues operating in a complex manner than as a question of engineering and oversight. The result is that the IMO became subject to a range of competing interests, largely pushed by private interests that were not held in check by the national filters. In fact, even three years after piracy off the Horn of Africa was identified as being a critical international issue, only eight nations responded to the IMO survey regarding priorities and measures taken in response to the issue. In examining the response of some nations, it can be described as little more than a simple reiteration of IMO guidance.

If one takes the position that the effectiveness and efficiency of international bodies can be impacted significantly by the nature and clarity of their authority and mandates, then there is an argument that loosely structured and overly participative bodies may expose their members to the vulnerabilities associated with undue interference that come from vested interests. This leads to a singularly controversial idea that the next evolution in the management of critical infrastructures (at least those that operate across international borders) is one that should see clearly empowered and defined international bodies taking a much more active role in the oversight of those sectors. This will not be an easy process.

The difference in outcomes can be linked to two very clear challenges. The first challenge is being able to identify the pool of experts that can identify the questions to ask without being influenced by political or other vested interests. For the electrical grid, these experts exist and are reasonably easy to identify. For the issue of maritime security, however, the lack of clearly defined bodies of knowledge, criteria that can be used to define expertise, and even the broadness of the topics involved can all lead to significant challenges in this respect. The second difference comes in the nature of each nation's oversight over the international body. NERC is certified by a federal entity to perform certain roles, as there are clear conditions to be met and specific criteria to be maintained. The IMO, however, is not overseen in this regard—operating more on a voting- and consensus-driven model than on a clear certification regime. The results are clearly evident in the time and utility of the activities to date.

This challenge is also apparent when one looks at the differences illustrated in the efforts across safety, pollution control, and security issues. Admittedly, the security issue can be described as both complex and complicated. It is complex in that there is significant interaction between the various elements of the challenge. It is complicated in that the various parts have not yet been defined in totality or even their individual nature. The end result has been an operational environment that can be defined in terms of unclear expectations, competing interests, and uncertain progress toward less than clear final outcomes. When we look at the more traditional roles of the IMO—safety and pollution control—it is a significantly different environment. Structures exist, parameters of involvement are well defined, and the outcomes are reasonably clear and focused.

This leads to the second vulnerability that will need to be addressed in the realm of critical infrastructure management at the international level—the need for expertise that can operate above national or other forms of vested interests. This, in itself, can become a self-defeating prophecy. Associations or communities of like-minded experts are needed to form a clear body of knowledge. At the same time, the formation of this body of knowledge leads to associations taking on more and more of a political role as they attempt to promulgate and promote that body of knowledge. We see this happening across a range of certification programs, pressures to adopt certified professionals only in the contracting process and similar measures. Arguably, it cannot be the various associations that lead this charge, but rather the academic communities that apply critical thinking and academic practices but address issues associated with "real-world application" through the recognition and inclusion of groups or even individuals that possess verifiable experience.

This structure operates at both the international and national levels—but answering different questions. At the international level, the academic and research communities answer questions that are based on establishing requirements that lead to conditions most conducive to success. At the national level, it focuses on analyzing courses of action and clearly defining outcomes without becoming embroiled in the political positioning associated with vested interests. It essentially becomes a *trusted advisor.* To achieve this trusted advisor status, it must be able to demonstrate that it maintains a field of view, attention, activities, and experience that operate at that level.

For the private sector entity, this shift in dynamics leads to a shift in organization but not necessarily in management. The organizational shift stems from understanding the source of requirements having changed. It means the potential for an increased involvement of international actors—complete with issues associated with appropriate delegation and information sharing, particularly where the use of foreign nationals is involved. These are issues that would require clarification within each national structure. The management, however, is not likely to shift significantly—private sector and other individual entities are still likely to see lists of requirements to be met, a national structure that ties it to either criminal, regulatory, or administrative law, and the need to allocate resources and effort (time, etc.) in meeting those requirements in an inspectable and auditable kind of way.

At a national level, the participation in this structure will not change significantly. The NRF was not written by the government in isolation. This document reflects extensive coordination as well as input from state- and local-level management, emergency management, and private organizations across the country; essentially, the very people who will be using the plan are the ones who have devised it. Thus the NRF is not a federal plan; it is a national strategic document encouraging and ensuring that everyone involved for a given response effort is working on the same strategy.

The NRF builds from a set of core principles that:

1. Stresses the need for partnerships across both government and private sector organizations.
2. Emphasizes a bottom-up approach recognizing that most incidents are managed locally, and that incidents should be handled at the lowest jurisdictional level possible.
3. Is designed to be scalable in such a manner that it can be expanded or narrowed based on the scope and nature of the incident.
4. Is flexible, but adaptable to varying types of disasters.

5. Recognizes that successful emergency preparedness and response management depends on the unity of command as well as a clear understanding of roles and responsibilities among all involved.

6. Stems from the concept that the NRF is always activated and encourages a forward-leaning posture by emphasizing a more proactive approach to preparedness planning, organizing, training, equipping, exercising, and applying lessons learned from all exercises and events. Planning ahead for a disaster is critical for its successful response, and thus the NRF encourages such and similar coordination; the phrase "expect the unexpected" can and should apply in using the NRF.

The most significant change in this regard will be that the NRF structure, reflecting national priorities, will likely be subject to additional (academic) scrutiny and then taken to the international level. The returns back from the international level would most likely form additional requirements unless they conflicted directly with the NRF that was submitted to the international level.

3.7   HOW DOES THE NRF TIE IN WITH LOCAL ACTIVITIES?

As noted earlier, this shift may involve some slight shifts in specific requirements but not in how an organization has to respond to the overall requirements. We see this level of organization within the NERC structure, where the NERC acts as a body essentially representing federal entities. This provides a clear link to the national legal structures and oversight that is necessary to maintain sovereignty and the rule of law. The mechanisms may be slightly different.

As for the assignment of resources, delegation of persons, and allocation of resources, the individual entities are not as likely to see substantial changes. The ultimate accountability for the corporate response would still remain the CEO or senior officer of the company, while the company would still be required to maintain the ability to clearly mitigate, prepare for, respond to, and recover from various different kinds of incidents and changes in conditions.

The most likely change would be in how the national level identifies its requirements. The current structure is caught in a no-win[16] situation. Regulators go to the industry to try to find out where the system is vulnerable through a process of consultation. In participating in this kind of structure, however, the private sector entity is:

1. Putting itself in a position that could lead to it becoming subjected to more regulatory requirements and scrutiny by regulatory bodies
2. Putting itself in a position where it has essentially made itself more vulnerable to action on the part of the regulator by giving that regulator expanded access to its operations and the conditions surrounding them

This situation is further exacerbated by national policies that restrict the various forms of inspectors from "turning off" their powers in the interest of maintaining the appearance of fair and consistent application of the law.[17]

The use of centers of expertise and the academic community provides a compromise solution to this impasse. This allows for the collection of data and their credible analysis on the one hand (the need for source collection, etc.), while also providing the analytic function that serves to sanitize that information. This addresses the majority of both concerns.

This structure is not without its own challenges. While the academic community may be structured in such a way that would keep it apart from the regulatory inspection process, it is often asked to be able to "show its work." This basically involves being able to communicate what, where, and when something was exposed to the academic team. Where this information is provided to the regulatory body, it can become the reasonable grounds for the initiation of some form of enforcement action. The individual entity then has to ask why it would expose itself to additional legal, operational, and often financial risk in order to maintain its own corporate responsibilities. The answer is that it would not, and the communications line is broken.

Resolving this issue is likely to continue to be one of the most significant challenges in the critical infrastructure assurance and critical infrastructure protection domains.

3.8   AREAS OF POTENTIAL RISK OR CONCERN

Of particular concern is the potential shift of requirements from state control to private industry control. This shift is subtle in nature. Under the national systems, private sector entities would contribute to national systems that would then render out the national priorities and cycle them back as requirements, based on public priorities. With the rise of private sector associations, the nature of control is shifting, and in circumstances where less robust international controls are in place, private sector controls become more prominent.

There are two vulnerabilities that contribute to this scenario. The first involves the lack of credible expertise that operates on behalf of the national bodies (that would check the progress of requirements falling into this category) or at least with no vested interests. The second involves organizations that have allowed themselves to become too participatory in nature, essentially shifting their focus from coordination to one of accommodation. Where these conditions can be found, private sector entities can, through their associations, move to have their own requirements (based on profit and not public interest) communicated back to the national bodies that have agreed to adopt them. This can lead to conditions where private interests are able to influence laws without having to go through the necessary checks and balances associated with the national system.

With an increasing understanding that many of the infrastructures operate internationally, this risk, even if remote, must be watched for carefully. This is particularly true during difficult economic times and credit restructuring, where private sector entities will seek to gain or establish any advantage that they can.

NOTES

1. The phrase "here be dragons" symbolizes areas that are considered dangerous or are unexplored territories, and is usually represented through demonstration of the practice of putting mythological medieval dragons, sea serpents, and other mythological creatures in uncharted, unexplored areas of maps and sea charts.
2. http://www.dhs.gov/canada-us-action-plan-critical-infrastructure (alt URL: http://cipbook.infracritical.com/book5/chapter3/ch3ref3.pdf).
3. http://www.publicsafety.gc.ca/prg/ns/ci/cnus-ct-pln-bkgr-eng.aspx (alt URL: http://cipbook.infracritical.com/book5/chapter3/ch3ref4.pdf).
4. http://www.dhs.gov/xlibrary/assets/ip_canada_us_action_plan.pdf. (alt URL: http://cipbook.infracritical.com/book5/chapter3/ch3ref5.pdf).
5. http://www.dhs.gov/xlibrary/assets/ip_canada_us_action_plan.pdf. (alt URL: http://cipbook.infracritical.com/book5/chapter3/ch3ref5.pdf).
6. http://www.publicsafety.gc.ca/prg/ns/ci/cnus-ct-pln-eng.aspx (alt URL: http://cipbook.infracritical.com/book5/chapter3/ch3ref1.pdf).
7. http://europa.eu/rapid/pressReleasesAction.do?reference=MEMO/06/477 (alt URL: http://cipbook.infracritical.com/book5/chapter3/ch3ref6.pdf).
8. http://europa.eu/legislation_summaries/justice_freedom_security/fight_against_terrorism/l33260_en.htm (alt URL: http://cipbook.infracritical.com/book5/chapter3/ch3ref2.pdf).
9. Utilizing the analogy of dragons and sea serpents on maps and sea charts.
10. http://www.nerc.com.
11. Ibid.
12. The August 2003 blackout was significantly different in that while electrical events in the past had been investigated by regional councils, the size and scope of this event (affecting three NERC regions) led to the NERC assembling a group of international experts to investigate. This can be found in the North America Electric Reliability Council's *Technical Analysis of the August 14, 2003 Blackout: What Happened, Why and What Did We Learn?* July 13, 2004, as found at http://www.nerc.com/docs/docs/blackout/NERC_Final_Blackout_Report_07_13_04.pdf.
13. http://www.imo.org/About/Pages/Default.aspx.
14. https://www.bimco.org/en/About/About_BIMCO.aspx.
15. In this context, the Baltic and International Maritime Council (BIMCO) met in a limited group to generate a standardized contract referred to as Guardcon. It was revealed in the explanatory notes to Guardcon that a number of the requirements were put in place in order to affect changes in the industry that BIMCO had been pushing forward, including reducing the number of smaller security companies offering antipiracy services. Once Guardcon had been circulated broadly throughout the private sector clubs, the lack of resistance by IMO became the tacit approval for its use.
16. A no-win situation, also referred to as a lose-lose situation, stems from a scenario in which a person has choices, but choosing no choice leads to a net loss regardless of the choice. This may also represent unavoidable, perhaps unforeseeable, circumstances giving rise to a negative situational change after a decision has been made, again reinforcing the net loss regardless of the choice or decision made.
17. This is not to say that inspectors should be able to arbitrarily switch off their powers or that the state should give a free pass to companies that have failed to meet certain requirements associated with public safety. The problem here lies in the desire to maintain absolutes—the ability to conduct business or the ability to maintain oversight—without having considered this kind of interaction at the start of the process.

4 Public-Private Partnerships

4.1 INTRODUCTION

This section focuses on the concept of public-private partnerships (also referred to as PPPs or P3) and how they can have a significant influence in the critical infrastructure protection (CIP) and critical infrastructure assurance (CIA) domains.

CIP efforts, as the reader will recall, focus on protecting our infrastructure. They deal with a structure that essentially protects an asset from some kind of harm caused by a threat when it exploits a vulnerability.

Furthermore, CIA efforts also focus on the ability to assure that a critical service is actually being delivered. The protection of infrastructure (CIP) is a subset of activities under a CIA program that tends to be better described in terms of the ability to *mitigate, prepare for, detect, and respond to* disruptions in the delivery of critical services or unacceptably high losses in the quality of those services.

When looking at critical infrastructure, the goal is critical infrastructure assurance, while the various objectives that need to be accomplished to achieve that goal can be described as critical infrastructure protection.

4.2 WHAT IS A PUBLIC-PRIVATE PARTNERSHIP (P3)?

A public-private partnership (P3) can be described in a number of ways. There are some common themes that run through all of them:

- It is cooperative in nature (between the public and private sector).
- Each partner brings forward specific knowledge, skills, abilities, resources, or expertise.
- It is intended to meet public needs.

The reason there are a number of different descriptions regarding public-private partnerships is because this label describes a number of different arrangements. At one end of the spectrum one can find the contracting out of services, and at the other end one might find the concept of privatization. The former represents the traditional way that government would engage the private sector, while the latter represents how government would essentially shed its accountability for certain kinds of infrastructure and operations (divestiture).

What should be clear is that this concept represents a further privatization of certain types of infrastructure. While the private sector continues to own a significant percentage of the critical infrastructure, certain kinds of infrastructure (water treatment plants, etc.) remain in the hands of national and regional (state, provincial, etc.) governments. This approach represents a deceleration in terms of the movement of infrastructure of public to private hands, but by no means a reversal.

This trend is likely to continue. Certain countries (Canada, Australia, and the UK, among others) have established government entities to assist in coordinating this activity.

4.3   THE P3 SPECTRUM

The P3 spectrum describes that range of activities that fall somewhere between the basic contracting services and full divestiture through privatization. This is more than simple construction. It can involve any one or more of the following in various combinations:

- Financing (banking arrangements)
- Design (engineers, architects)
- Construction (surveyors, engineers, build teams)
- Operations (facility management)
- Maintenance (repairs)

The first set of requirements to understand involves being able to answer questions that describe the nature of the operations being undertaken and the balance between the public and private sectors.

The first question involves who will be delivering the services. Given that CIA does not allow us to consider simply shutting down the services, the response will generally fall into one of the following categories:

1. **Private sector (entirely).** In circumstances where there is no apparent need for oversight, short-term revenues may be generated through the sale, long-term budget pressures may be relieved, and the critical service can be reasonably assured.
2. **Private sector with public sector oversight.** In circumstances where the private sector may be in a better position to offer the service, longer-term budget pressures are relieved, shorter-term revenues may be generated through licensing, and the critical service can be reasonably assured, with oversight in place to assure quality.
3. **Public sector with private sector support.** In circumstances where there are specific government responsibilities that cannot be maintained adequately if passed to the private sector, certain longer-term costs are reduced by transferring responsibilities to apparently less costly mechanisms, and critical services must be maintained.
4. **Public sector with private sector contribution.** Where it is not appropriate that the private sector be involved in the delivery of the service, short-term costs are overcome through private sector funding, longer-term shortfalls are overcome through temporary arrangements, and there is a need to deliver the service.

The latter of these circumstances speaks to a potential situation that is particularly troubling—where the costs associated with maintaining the life cycle management routines for the infrastructure have outpaced the ability of the government to pay. We see this circumstance in situations where the public sector must enter into an agreement with the private sector to raise the necessary funds to complete a project because constraints within government do not allow for the spending. This should be at least an indicator of a potential issue in priority setting.

4.4   ESTABLISHMENT OF NEW CAPACITY

As noted in previous versions of this work, there is a need to maintain a balance between demand and capacity. This is not strictly a one-to-one ratio. The balancing point involves the demand being in balance with the capacity when taking into account the need to maintain the resiliency of the overall network delivering the service.

When looking at private sector involvement in the management of infrastructure, one must remain cognizant that the private sector's focus is not on the public good. It is on the generation of wealth and specifically profit. Profit, in general terms, can be influenced by either reducing costs (such as maintenance, etc.) or by increasing revenues.

Two examples can be used to illustrate this point. The first involves the transportation sector and the construction of new roads. The 407 ETR was constructed to relieve traffic congestion in the Toronto, Ontario, Canada, area and runs approximately 108 km from Burlington to Pickering. The highway was the result of a tender that generated slightly over $3.1 billion (Canadian) for the provincial government.[1] In return, the corporation is able to bill on a pay-per-use basis with light vehicles paying a per-kilometer fee to the corporation in return for traveling on the highway.

While the initial revenue generated for the province appears to be substantial, it must be put into the context of the tolls that are collected by the road operator. In 2010, the total number of kilometers traveled by all commuters was $2.336 billion.[2] Considering that the revenue per trip is slightly over $5.00 per trip, while the expenses per trip were approximately $1.00, with approximately 114 million trips recorded in 2010, profits can be estimated at slightly under half a billion dollars. A quick look at the bond maturity profiles provides a very clear example of the profitability of the infrastructure.

The Illinois Tollway provides another example. In 2010, the Tollway had revenues of approximately $673 million (USD), while the allocations are approximately $686 million. It should be clear, however, that this number includes approximately $206 million for renewal, replacement, and improvement, and $255 million for maintenance and operations.

What can be seen when comparing these two sets of numbers is that the Ontario 407 ETR is far more open in declaring itself to be well-run business venture. Profits are generated, there is a clear return on investment, and there is an attempt to gather further business (profit) by portraying enhanced services to its clients. On the other hand, the 2010 Illinois Tollway presentations tend to focus more on portraying a break-even status, with an emphasis on social responsibility and participation.

4.5   MAINTENANCE OF EXISTING CAPACITY

While new capacity may be needed to meet increasing demand, this does not absolve organizations of their need to maintain the existing infrastructure. Perhaps one the best examples of this challenge comes from the electrical sector and the conversion of Ontario Hydro into its five companies (later known as Hydro One, Ontario Power Generation, Independent Electricity System Operation, Electrical Safety Authority, and Ontario Electrical Financial Corporation). This transition proved to be particularly challenging.

The challenge lies on two fronts. As part of the transition, the decision was made that the previous debt had to be serviced outside of operating costs. The result was a debt retirement charge that is intended to pay down approximately one-third of the former debt and includes an additional 0.7 cents per kilowatt hour with certain exceptions.[3] This charge is included on the bills for most consumers.

The second challenge lies in the ability to achieve profitability. The majority of revenue comes from the payments made by electrical consumers. The rates paid by consumers are closely regulated by the Ontario Energy Board that sets prices for off-peak, mid-peak, and on-peak periods. The end result for consumers, however, was a cost that was broken down to include the costs of generation, transmission, debt retirement, and other costs.

So what does this mean in terms of critical infrastructure assurance? CIA refers to the ability to assure that critical services are being delivered. The public sector management approach was failing in this respect, or could even be argued to have failed, because the government, in order to reduce costs, divested itself of the infrastructure and decided it could no longer deliver the service. The for-profit model ensures, with sound management, that the resources required to run the infrastructure are appropriately balanced with its costs, addressing this particular vulnerability in terms of a lack of financial stability.

From the critical infrastructure protection perspective, the for-profit model also makes a level of sense. By ensuring that the revenues and costs remain at least balanced, each individual infrastructure generates revenue essentially based on the demand being placed on it. Similarly, the silo that is created through user fees means that infrastructure costs can be balanced in such a way that significant underperformers do not put a drain on the whole system or overall network.

4.6   NETWORKED USER FEES AND THE NEED FOR OVERSIGHT

For the public, the general conclusion above should cause a level of concern. As shown by the Ontario Hydro example, the transition from public utility to private entity came with a significant price tag. It is unlikely that private sector entities would waive their requirements for debt to somehow be managed outside of their envelopes, meaning that the cost would likely be passed on to the consumer or absorbed by the public debt. In all cases, the end result is an increased burden on the end consumer, which, in itself, can lead to inflationary pressures.

At the same time, care must be taken to monitor the level of profits in the P3 relationship. Consider two other highway toll roads. The 407 ETR advertises a length of

108 km, which can cost 19 cents per km, for a cost of approximately $20.52. I-476 in the United States, however, cost $42.05—a significantly higher amount—until it is noted that it is for a distance of 442.7 miles, or about 708 km, for a cost of slightly under 6 cents per km. As with the Illinois Tollway, the focus of I-476 is not on business or the generation of wealth.[4]

This has the potential to create significant inflationary pressure on the cost of goods, particularly through the cost of transportation. For example, if the good had to travel 100 km to market, there would appear a charge for that 100 km that would have to be integrated into the shipping cost. While this may not have a significant impact on communities that are essentially self-sustaining, major urban centers would likely see significant increases in terms of the cost of fuel, food, and other commodities that may have to be imported or travel significant distances through the network.

The remedy to this situation would logically have to involve a reduction in various taxes that are paid by the public and which were intended to maintain the same infrastructure. For example, the cost of gasoline has a charge in it for the maintenance of roads. Similarly, other infrastructures that are maintained by the public purse have also had taxes collected for their operation, but channeled into general revenues. Essentially, as this privatization continues, a condition of double taxation would gradually evolve, where the taxes of the public sector and the user fees collected by the private sector overlap. From the perspective of consumers, this would essentially mean that they were paying twice for the same service.

In Western countries, the taxpayer actually does not pay twice because of how taxes are collected. While the price of gas at the pump includes a cost for road maintenance, those funds are collected and committed to general revenues. Those general revenues can then be assigned across any number of government priorities, but do not have to be allocated for the purposes for which they were collected. In short, if a higher priority than road maintenance were to appear, the money collected for road maintenance would simply be repurposed.

Given the number of government spending priorities—ranging from an aging population to war—a vast majority of the general revenues have been assigned to special priorities and not the day-to-day upkeep of the infrastructure. When looking at this from a short-term perspective, this does not appear to be a terribly significant issue and can be easily rectified. Having fallen into this trap several times over, however, the costs needed to rehabilitate and then manage the infrastructure at levels that would meet the demands placed on it are now at a level where they are almost unattainable. In short, like the credit crisis, several infrastructures within the public sector management are now at critical levels.

The remaining alternative therefore requires that the public sector element monitor the performance of the private sector element, not only in terms of maintaining the infrastructure, but also in terms of ensuring that the public is protected against profit taking. This can only be accomplished by setting clear expectations during the conceptualization and design phases of the agreement and understanding that where the government imposes restrictions on the return on investment, it will have to make some effort to ensure that those restrictions remain in force.

4.7 OTHER FORMS OF PUBLIC-PRIVATE COOPERATION AND THE EROSION OF GOVERNANCE

The need for this oversight also extends into the development of laws, regulations, and policies. Each of these has traditionally involved a consultative process that is used to gauge the impact and benefits associated with the development, implementation, monitoring, and review. This consultative process is often used by various interest groups, associations, organizations, or even individuals to present points of view in the hope of making a convincing enough argument that they suffer less disruption or are able to gain some benefit from the new measures.

This structure assumes that there is a clear understanding of the roles and responsibilities of each group. The government is there to conceptualize, design, implement, monitor, enforce, and if appropriate, adjust the various controls on persons and activities that fall within its jurisdiction. The private sector is there to provide an understanding of the potential consequences of those decisions and, in some cases, propose alternatives for consideration by the governing body.

This has been shifting toward the private sector's advantage over time in a number of industries—often those that are involved in the self-regulation exercise or in terms of performance-based regulation. These structures allow for the private sector entity to put forward its own requirements as long as it meets certain goals. Given that these goals are often aligned with the need to prevent or respond effectively to situations that would disrupt the infrastructure or cause injury to society, including the local population, there is a very clear need to define what the outcome should be and then to test, in a credible manner, whether or not that outcome is being achieved.

The requirements communicated out of the private sector have used a structure that relies upon the conduct of risk assessments and the development of plans—followed by the verification that the plans are actually in force. The assumptions in this structure are that the risk assessment has identified at least the threats, vulnerabilities, and risks of most significant concern, and that the plan is adequately able to appropriately mitigate, prepare for, respond to, or recover from the events associated with those conditions. This structure is becoming more and more apparent in the transportation, energy, and communications domains where the private sector has been increasingly relied upon to provide technical input into the formation of the various forms of regulation.[5] Where the inspection process is based upon the legal or administrative requirement to "have a plan and put it in place," the public sector element runs a significant risk of shifting onto a structure that simply verifies that the plan is in force but fails to determine if the plan is valid or appropriate in the first place.[6]

This system can be overbalanced in the other direction. Prescriptive regulations, including management by set standards and best practice, can lead to conditions where a false sense of security becomes a risk of its own. Again, the assumptions being made are that:

1. The prescriptive standard is, in fact, the best option with respect to dealing with certain risks.

2. The prescriptive standard is actually applicable and took into account the ranges of conditions associated with the threat and operating conditions.

In these structures, CIA and CIP activities become standards driven. This has been particularly applicable in the information technology domain and certain other regimes that are subject to technical or legal liability, including insurance-related challenges.[7] Arguments associated with cost, efficiency, and regulatory compliance, particularly where audits and inspections are involved, factor significantly. The overseeing body, in some cases even a third-party certification body, provides checklists of what is to be presented. The private sector entity then ensures that each item on the checklist has been addressed and recorded—a practice that greatly facilitates the oversight process, but that can lead to the inspection or audit cutting corners when looking at the issue from a whole assurance or whole compliance point of view.

4.8 BALANCING POINTS

These challenges point to a critical need for the P3 to operate in a balance between the public and private sectors. This balance must exist in at least the following:

- The use of a common definition base
- Education, training, and expertise
- Roles and responsibilities
- Governance and enforcement

This balance is needed to achieve clear communications that attain the necessary balance between prescriptive (ensuring that baselines are met) and performance based (ensuring that assurance, resiliency, and protection goals are achieved). This begins with the basic definitions that are used. One challenge is that there are still a significant number of definition bases being used, and in some cases, persons have become involved in the system who lack the knowledge, skills, training, or experience, singly or in combination, and who, by virtue of their position or simple rhetorical ability, create their own. Without having that clear understanding of the basic definitions, a condition similar to the "fruit of the poisoned tree" comes into play—the confused definition base providing a foundation for unclear or even convoluted communications.[8]

With a common definition base, there is a need to establish a common and accepted approach or doctrine. Again, the assurance and protection communities are at a stage in their maturity where this is not a simple task. Those who have been involved in the asset protection and security domain will be very familiar with the competition between disciplines in the information security, physical security, business continuity, and other domains. With each discipline continuing to operate within its silos and attempting to promote its own view of the others from within that silo, one might comment that the arguments that arise, from a senior management perspective, are best described in terms of an unhealthy sibling rivalry that draws attention and efforts away from the running of the corporate family.

This is particularly true in the P3 environment where government policies and private sector practices can come into conflict. On one hand, policies such as the Policy on Government Security in Canada provide a structure or set of frameworks that government security programs and those doing business with the government are supposed to recognize and adhere to. Depending on whether or not these policies, including any supporting standards, are kept up to date, they can have varying degrees of utility, as they are written with a government-centric focus. The private sector element to the equation has more flexibility and may opt to follow no specific path, a path along the line of a professional or trade association, or a combination of approaches that allow it to demonstrate enhanced capabilities within a set of apparently valuable domains through membership or certification. While the private sector is vulnerable in terms of the requirement to be subjected to many regimes, it has the flexibility to make certain decisions within its own management as to how it will approach those challenges.

While the private sector may be vulnerable in terms of the number of regimes it can be subjected to, the public sector has a dissimilar challenge. Most persons involved in the inspection and oversight process are employees that are protected through collective bargaining or similar arrangements. The result is that certain organizations tend to focus on the training directly associated with the job process, but not necessarily the discipline involved. This places the public sector organization into a difficult position as the individual in the field:

1. May not be able to recognize measures that may not work
2. Understand how the measures function individually or as an integrated system
3. Understand the extent and nature of the risks inherent in the environment the public sector is attempting to regulate

The final result, particularly if the public sector fails to keep up the training for its personnel, is an inspectorate that deploys into the field simply to have preformed questions answered while exposing the private sector entity to officially induced errors.[9] There is an imbalance between the private sector, which seeks out the most skilled and valuable person for the organization (usually represented through enhanced education, training, or experience), and the public sector, which may, if not prudent, allow persons to become stagnant in their knowledge, skills, and abilities.

While this may seem inconsequential to some, the disparity is significant when looking at how many regulations are enforced. While some fall under systems similar to those used in criminal or civil proceedings, regulations are generally enforced through administrative tribunals. These administrative tribunals allow for slightly broader or relaxed standards with respect to evidence and the provision of expert opinion. To give an expert opinion, however, the individual must be able to show an appropriate level of knowledge, skills, and experience. Where there are two dissenting opinions, favor may be given to the expert that can better demonstrate the more enhanced level of education, training, or experience. When this is combined with a regulatory regime that does not have very clear and measurable criteria to meet, the outcome can be a balance that shifts significantly toward the private sector entity that can demonstrate that its personnel have enhanced levels of third-party accredited training and experience in the field as opposed to public sector workers. This in turn shifts the balance of probability that the private sector will be successful in its presentation to the administrative tribunal and degrades the ability of the regulator to enforce its own regulations without being constantly pulled into the administrative legal system.

4.9 AUTHORS' NOTES

The P3 does offer significant opportunities for the public and private sectors to operate more efficiently. It is also one that must be understood in terms of the potential risks involved. The first step is to understand the nature of the operations involved and how that may influence the long-term relationship between the public and private service when delivering the product.

It also means ensuring that the roles and responsibilities of the public and private sector are clearly defined, and that these roles and responsibilities, at a minimum, also identify the requirement to ensure that each side is able to interact (if only doctrinally) by using common and trusted frameworks. It also means that while the public sector may be enjoying some immediate benefits, it has responsibilities to oversee the operations in general (to protect the public from gouging or other unscrupulous trade practices) and to maintain the necessary expertise to be able to oversee those operations. These responsibilities must also be looked at in terms of the enforcement mechanism that will apply in the P3 arrangement if it is to be applied successfully.

In essence, the P3 can be described as a potentially more streamlined manner by which CIA and CIP activities can take place, but is by no means a "cure-all" or "magic bullet" when looking at the broad range of effort needed to maintain the agreement.

NOTES

1. http://www5.407etr.com/about/background-information1.html.
2. Ibid.
3. http://www.fin.gov.on.ca/en/guides/drc/101.html.
4. Tolls were calculated using the online tool for the Pennsylvania Turnpike as found at http://www.paturnpike.com/toll/tollmileage.aspx.
5. In the maritime security regime (an example of performance-based regulation), the public sector identifies certain goals to be achieved. The private sector then conducts the security assessment (risk assessment or question) and develops the security plan (risk management or answer) to achieve those goals. Given that these regimes are generally inspected against the plan, this results in a significant vulnerability in the structure, as it is premised on the assumption that the assessments and plans were developed in good faith and were kept free of attempts to reduce or otherwise manipulate conditions to the private sector's advantage. Several nations were involved in discussions with industry that saw regimes, such as the ISPS, become limited in scope to certain activities (such as ships in port and not in transit) despite sound security practices and doctrine that establish baseline controls that must be maintained at all times.

6. The counterargument used by regulators is that this approach allows businesses the flexibility to balance security and operations. What is less communicated is that this approach also includes rationalizations that the approach reduces the legal liability to the government because it did not direct a specific measure, and therefore the due diligence associated with specific measures is shifted back onto the private sector.

7. Several groups clearly indicate that their security programs are managed according to a range of standards in the energy, financial, medical, transportation, and communications sectors. For the reader, a review of public Web sites can provide a clear indication as to how deeply this approach has permeated into certain industries.

8. The fruit of the poisoned tree refers to a legal principle in which evidence or information that is the direct result of some action that is deemed to be inadmissible also becomes inadmissible.

9. The concept of officially induced error involves situations where a regulated organization receives information from an authoritative source (the regulator) that actually causes it to come into conflict with the regulations in question or with the regulations in another domain. The company, in following the official's guidance, is punished for following that direction because it contravenes the requirements of another regulating body.

5 The Reinvention of Information Sharing and Intelligence

5.1 INTRODUCTION

This chapter examines the role of information sharing within the critical information protection (CIP) and critical infrastructure assurance (CIA) domains. The distinction between these two activities is profound—protection focusing largely on the activities of an organization to be adequately robust and resilient in their operations and assurance focusing on the ability of the system to continue to deliver critical services at levels that meet or exceed the demand for those services. This latter part incorporates critical infrastructure protection and a range of other activities.

The first step in addressing any critical situation is being able to detect and identify what and where that situation is. While this statement may seem simplistic, it is one of the greatest challenges in the industry today, where the challenges associated with isolated administrative processes, incompatible processes, competitive influences, regulatory approaches, legislation (including the laws of other countries), and even personal interpretations come into play. Those that have worked in the establishment of information sharing centers (or similar entities) will be all too familiar with the sheer volume of work and complexity of identifying who should be at the stakeholder table.

This chapter therefore looks at some of the core elements of information sharing that need to be in place when addressing these challenges.

5.2 DATA VS. INFORMATION VS. INTELLIGENCE

When approaching the issue of information sharing, one needs to understand the difference between data, information, and intelligence. This is a matter of nuance and subtlety that is often not apparent.

Data involves a set of singularities and is the absolute basic building block when looking at the data, information, and intelligence hierarchy. Data represents a single unit and is often highly empirical in nature. For example, one can confirm that a runway is a particular length. This can also confirm that a person holds a certain opinion.

Because data is empirical in nature, it can be described in terms of completeness, accuracy, and repeatability. The length of the runway should remain relatively constant over time. An opinion may change over time, but the changes can be detected by going back to the person and confirming what his or her current opinion is.

It is at the data level that inspections and audits factor most significantly. Gaps or errors in the collection, handling, distribution, or retention of data factor heavily in audit reports. This is because data is the basis of decision making—the foundation upon which the management structure rests.

When data is collected and organized, it moves into the realm of information. For example, the length of the runway may be data, but the overall description of how the airport is laid out would be considered to be information. In another context, a sensor may record a certain voltage in a wire, but when the information from all sensors is brought into the control room and presented on the main viewing panel, we have moved into the realm of information.

Information is assessed on completeness, accuracy, and repeatability at one level (often in terms of confirming the data) and reliability and credibility at another. For those familiar with the various forms of information gathering, like the Admiralty Code, reliability is basically a technical assessment that describes whether the source of the information has the ability to collect, gather, and present it. Credibility, on the other hand, refers to the ability to corroborate the information through other sources. Depending on the nature of the information collection exercise, these two factors will present a relatively clear view as to whether or not information can be acted upon.

Finally, intelligence is used to describe information that has been brought together, collated, assessed, and prepared for dissemination. This is a formal process that is used to answer the fundamental question of "So what?" Returning to our example of the runway, intelligence may look at the layout of the airport and come to the conclusion that "based on the information at hand and the conditions today, the layout of the airport points toward there being an increase in the number of heavier aircraft at the airport. This is assessed as being the result of a desire to increase air freight movement activities."

These three layers are very much interconnected. Bad data can lead to unreliable or perhaps incredible information, which can lead to bad intelligence. This bad intelligence is then fed into the decision-making processes and leads to the organization either making the wrong decision or failing to make the right decision. In either case, it exposes the organization to various levels and kinds of risk.

5.3   THE IMPORTANCE OF BACKGROUND TO CONTEXT

As stated earlier, while data is relatively empirical in nature, context plays a much more significant role when looking at the transitioning process from data to information, and provides a critical role when looking at the transitioning process from information to intelligence.

The transitioning process from data to information involves data being organized. How that organization will be structured will be based on the mission of the organization and how success is measured. A container facility that needs to move so many containers through its facility per hour will likely measure things in terms of either containers processed or time. For example, if the loss of an information technology system means that the processing of containers has to happen manually, the impact is likely to be assessed in terms of the reduced number of containers that can be processed with the same assurance that they are being moved appropriately. Similarly, an electric generating station that needs to generate so many volts of electricity may measure its impacts in terms of the amount of electricity it can generate while maintaining the assurance that it is generating clean electricity that can be pushed onto the electrical distribution grid. Medical facilities may measure impacts in terms of the rate and accuracy of diagnosing and treating patients effectively. The reason for this approach is simple—each organization is expected to contribute to the overall success of the organization, and senior management measures the performance of the organization in terms of its ability to meet goals that it sets.

Organizations can fall into a trap by attempting to keep information as empirically grounded as data. Consider the drawings of an airport. The engineering diagram is required to be empirically accurate, and as a result, it can simply be a collection of the various data elements (runway dimensions, taxiways, etc.). The filters being applied to the information simply focus on clearly relevant data. What if those requirements are less empirical in nature? This would pertain to situations where individuals are asked to apply judgment or where the scope of the information is less clear. For example, what if an individual was asked to provide a map of dirt roads and overlay the weather conditions over that map? At this point, the individual has the ability to interject his or her own judgment in terms of what is needed because the needs can be interpreted in different ways.

This is even more apparent when looking at the transition point between information and intelligence. Again, the filters being applied are those that sift through the credible and reliable information to find those bits that are relevant and timely. In this case, there is an additional layer of complexity. The individual is not only asked to consider the full range of available information, but also asked to assess the import of that data.

At this point, the knowledge, skills, abilities, and experience of the individual will factor significantly. These are the foundations upon which the individual will make the determination as to what is worthy of consideration (information) and how it is important (intelligence). An individual who has an engineering background will base these decisions off of different thinking than an individual that has a liberal arts background. The engineer may be much more precise and process driven but unable to grasp the less tangible issues that the individual with the liberal arts background can. Conversely, the individual with the liberal arts background may not possess the mathematical or similar analytic skills to be able to identify the connections between things that are not apparent on the surface. The result of these differences is that the data-information transition may not be equal at all times, and it is less likely that the information-intelligence transition will be equal.

When this is extended beyond the realm of intelligence, the organization's decision-making processes can be affected. Management bases its decisions on two major activities. The first involves risk management or the manipulation of conditions so that an organization's exposure to loss (a factor of probability and impact) is reduced to acceptable levels. For example, management may determine that it is not willing to accept a project incurring financial losses after a certain period of time. The second part of the process is the cost-benefit analysis that will look at the net return on investment associated with the various alternatives. This is where things can become difficult because the impacts against an organization can be assessed, but not necessarily measured. This may be the result of different persons assessing the scope of an impact differently (immediate losses vs. future earnings, for example) or the result of factors not having precise values (such as impacts on an organization's branding or credibility).

5.4   CONTEXT AFFECTING SENSITIVITY

It is impossible to assess sensitivity without understanding the context. The concept of sensitivity is directly linked to the impact that an organization accepts as arising should the asset fall outside of appropriate care and control. This impact, often referred to as an injury in the asset protection and security domain, is factored with the probability of such an occurrence arising to give an idea of the risk involved. This risk is the same risks that are prioritized and given to management for their consideration and, if warranted, decisions with respect to managing that risk.

As part of this calculation, the organization must remain aware of how the context is affecting the process that leads up to the prioritized list of risks. This may include the following:

- **Impact.** The context may result in an individual assigning a higher, lower, or appropriate value to the asset. Where assets are overvalued, the risks associated with it will naturally appear more significant and the organization may waste resources in responding. Where assets are undervalued, the risks may be understated and leave the organization exposed to unforeseen losses.
- **Probability.** The context may result in the probability of certain scenarios being overvalued, undervalued, or even discounted. Consider personnel with military or law enforcement backgrounds. These groups have been in direct contact with certain kinds of threats and significant amounts of information regarding those threats that are not readily available to the public at large. Because of this experience, the context in which the information and intelligence is presented is often different from that held by management—sometimes leading to conflict as management refuses to accept the probability of certain scenarios.
- **Vulnerabilities.** These are indicative of the lack of something or incomplete application of something that allows a threat to cause injury to an asset. These are heavily contextual in nature and frequently challenged. They are often identified by an individual based on his or her knowledge, skills, experience, or motivation. Similarly, the operational, environmental, financial, regulatory, and threat contexts may make certain vulnerabilities more relevant than others.
- **Thresholds.** Risk management is based on the risk being perceived as crossing certain thresholds. Often these thresholds are imprecise or range based on the personal tolerances of management. Where the context changes, such as new financial restraints or conditions, threats to operations, regulatory requirements, etc., management decisions regarding how to approach the risks may also change.

Context, however, is more than the physical environment. The legal, regulatory, environmental, operational, cultural, and threat environments also factor significantly. These all become part of the larger context that encapsulates management decisions. It is this combination of context and the characteristics of the individuals involved that come together to form the perception of risk.

The mechanics of this influence, touched upon above, can be described when looking at the roots of risk. Begin with the five major categories of sensitivity:

- **Confidentiality.** The need to restrict access to something so that it is only available to an identified, authorized, and appropriately trusted community.
- **Integrity.** The ability to ensure that something has not been added to, changed, or deleted from without appropriate checks and balances being met and only using trusted processes.
- **Availability.** The ability to rely upon something to be available for use upon demand and to have it function as intended.
- **Relative value.** In terms of the dollar value or equivalent of something.
- **Social value.** The importance of the asset to the community or population.

What needs to be clear is that the value of an asset is often stood on its head as a means of rapidly assessing the impact associated with some kind of threat. While this does offer a method for assessing the impact, it often fails to accurately describe the overall impact of something. Consider the electronic control chip for modern vehicles. Such a chip may only cost a hundred dollars or so to produce and may only be marked up slightly due to the volume of sales, but the loss of the chip has two major contexts. The first is the lost revenue to those that manufacture the chip and sell it to the automaker. The second, and less apparent, involves the loss of production and delay in sales that results when an inexpensive but critical component in the vehicle is missing.

It should be clear that the concept of perspective and context are intertwined. Individuals have perspectives that are formed through their education, training, experience, and motivation. This perspective forms the basis of how they interpret the data, organize it into information, and build the context around them. That perspective and context drive how we assess the value of assets, and this in turn feeds into the risk management and enterprise management decision-making processes.

5.5 ENTER THE CLOUD

So how does one break free of this trap? There are two possible solutions. The first involves building a system that attempts to take as much of an individual's prejudices or perspectives out of the equation. This approach is difficult in that it is nearly impossible to validate and it is nearly impossible to apply consistently. The second is to use a number of perspectives and a Delphi kind of approach to look at the perspectives, contexts, and ultimately, risks to the organization.

This is where the concept of cloud computing comes into play. There are really three elements to the cloud that come into consideration. The first is that data is held in such a way that it is accessible across a broader community. In its purest form, cloud data would be accessible to everyone, but this is, quite frankly, not realistic.

The second is that the computing power, the analysis of the data, and its organization would actually be subjected to a number of intermediary processes on the way to being transformed or translated into information. The third element is that the information, produced in a cloud format, would likely be more accessible and, as a secondary element to this, also likely available in its interim form and not simply in its final form. Each of these needs to be understood, including the potential impacts associated with misuse or even hostile use, before an organization decides to move its data into a cloud format.

The first element is the result of a gradual shift in terms of how data, information, and intelligence are handled by organizations. While intelligence, particularly in its most sensitive forms, is still guarded closely, the raw data and information have been the subject of a gradual loosening of controls. Consider the period around Y2K—organizations largely held their data, information, and intelligence on proprietary systems. Those proprietary systems needed to be maintained and protected at the cost of the company—sometimes an expensive endeavor. Gradually, organizations sought to realize efficiencies by outsourcing, first, parts of the ability to hold data and information. Off-site storage centers and data repositories, particularly for use as backup sites, became more prevalent. This in turn led to organizations seeking to make arrangements with third parties that could handle certain parts of the processing of data and management of information. Finally, we now see network-based organizations using third-party suppliers entirely for their data holding and information management requirements. This transition has significant impacts when looking at the overall ability of an organization to protect and ensure the services it delivers.

This migration has forced organizations to adapt how they look at controlling their data, information, and intelligence holdings. In the more traditional models where organizations controlled the personnel, assets, facilities, information, and supporting infrastructure, the focus was ensuring that the organization applied the necessary administrative, physical, procedural, and technical security controls. As certain parts of this processing and storage capability were moved to known third parties, the only significant element that changed was the span of control that the organization exercised when planning, designing, implementing, monitoring, and adjusting these controls. As a result, outside networks needed to be certified against certain criteria, and a risk management decision was made through the accreditation process.

5.6 THE CLOUD AS AN AMPLIFIER

The integration of the cloud into the computing base (note that this is not necessarily the trusted computing base) will simply be an amplification of this principle. The main challenge for executives and managers with responsible charge positions will be to maintain their focus on their own mission and determine to what extent the cloud's capabilities can be exploited. This includes asking the following questions:

- Has the organization appropriately identified the sensitivity of its data, information, and intelligence from *both* an operational point of view and the means and opportunity it can provide a competitive or hostile entity?

- Has the organization appropriately identified the requirements that must be met to appropriately manage the risks associated with the confidentiality, integrity, availability, relative value, and social value of the data, information. and intelligence?
- Has the organization designed and implemented a strategy that will allow the organization to ensure that these requirements are met and maintained? As a second part of this, has the organization also implemented a strategy that ensures that, once in place, they remain in place?
- Has the organization put in place the necessary administrative, physical, procedural, and technical controls so that it can monitor the location, condition, and access to its data, information, and activity? Can it exert the necessary influence to control the same?
- Finally, has the organization designed and implemented the necessary administrative, physical, technical, and procedural controls so that it can recover its data, information, or intelligence at the same level of confidence or trust?

This reflects the perspective that organizations may seek to exploit the capabilities offered by the cloud, but prudent managers, often linked to accountability, will look at the cloud as a tool that serves the organization as it attempts to accomplish its goals and achieve its objectives.

Perhaps the greatest challenge for those seeking to protect and assure critical services will be to identify, achieve, and maintain an appropriate balance when looking at exploiting the opportunities offered by cloud computing. This will rely heavily on those that can assess the sensitivity of data, information, and intelligence to the organization, and the opportunities that the same data, information, and intelligence would offer competitive or even hostile entities. It will also involve a significant effort to manage the expectation of clients and users who will have been inundated with communications extolling the latest and greatest capabilities associated with cloud computing.

5.7 CLOUDS AND CONCEALED CONDUITS

In this context, identifying the cloud as a concealed conduit may be of some value to the protection or assurance practitioner. This concealed conduit does not necessarily mean that the cloud penetrates the access control measures around the known network. It can also latch onto points where data, information, or intelligence is passed outside of the trusted network infrastructure.

For the protection and assurance practitioner, some of the questions that should come to mind are the following:

- Does the organization share infrastructure with competitive or hostile parties? Is the infrastructure kept separate?
- Does the cloud, when establishing the resources necessary to store or process data or information, establish a partition that can be protected against outside interference, intrusion, or monitoring?

- Does the cloud, when communicating data, information, or intelligence, maintain an appropriate level of protection so that only trusted parties receive or have other access to it?
- Does the cloud create duplicates or copies of data, information, or intelligence, and are these protected to the same extent?
- Does the management of the cloud's storage, processing, or communications routines or processes ensure that only those persons identified by the client as meeting certain criteria have access?

What we are essentially discussing here is the trusted computing base (TCB). This can be described in terms of that infrastructure under control where the hardware, software, and firmware involved operate at a level where management does not face any significant risks associated with losses of confidentiality, integrity, or availability of data or services.

Dealing with cloud-based issues, when put in this context, is a fairly simple exercise contextually but may pose some challenges in terms of implementation. Integration of the cloud simply involves expanding the trusted computing base in terms of processing and storage. In mature systems where there is an implemented certification/accreditation regime in place, this is a simple matter of activating the appropriate change control protocols. At this point, the issue becomes complex and offers the opportunity to open up concealed channels.

The first issue involves identifying the scope of infrastructure that may be involved. This can be divided into a series of questions:

- Where can data be sent or stored as part of the processes directly involved in the computing or storage processes? For example, what servers and lines of communication are identified as being able to handle the data?
- Where can data be sent or stored as part of the processes that are indirectly involved in the computing or storage process or, in other terms, may be involved in supporting the overall operations of that infrastructure? For example, does the infrastructure involve backup routines or systems that will copy the data and hold it in other locations?

The second involves being able to trust what we know about that infrastructure. In the information technology realm, this generally involves the concept of certification and accreditation. Certification involves an expert determining the level of compliance, or adherence, with specific standards. Accreditation involves management looking at the level of adherence to those standards, determining specific steps needed to manage any unacceptable levels of risk, and then commissioning the network to operate within certain constraints.

This leads to two kinds of concealed conduit. While both involve the actual conduit being present, the difference comes from whether or not the accrediting body detects those concealed conduits. In cases where there is an appropriately conducted threat and risk assessment, inspection, and other forms of checks, the conduit may be fairly apparent to the accrediting body. That is because of the work that was done to identify it and communicate it. The second comes from situations where the conduit is there, but remains undetected for some reason. This could be the result of a number of factors, including the following:

- Failing to identify the appropriate criteria to be met
- Failing to use appropriately capable persons (expertise)
- Failing to conduct the full assessment
- Over-relying on end documentation (such as certificates)
- Refusing to accept what is presented in the technical reports

The overreliance on certification documentation has a number of elements to it. The education industry has often been challenged by the following:

- Programs that are not accredited but hold themselves out to be
- Institutions that hold themselves out to be competent and capable but that operate without oversight
- Simple business enterprises that will sell an official-looking certificate that can be used to fraudulently bypass hiring or similar controls

We also see this practice entering into other certification regimes. This also comes in various forms—ranging from unethical practitioners to disreputable business enterprises.

It is this latter element that poses the most significant risk to those looking at the issue of cloud computing. This is because the organization may well take steps to mitigate the risks associated with certain detected and assessed vulnerabilities, but it may well fail to act if those vulnerabilities are not identified. This failure to act means that the overall process has not delivered the value that it should have, and also leaves the organization, and potentially the overall system, vulnerable.

5.8 LINKING THE TRUSTED COMPUTING BASE AND USER COMMUNITIES

When looking at information sharing, one has to look at who is sharing the information, what is the information being shared on, and is it appropriate to be sharing the information. These three elements are the core of any effective information sharing structure—ranging from conference calls to multi-million-dollar fusion centers.

Having looked at what the information is being shared on, we need to return to the authorized user community. This community has three things in common:

- They are identified, and that identity is authenticated through trustworthy sources.
- They are authorized to have access to the assets involved, ranging from the TCB to the information held on it, after having undergone a formal authorization process.

- They are all bound to abide by certain conditions, generally set down as part of the certification and accreditation process.

This community represents more than simply the end users and managers of the TCB. It also includes a range of support services and other secondary roles that may have incidental access to the system or the data contained on it.

There are potential conflicts that need to be overcome when looking at information sharing and the TCB. The first involves the philosophy of how the authorized user community should be defined. The TCB sets these definitions in terms of the need to know—limiting access to those who have met the criteria defined above.

People, however, do not operate based on the need-to-know principle. They operate on the basis of what might be more appropriately termed the need to share. This does not mean that the user is compelled through some feature of character to give away secrets to all under the sun. It means that the user evaluates individuals on a case-by-case basis and ultimately makes a personal judgment call based on (1) personal trust and (2) the need to share the information in order to accomplish the goals.

This does not represent an attack on the concept of the need to know. That concept is still being preserved under the need-to-share regime. It does represent, however, two shifts in doctrine. The first is that it moves the need-to-share information back to the user/operations level and away from the administrative level. It also means that the need-to-know decision becomes decentralized, with the authority being taken by the user level and often justified through the argument that the sharing was vital in order to reach the objectives and maintain the goals of the organization.

This decentralization of the decision to share information, sometimes even outside of apparently normal practices, means that those overseeing the information sharing arrangements and the TCB must place significant emphasis on education, training, and oversight. This applies through the entire cycle that an individual may have access to the information and the TCB, including the following:

- Background screening as a mandatory part of selection
- Training
- Ongoing familiarization
- Active monitoring of the individual and use of the network

Having selected the individual and before granting access, the individual must be made aware of the various restrictions that operate within the system. This is a basic principle linked to the concept of natural justice—before enforcing something there must be a reasonable expectation that the restriction is well known and understood. This also applies to the consequences associated with violating the consequences. This requirement is often overlooked or bypassed in large or distributed organizations, leaving the organization vulnerable in terms of a lack of ability to enforce its own requirements with those with access.

Meeting this requirement in the need-to-share environment requires more than simply having signed statements on file. As the user has additional responsibilities in terms of the decision to share information or allow access, he or she must also be well educated and competent in making decisions that remain in line with management's intent. It also requires the user to have the confidence necessary to make the appropriate decision to share or not to share. A significant part of this is understanding that the management involved applies rules consistently and fairly on one hand, but on the other hand does make decisions and exercise judgment when individuals can be clearly shown to be operating in a way that takes appropriate precautions and meets management's intent.

Corporate culture and how it accepts or rejects the risk environment will also factor heavily in this. Where an organization's corporate culture is well aware of the threats, vulnerabilities, risks, and consequences, it is much more likely to ensure that various restrictions stay in force and will limit its decisions to those that align with both the intent of the restrictions and operational needs. An organizational culture that does not accept these will not abide by the restrictions except in circumstances where it believes that individuals will be detected and punished. While this may be adequate in the eyes of some management, it is a weak posture.

From the perspective of information sharing, this means that a balance exists with respect to access within the user community and TCB and the privileges that can be exercised as part of the need to share.

This balancing point will be weighted as a result of a number of decisions with respect to how risk is managed. These decisions and requirements will be the result of requirements including, but not necessarily limited to, the following:

- Laws, regulations, and similar measures that generally cannot be risk managed except by the most senior levels of government with the support of the courts
- Overarching policies that are the result of parent organizations making risk management decisions
- Restrictions that are the result of information sharing or asset sharing agreements
- Internal decisions that are the result of management's decision to manage risks in a certain way

It is important to note that the principles of risk management are an important element in the need-to-share principles. One of these principles is that it is only the owner of the risk management decision that has the authority to make decisions that run contrary to his or her previous direction. This is that individual who bears the accountability associated with the appropriate protection or use of the assets involved and, as a result, holds delegated authority from the more senior layers of management—usually the highest levels. Those that decide to manage risks differently for their own purposes without first seeking the consent of that delegated officer or individual run a significant risk of running afoul in their decision making.

Ultimately the requirements and constraints placed on individuals must be clearly communicated. This is once again accomplished through the inform-and-acknowledgment process. The individual is informed of the sum total of the requirements, the relevant consequences, and the method of clarifying issues. The individual then acknowledges that he or she has been informed, assents to being subjected to the sanctions that may arise from breaking them, and acknowledges the process by signature or some other attestable means.

5.9   BARRIERS TO INFORMATION SHARING

The key barriers to information sharing come from a lack of trust and teamwork between the government, industry, and academic parties. The level of trust will vary from interaction to interaction, but the lack of trust between institutions is clearly evident.

From the government perspective, the reasons the private sector refuses to share information can be reduced to the following:

- The desire to conceal information that may lead to the government detecting shortfalls in regulatory compliance
- A lack of trust that assurances given by the officers in one part of government will be adhered to by officers in another part of government
- A lack of confidence that information provided in confidence will be maintained in confidence due to public disclosure rules

From the private sector perspective, concerns surrounding the sharing of information rotate around a number of core issues. These include the following:

- That information shared in consultative processes may be used by the government as part of a regulatory enforcement action
- That information shared in a consultative process can make it to the hands of the competition, causing loss of market position
- That information shared in consultative processes can end up in the hands of the public and lead to a loss of public confidence or brand credibility

The academic community has been proposed as one potential alternative to break this stalemate. The academic community is seen as being free of vested interest and can be trusted, when appropriately directed, to remain free and clear of competitive issues. One significant concern, however, is that the academic community is also subject to a number of laws requiring the disclosure of information, and this could again expose the information.

If looking to build communities that allow for the sharing of information, a change in many of these attitudes will be required. Government regulators, often overly concerned with practices to ensure absolutely equal fairness, will need to understand that such practices may need to be adjusted somewhat if the private sector is going to expose itself to additional risks. Similarly, all parties will need to understand that any information revealed during these processes must be protected against disclosure, even if under the authority of exceptions to existing disclosure information or under the authority of new legislation.

The final barrier to information sharing lies with organizations that seek to advance their position by having access to data, information, or intelligence that others do not. Administrative processes, including security clearances, will need to be adjusted to allow for regional (provincial, state, territorial) and municipal governments' participation. Many of these barriers are in need of adjustment to reflect new operational and CIP/CIA realities. The focus, particularly in a world where joint operations and international teams are involved, must be on the ability to share data, information, and intelligence in such a way that the overall parameters for mission success are achieved.

5.10 THE RISE OF OPEN SOURCES

Open-source data and information comes from the computer industry's use of open-source software or software where the code is freely available. Organizations are now placing more and more information into the public domain, often as a tool to attract business or to demonstrate their own capabilities. Researchers access this data and information to perform research that would have been impossible in the past.

The vulnerability associated with open sources comes from the potential for researchers to fail to apply quality controls or checks to the data. While governments and academic institutions have often limited the overall access to information, treating it as a marketable commodity, they have done so with an understanding that such data was only published after undergoing stringent checks ensuring its reliability and credibility.

The risks associated with open sources, as a result, involve a loss of credibility of the research at one level or, at a more fundamental level, a loss of accuracy or completeness. It should be clear, however, that these risks can be mitigated and addressed through the formation of networks of private researchers. Several organizations, ranging from formal associations (ASIS International and the International Association of Maritime Security Professionals, to name a few) to less formal networks (SCADASEC and similar research lists), form networks of persons who can comment on the validity and context of the data and information while the data is on its transformative process to information and ultimately intelligence.

5.11 OPEN-SOURCE INFORMATION AND INTELLIGENCE

What researchers need to be cognizant of is the difference between open-source information and open-source intelligence. The difference between the two parallels closely the difference between information and intelligence. Open-source information is intended to provide facts, but not to explain the importance of such facts. Intelligence, on the other hand, is data and information that have undergone that formal process of collection, collation, analysis, and dissemination.

As with data and information, there is a need for the researcher to be cautious. There are several companies that indicate that they produce intelligence, where in fact they are simply regurgitating open sources of information. These firms are often little more than media monitoring companies that can provide lists of commentary. The second challenge is that those companies that do produce intelligence need to be understood in the context of what they deliver as business lines. In short, as with other information, the context in which it organized the data needs to be understood.

That being said, there is a notable increase in the number of organizations that sell or trade in what can be described as open-source intelligence. These involve organizations gathering together publicly available information and, with the assistance of specially trained or skilled individuals, working that information through the analysis process to become intelligence. Some of this intelligence is placed into the public domain in order to demonstrate the capability of the organization, while the rest is held on to in order to develop clients. These organizations may be less susceptible to certain kinds of contextual pressures, but still need to be understood in terms of their business contexts, including relationships with other clients or service providers.

A significant number of these groups have risen because of the need for credible intelligence in the private sector and, as noted above, the inability of the private sector to work through various information sharing requirements in a timely manner.

5.12   AN APPROACH TO INFORMATION SHARING—THE CONSEQUENCE-BENEFIT RATIO

As these organizations arise, there is an opportunity to change the model. At the grassroots level, open sources of information and intelligence can be supplemented by the more proprietary sources. The emphasis, however, would shift from those proprietary sources to publicly available sources that can be reviewed and quality controlled.

This open-source information can be brought together through various different forms of technology. For information that has no significant value in terms of compromise and sensitivity, the Internet and other wide broadcast tools may be appropriate. As information becomes progressively more sensitive, the shift may be toward the more traditional restrictions.

Ultimately, however, to break out of the current deadlock, the government needs to look at information sharing in terms of cost and benefit. Where the consequences can be mitigated and limited to areas that do not overly affect the safety, security, and economic well-being of citizens, the benefits in terms of contributing to operational success can be weighed. If there is sufficient imbalance in favor of operational success, then the information is shared within the trusted community or, as a second tier, the community that is working toward the common interest.

6 Emergency Preparedness and Readiness

6.1 INTRODUCTION

This chapter discusses some of the challenges associated with the structured methodologies that are used to respond to acts of terrorism, major crime, food safety events, or natural disasters.

6.2 THE RISE OF CORE OFFICES

Over the past years, we have seen a number of restructurings take place with respect to how nations prepare for certain kinds of major incidents, calamities, or natural disasters. One of these restructurings has resulted in the formation of umbrella departments, such as Public Safety Canada and the Department of Homeland Security. These organizations tend to coordinate and oversee a number of specific efforts that are intended to mitigate, prepare for, respond to, or recover from major events.

In Canada, Public Safety Canada oversees activities that include emergency management, national security, crime prevention, law enforcement, and corrections.[*] Within the realm of emergency management, the department openly indicates that it develops national policy, response systems, and standards on top of operating the Government Operations Center, issuing alerts and similar activities associated with Canada's critical infrastructure.

Within Canada, the core documentation is the Emergency Management Framework. This framework establishes the core framework, principles, governance mechanisms, coordinating instruments, and next steps.[†] Within this framework, the Federal Emergency Response Plan defines a number of roles and responsibilities of federal entities and sets down the strategic directives that range from the saving of lives to the maintenance of public confidence.[‡] What should be clear in this structure is that the national umbrella organization in Canada has a role that oversees both the activities of federal entities and the relationship between the federal and territorial entities as they are brought together under the National Emergency Response System.

Within the United States, the Department of Homeland Security plays a similar role. Perhaps the greatest notable difference between the two organizations is that in Canada, the Royal Canadian Mounted Police (Canada's national police body) and the Canadian Security Intelligence Service (Canada's national intelligence body) are integrated into the overall Public Safety Canada entity, while in the United States,

---

[*] http://www.publicsafety.gc.ca/index-eng.aspx.

[†] http://www.publicsafety.gc.ca/prg/em/emfrmwrk-2011-eng.aspx.

[‡] http://www.publicsafety.gc.ca/prg/em/ferp-eng.aspx#a18.

the Federal Bureau of Investigation and the Central Intelligence Agency actually remain outside of the Department of Homeland Security.

While these organizations play important roles in terms of ensuring that the appropriate organization, framework, structures, and mechanisms are in place, the importance of the first responder cannot be overlooked.

6.3 FIRST RESPONDER

It is as important to have an effective response as it is to have coherent frameworks and policies. On one hand, the frameworks and other more strategic efforts are what allow for the effective management and administration of the efforts to mitigate, prepare for, respond to, and recover from events. On the other hand, the education, training, abilities, and commitment of those on the ground must align with the challenges confronting them, but also be able to act as the knowledgeable eyes and ears for various levels of risk management. First responders must be able to function both vertically across various layers of government within their craft and horizontally so as to ensure that the response to incidents is handled as gracefully and effectively as possible.

The term *first responder* refers to those individuals who in the early stages of an incident are responsible for the protection and preservation of life, property, evidence, and the environment. This definition includes emergency response providers as defined within Section 2 of the Homeland Security Act of 2002 (6 U.S.C. 101), as well as emergency management, public health, clinical care, public works, and other skilled support personnel (e.g., equipment operators) who provide immediate support services during prevention, response, and recovery operations.[5]

In Canada, the term *first responder* refers to "a trained and officially mandated responder involved in a response to chemical, biological, radiological, nuclear or explosive event."[5a] The general definitions also include the concept of the *first receiver*, which is defined in terms of healthcare workers who assist the victims of CBRNE events (including events involving contagions) after exposure but prior to hospitalization.

Regardless of the difference in how the umbrella organization defines first receivers/first responders, those responding to various forms of events face unique and difficult challenges that require coordination and cooperation among the various levels of government, or even international entities.

6.4 FIRST RESPONDER CLASSIFICATIONS

At the time of drafting of the second edition of this work, the various classifications of first responder were growing into a rather long and comprehensive list. Depending on the nature of the incident and a given emergency situation, environment, or hazardous condition, the following groups were first seen as being reasonably indicative of the functions required by communities:

Law enforcement
Fire services

Emergency medical or ambulatory services
Emergency management including emergency preparedness
HAZMAT and containment
Public works

This list was quickly expanded to include a range of private organizations and entities that could bring special knowledge, skills, abilities, or resources to the event. Given that the list of potential incidents itself was very broad, the list of potential first responders also grew significantly, and to the point where one might argue that it would be easier to identify who was *not* a first responder to some kind of event rather than who was.

It became apparent that there needed to be some understanding that the list of responders could be flexible. This was already understood within the concept of the incident command system that saw personnel moved into and out of the command structure as needed. What also became apparent was that the incident commander was better defined in terms of being the first person on the scene and responsible for setting in place the conditions that would facilitate the arrival of follow-on responders than for necessarily solving the issue at hand.

Even as this concept of flexibility was becoming better understood, the concept of interoperability was becoming more important. While the importance of compatible and interoperable communications equipment was given particular attention following 9/11, this gradually expanded to a more holistic view of interoperability that took into account common standards, cross-training in policies and procedures, joint exercises, and a range of other activities. While the utopic end state of completely interoperable systems and organizations is still in the future, significant progress has been made in this regard. As a result, the administrative definition of *first responder* has become blurred through an increase in community involvement and cross-training.

6.5 GUIDELINE CLASSIFICATIONS

The role of the guideline is to provide the first responder community and interested stakeholders with varying degrees of information, developed by competent organizations that would assist them in maintaining the expected level of capability and interoperability. While the first responder community is generally primarily interested in their own guidelines, the guidelines are often shared between organizations that work together or train together so as to promote the interoperability of the organizations.

Guidelines are broken down into three definitive areas:

1. Awareness-level guidelines
2. Performance-level guidelines
3. Planning- and management-level guidelines

While these guidelines were originally intended for first responders and provided a level of knowledge that was more commensurate with advanced knowledge, skills, abilities, and resources, certain guidelines soon spread into the public domain.

6.6 EXAMPLE: *NORTH AMERICAN EMERGENCY RESPONSE GUIDEBOOK*

The *Emergency Response Guidebook* (ERG) was developed jointly by the U.S. Department of Transportation (DOT), Transport Canada (specifically CANUTEC), and the Secretariat of Communications and Transportation of Mexico for use by firefighters, police, and other emergency service personnel who may be the first to arrive at the scene of a transportation incident involving a HAZMAT.[6]

The aim of this guideline was the following:

  Assisting in identifying potentially hazardous materials quickly
  Assisting in identifying the appropriate steps to be taken to protect persons, property, and operations

Since the drafting of the second edition, the various national entities in Canada, the United States, and Mexico have made progress with respect to improving the online system. This has included a much improved online portal that can be accessed at http://wwwapps.tc.gc.ca/saf-sec-sur/3/erg-gmu/erg/ergmenu.aspx. While the updates for the work may be processed every three to four years, the online version allows for a level of confidence that up-to-date information is being accessed.

6.7 AWARENESS-LEVEL GUIDELINES

The awareness-level guidelines address training and awareness material for personnel who are likely to come across situations that pose a risk to the safety, security, or economic well-being of those in the area. Within this context, the priority of work is often to take steps appropriate to preserve life, identify the nature of the event, communicate the need for assistance, take immediate steps for containment, and facilitate the arrival of those who are in a position to best respond.

While the previous guidelines focused on various forms of HAZMAT incidents, there is a need to broaden the six traditional areas to include a range of evolving issues. These include the following:

* Recognize incidents
* Know the protocols
* Know the measures for self-protection
* Know procedures for protecting potential incident scenes
* Know and follow the on-scene and security protocols
* Possess and know how to properly use equipment to contact dispatcher or high authorities to report information collected at the scene and to request additional assistance or emergency response personnel

While these six topics originally focused on the HAZMAT issues, they can be expanded to include a range of evolving threats, including the following:

* Disease (particularly in the transportation sector)

- Invasive species (damaging agriculture, water supply, etc.)
- Counterfeit goods (particularly in the high-tech sectors)
- Climate change-related issues (drainage and drought)
- Cyber-related and telecommunications (in terms of converged technology)

There is some discussion about whether this level of training would be beneficial to the community at large. Although first responders are generally the first official response on the scene, it is often the victims of the event who have first contact with it. The authors propose that there is a benefit to ensuring that members of the community are encouraged to undertake similar levels of training or that publicly suitable awareness programs or packages be made available to its citizens free of charge.

6.7.1 Recognize Incidents

For each of the topics above, there is a significant need to be able to recognize incidents. Recognition of incidents is critical to being able to identify, categorize, and initiate the response to conditions discovered on the ground. The following areas are important when looking at the recognition of incidents:

- Understanding what the various threats are, what vulnerabilities they can exploit, and what risks they are associated with
- Being able to identify if any of those threats are present at the scene
- Being able to use the appropriate guides and other reference materials
- Understanding the potential outcomes or consequences for an emergency when one or more of the threats are discovered

If the goal is to be able to detect, identify, and categorize something quickly, then the individual should not have to rely on reference material to identify common threats, vulnerabilities, and risks. Similarly, he or she should not have to use reference materials to identify the key sources of information.

6.7.2 Basic Protocols

When looking at the response to any incident, there are those steps that must be almost automatic and those steps that are taken as a result of the situation on the ground. These are generally defined in protocols that first responders use when arriving on the scene and in order to prepare to conduct work at the scene. First responders should be very familiar with the following protocols:

- Being able to clearly identify the core risks and consequences associated with the conditions on the ground
- Preparing for movement to the site (who, what, where, when, how, and why to move)
- Movement to the site (how to move, when to stop, etc.)
- Identifying the safe areas from which to work

- Communications with subordinate, parallel, and superior organizations and, by extension, the limits on communicating with the press or people other than those responding to the incident
- Immediate steps to be taken in terms of the protection of persons and the protection of the public (including situations in which individuals are contaminated and the risk of further contamination is not acceptable)

The need for this level of familiarization with protocols cannot be overstated. The first responder must not only be comfortable with his or her own ability to follow these protocols through, but must also appear to be in control of the situation and comfortable with the steps that are being taken. Should the first responder exhibit signs of stress, discomfort, or discontent with the actions on the ground, there is a risk that those sentiments will raise concerns in those around them—including the victims of the incident.

6.7.3   KNOW SELF-PROTECTION MEASURES

As the first responder is arriving on the scene, he or she must be aware of potential threats in the environment and be taking appropriate precautions, including the use of personal protective equipment (PPE). This may be full-body biological suits, various forms of breathing apparatus, or even weapons. The protective equipment will largely depend upon the nature of the situation and the nature of the first responder in terms of what equipment makes up the basic load for each person.

There is a balance that must be established. The first responder acts as a trained set of eyes and ears on the ground while also acting as a symbol of the response to the population. As a result, the first responder must be able to strike a balance in terms of self-protection that preserves his or her ability to meet mission objectives while also communicating, through his or her actions, in such a way that the population affected gains a sense of comfort or confidence in the overall response. Ultimately, however, the first responder must keep the mission first and understand that the mission is intended to save the greatest number of persons and greatest extent of property possible.

In looking at the needs associated with self-protection, the following factor significantly:

- Understand the hazards (safety) and risks (security) to human life, property, and operations.
- Recognize the signs, symptoms, indicators, and warnings associated with those hazards and risks as they begin to appear on persons and equipment.
- Know what PPE is needed for one's own protection and what may be needed to support anticipated casualties.
- Know the limitations associated with that equipment.
- Know how to procure, receive, configure, use, maintain, store, and dispose of such equipment (including potentially contaminated equipment).
- Know the procedures that are to be followed with respect to inclusion, separation, or isolation of casualties or potentially affected persons (including safe distances and rates of exposure).

The other aspect of self-protection is often overlooked. This is the mental and psychological preparation that must be made, often years in advance, in order to remain effective during and after the incident. The first responder must be prepared, depending on the nature of the incident, to be exposed to images that include human casualties, animal deaths, destruction, or damage of cherished points. It is becoming more accepted that first responders can be subjected to operational stress injuries from their exposure to these kinds of situations in the field, and the first responder organization should establish programs that provide tangible support intended to prevent this issue or respond effectively to it.

6.7.4 KNOW PROCEDURES FOR PROTECTING INCIDENT SCENES

The three different aspects regarding the protection of incident scenes are:

- Protecting the scene from outside influences that may seek to enter the scene for malicious or inappropriate purposes
- Protecting the scene from inside influences that may seek to cause further damage
- Protecting the scene in terms of being able to gather the data and information necessary to form a credible intelligence picture and understanding of the event for use in the intelligence cycle or the courts

One aspect of this involves inter-entity cooperation. For example, within the transportation sector, much of the infrastructure is protected under a range of several security regimes. Infrastructure used for that purpose can become invaluable—particularly in terms of closed-circuit video equipment recordings, access control logs, and similar documentation. The challenge here is to ensure that the necessary lines of communication between entities have been established such that administrative controls on information have been resolved before the event, and do not become another challenge during the initial response.

6.7.5 KNOW SCENE SECURITY AND CONTROL PROCEDURES

The goals for scene security and control procedures are defined above. Ultimately, the goal is to be able to protect persons, property, and critical operations while preserving enough data and information so as to be able to form a clear picture of the incident. This clear picture is necessary if the organization wants to learn from the event and make any adjustments to its own measures.

For the first responder, this means that he or she must be able to perform any of the following:

- Understand the department or agency site security and scene control procedures for awareness-level trained personnel.
- Follow those procedures outlined for ensuring scene security and for keeping unauthorized individuals or personnel away from the incident scene

or adjacent hazardous areas; this includes cordoning off any such areas to prevent anyone from inadvertently entering the incident scene.

- Maintain incident scene security and control until a higher authority arrives at the incident scene.
- Be familiar with the department or agency incident command procedures.
- Protect any physical evidence, such as footprints, any relevant containers, papers, etc.
- Know the department or agency procedures for isolating individuals from danger areas.
- Know how to deal with contaminated individuals until a higher authority arrives at the incident scene.
- Recognize that the incident or event scene may be deemed a criminal scene, and that evidence must be protected and left undisturbed until a higher authority arrives at the incident scene to take control.

6.7.6 KNOW HOW TO USE EQUIPMENT PROPERLY

Knowing how to use the equipment properly consists of a number of sub-elements, including:

- Knowing when the equipment is to be used
- Knowing the limitations of the equipment
- Being skilled in the operation of the equipment
- Being skilled in the basic maintenance and troubleshooting of the equipment

Those coordinating this set of activities should be aware that this is not something that can be accomplished hastily. It requires adequate preparation time beforehand, since the first responder is likely to be operating the equipment in less than optimal conditions.

Education and training can take a number of forms. These include the following:

- Basic training in the operation of the equipment (under normal conditions)
- Advanced training in the operation of the equipment (austere or difficult conditions)
- Basic maintenance in support of operations in the field
- Refresher training to keep skills up to date and practiced

As an expansion of the knowledge of equipment identified in the previous edition, the following ought to be considered:

- Knowledge of how to use communications equipment (two-way radio, cellular phone, satellite phone, Voice over Internet Protocol (VOIP) or similar systems, Web mail, email, and proprietary texting/Short Message Service (SMS) systems).
- Knowledge of how to request additional personnel, equipment, space, information, or support/assistance that will assist in dealing with managing the

incident, managing casualties, controlling the environment, or communicating with outside/external organizations.

- Knowledge of how to accurately describe the threat discovered in the environment using appropriate terminology and to a level of detail where second-line or supporting responders/receivers can assist. This also includes being able to identify the appropriate response entities and capabilities within the affected jurisdiction.
- Knowledge of when and how to request additional assistance, escalate requests for support, and the levels of delegation or authority associated with the command structure.
- Knowledge of the department, agency, or other entity emergency plans and procedures for all roles that they are assigned to, the role of their supervisor, the role of their subordinates, and how to establish an incident command structure.
- Knowledge of how to notify the communications center and how to establish communications with alternate communications centers so as to be able to report information regarding actions taken, hazards assessed, or potential emerging issues of concern.

6.8   PERFORMANCE-LEVEL GUIDELINES

This level is divided into two sections, each with a separate set of training guidelines. The training guidelines for the respondent at the performance level target personnel who will likely respond to the scene of the incident, most likely involving dangerous organisms or chemicals. Responding personnel, if properly trained and equipped, will conduct on-scene operations within a non-safety area that has been set up on the scene, to control and close out the incident. It is expected that those personnel trained for Level A performance levels will work within both non-safety and safety areas, supporting personnel who are working in a non-safety work area. Personnel trained for Level B performance levels will work within non-safety areas, and in other areas set up on the incident scene or event as needed.

6.9   OPERATIONAL LEVELS DEFINED

Level A is the *operations level*; Level B is the *technician level*. Sections 6.10.1 through 6.10.3 refer to Level A; Sections 6.11.1 through 6.11.8 refer to Level B; both levels are specific to the performance level, as outlined. Portions of these procedures may have sections or parts of their sections added or removed; this was necessary to generalize the overall procedural efforts of on-scene crisis management.

This structure may vary depending on the various organizations. What is being communicated is that there are two clearly distinct categories associated with the operational level.

6.10   LEVEL A: OPERATIONS LEVEL

6.10.1   Have Successfully Completed Awareness-Level Training

This training for responders involves possible handling of dangerous organisms, chemicals, and other materials in addition to other specialized training. It includes the following:

- Complete training (or have equivalent training and experience) in and understanding of the guidelines at the awareness level for the function specific to the respondent.
- Understand terminology, classes of materials and agents, toxicology of HAZMAT, weapons of mass destruction (WMD) agents, or materials, classification or other categorization of dangerous organisms, and anything not previously mentioned that would be considered hazardous to human life or property.
- Be aware of any potential targets for possible attack by any individual(s) having or using any WMD agents or materials.
- Know the preplans to be used within the department or agency emergency response plan for those locations listed (i.e., know what to expect and do for a chemical storage facility, fuel depot, etc., in case of an emergency).
- Know how to collect and forward any intelligence gathered regarding potential terrorist or criminal activity or actions involving possible WMD agents or materials.
- Be capable of coordinating and gathering any relevant intelligence from any sources, organizations, etc., that may be found at the incident scene or event.
- Demonstrate skills and knowledge in the preparation of any hazard or risk analysis of a potential WMD target within the local community or target area.
- Know how to assess the consequences for different threats, as well as collateral damage effects resulting from the implementation and enactment of those threats. This includes being able to make a hasty assessment of how the environment can lead to changes in consequences.
- Participate in joint training exercises or drills with other emergency response organizations, departments, or agencies, which are expected to participate as part of the response to potential WMD events within the target area.

6.10.2   Know ICS Awareness Procedures

In this step, within this level, it is essential for the responder to know the ICS and be able to follow the unified command system (UCS) procedures for integration and implementation methodologies of each system. In the following section, detailing some of the requirements to meet the above, note that all dangerous organisms, chemicals, etc., are intended to be covered (dangerous organisms should be considered as including invasive species):

- Know how systems integrate with each other and provide support for the incident as best as possible.

- Be familiar with the operations of both command systems' structures and methodologies, and be able to assist the UCS if/where needed.
- Know how to implement initial site management procedures following the department incident command system and emergency response plan. Such procedures include:
  - Establishing communications with dispatched communications or command center
  - Establishing control zones for the incident scene or event
  - Locating the command post
  - Forwarding any intelligence gathered that has been collected at the incident scene or event
- Be able to implement the ICS component of the department or agency emergency response plan for any given WMD situation or event involving dangerous organisms, etc.
- Be aware of any assets available from the department or agency, as well as from local departments or agencies that could provide assistance specific to a potential WMD situation or event.
- Know what procedures are required to be followed to get resources to the incident scene or event if/when as needed.
- Be familiar with any assets that could be made available from other emergency response organizations, local or otherwise.
- Understand and follow department or agency procedures for accessing other organizations' help specific to a potential WMD situation or event.
- Understand the purpose and function of the UCS.
- Know department or agency procedures for assisting in the implementation of UCS for incident scene or event management specific to a potential WMD situation or event.
- Be capable of assisting the critique and review of actions taken before, during, and after the complete response specific to a potential WMD situation or event.
- Assist with any documentation of lessons learned and activities from the critique or review as to how the lessons learned may be applied for future courses of action specific to a potential WMD situation or event.
- Understand the importance of and know how to terminate documentation specific to a potential WMD situation or event, to be conducted relating to, or specific to, the areas of activities while conducted before, during, and after the specific potential WMD situation or event.
- Know and follow department or agency guidelines specific to news media coverage.
- Know how to develop an incident action plan (IAP) specific to coordination activities with the on-scene incident command.
- Ensure that the IAP is consistent with the department/agency emergency response plan.

6.10.3 Know Self-Protection and Rescue Measures

This includes following any self-protection measures and rescue and evacuation procedures for potential situations involving risks of exposure to dangerous organisms or chemicals. The following should be considered within any structure:

- Know how and when to use appropriate personnel protective equipment (PPE) issued by the department or agency and to work within a non-safety area that is on scene specific to a potential WMD situation or similar event involving a risk of exposure or contamination.
- Follow department or agency policies for use, inspection, and maintenance of PPE.
- Understand hazardous situations and risks associated with wearing protective garments or clothing or other protective clothing and equipment.
- Understand and follow rehabilitation methodologies to assist other responders to reduce any levels of heat-related stress, exhaustion, issues associated with psychological responses to confinement, or losses of mobility.
- Know precautionary measures necessary to protect responders who are on scene.
- Know how to determine the appropriate PPE for protecting officers who will be entering non-safety areas on scene specific to a potential WMD situation or event.
- Know the protective measures that are necessary to protect individuals, other responders, and other department or agency personnel who are on scene specific to a potential WMD situation or event.
- Know the department or agency and on-scene incident commanders' plan for evacuation of individuals within the non-safety areas specific to a potential WMD situation or event.
- Be capable of rescuing and moving individuals specific to a potential WMD situation to a safety area for triage and treatment by emergency medical respondents.
- Understand the roles of Level A performance-level responders, and the roles of other levels of respondents within the department or agency emergency response plan.
- Know how to implement appropriate decontamination procedures for individuals, respondents, mass casualties, and equipment within, around, and surrounding nonsafety areas.
- Understand the importance of proper decontamination of any reused equipment.
- Know and follow department or agency procedures or practices for handling and securing any suspicious packages, articles, or items.

What is often overlooked in systems such as this is the background efforts that are needed to establish, validate, maintain, review, and adjust the various documents, including plans, standards, procedures, guidelines, and training material. For managers involved in this domain, it should be noted that significant effort may be required to accomplish this.

6.11 LEVEL B: TECHNICIAN LEVEL

6.11.1 KNOW WMD PROCEDURES

This is necessary in following procedures for working at on-scene situations specific to potential WMD situations or events. The following should be incorporated into the overall structure:

- Know how to conduct any investigation and protect and collect evidence in conjunction with department or agency procedures for chain of custody, documentation, and any specific security measures necessary to store evidential information, articles, or items, whether or not contaminated, or however contaminated.
- Implement the department or agency emergency response plan on-scene security measures and procedures. Procedures should include:
  - Providing security for command post operation
  - Controlling or monitoring activity into or out of on-scene areas (both safety and especially non-safety areas) specific to a potential WMD situation or event
- Know how to implement appropriate on-scene decontamination procedures for protection of individuals, members of the public, emergency responders, or others who may have been contaminated on scene by agents or materials resulting specifically from the potential WMD situation or event.
- Know how to implement basic life-saving and supporting procedures for protection and treatment of individuals, members of the public, emergency responders, or others on scene specific to a potential WMD situation or event.
- Know how to implement procedures and measures for minimizing the spread of contamination of hazardous agents or materials to other locations, individuals, or equipment not previously contaminated, either within or surrounding non-safety areas resulting from the contamination.
- Be trained in recognizing any potential acts of terrorism.
- Be capable of identifying possible agents or materials that could be present at a WMD situation or event.
- Understand the roles and jurisdictions of any federal departments or agencies specific to a potential WMD situation or event.
- Be able to coordinate and assist in the overall investigative process specific to a potential WMD situation or event.
- Be aware of any applicable laws, as well as privacy and security-related issues specific to the potential WMD situation or event.

6.11.2 HAVE SUCCESSFULLY COMPLETED AWARENESS AND PERFORMANCE-LEVEL TRAINING

This involves possible HAZMAT handling for WMD and other specialized training.

- Complete training (or have equivalent training and experience) in and understanding of the guidelines at the awareness and performance levels for Level A training for the function specific to the respondent.
- Know the terminology associated with WMD agents, chemicals, dangerous organisms, and with any equipment, mechanical or otherwise, that would be used in conjunction with any tasks or assignments specific to the skill sets or knowledge base of the respondents.
- Have knowledge of, and ability to use, any specialty equipment used in conjunction with decontamination procedures, containment, or transportation for evidential purposes.
- Know how to conduct risk analysis and assessment for any HAZMAT or any WMD agents or materials for on-scene situations and for preplanned potential terrorist or criminal activities within any given area. This includes being able to conduct hasty assessment with respect to the level of contamination or exposure to dangerous organisms and the potential spread of that organism given current, flows, winds, and tides both in the environment and associated with infrastructure.
- Have experience in some emergency medical basic life support treatment and rescue of individuals and responders, triage and decontamination of individuals and equipment, and transportation capabilities of individuals exposed to WMD agents, dangerous organisms, or materials.
- Participate with emergency response organizations in joint training exercises or drills involving specified tasks, mock-up scenarios, or working with mock WMD agents, dangerous organisms, or materials.

6.11.3 Know Self-Protection, Rescue, and Evacuation Procedures

This includes following any self-protection measures and rescue and evacuation procedures for potential WMD situations or events. The following should be included in any structure:

- Knowledge of how to develop, maintain, and follow plans and procedures associated with the response to various kinds of events:
  - Know how to develop site safety and a control plan initiative that coordinates activities with the incident commander, if qualified. That is, personnel conducting such tasks must be trained and experienced in these areas of safety and risk mitigation; otherwise, inexperienced personnel may cause further safety issues or concerns to those who are on scene.
  - Assist however possible with the implementation of the IAP on scene, or if requested, develop an IAP per directive from the incident commander.
- Be able to recognize potential threats:
  - Be able to recognize types of WMD agents or materials.
  - Know how to use and read results from diagnostic and sampling equipment and instrumentation devices.

- Understand the limitations of the detection or diagnostic instrumentation devices that are provided by the department or agency.
- Knowledge of PPE and supporting equipment, including the equipment proper, maintenance tools, supporting equipment, and supplies:
  - Know how to select and use the PPE[8,9] needed to work safely within non-safety or near non-safety areas that are near or on scene specific to a potential WMD situation or event involving dangerous organisms, chemicals, or materials.
  - Understand the limitations of the PPE. Follow department or agency policies and guidelines on how to use, inspect, and maintain the PPE.
  - Understand the hazards and risks in using protective clothing.
  - Understand and implement rehabilitation measures to help responders reduce level of frustration or heat stress. Take any other necessary precautions to protect on-scene responders or other individuals that are on scene specific to a potential WMD situation or event.
- Knowledge of steps to be taken to protect persons and remove them (as best able and appropriate to the threat) from immediate harm:
  - Follow department or agency safety procedures and practices for retrieving, handling, transporting, and disposing of any unknown or suspicious package, article, device, or item.
  - Follow department or agency precautionary measures and safety practices to safeguard personnel against contamination as best as possible.
  - Have experience in some emergency medical basic life support treatment, rescue of individuals and responders, triage and decontamination of individuals and equipment, and transportation capabilities of individuals exposed to WMD agents or materials.
  - Assist however possible any emergency medical groups that are on scene with the incident commander coordinating efforts of this type of support.
- Have experience to assist the incident commander in establishing any safety procedures for performing specialized tasks to lower the safety levels of the hazard from the potential WMD agent or HAZMAT.
- Be able to perform such tasks if assigned.
- Know how to plan for and implement coordination efforts with any emergency medical group, and to implement medical monitoring procedures for those individuals entering or leaving non-safety areas as needed.

6.11.4 Know and Follow Procedures for Performing Specialized Tasks

This includes knowledge to perform specialized tasks at the scene of a potential WMD situation, area of contamination, exposure to an invasive species, or similar event. The structure should include the following:

- Recognize the activities that will be coordinated with the on-scene incident commander.

- Know how to identify the appropriate PPE and specialized tools associated with CBRNE threats, including those posed by dangerous organisms:
  - Know how to select appropriate PPE for the specialized task to be performed on scene, and to establish safety procedures and practices to be followed as outlined within the procedures of the department or agency that is responding.
  - Use technical reference materials to assist in the selection process of the PPE that is appropriate for the tasks.
- Know procedures on how to operate equipment associated with detection, sampling, collection, or containment of dangerous chemicals, dangerous organisms, or other forms of contaminations:
  - Follow procedures for operating any detection or sampling instrumentation devices or equipment.
  - Understand the limitations for collecting solid (including granular or particulate materials), liquid, and gaseous substances for detection, identification, and classification of potential WMD agents or materials, and for the verification of such materials as needed, and including invasive species.
  - Know and follow procedures and best practices for retrieval of contaminated evidence and for the safe handling or transportation, storing, and securing of such evidence materials, items, articles, etc.
  - Use technical reference materials to assist in the tasks outlined as necessary.
  - Be able to perform similar tasks with respect to potentially dangerous organisms or contamination within the environment.
- Be able to mitigate any on-scene hazards and risks to responders and members of the public:
  - Assist the on-scene incident commander in developing and implementing strategies and tactics that will reduce on-scene risks for any responders or members of the public.
  - Be able to recognize any special threats, such as secondary incendiary or explosive devices that would otherwise be used to harm or kill any emergency responders, members of the public, any equipment used for the detection, decontamination, or removal of WMD agents or materials, or the vehicles to be reused.
  - Follow procedures and best practices for safely searching for suspected devices and, if found, controlling or removing these types of threats from the scene and away from those individuals, members of the public, and any responders or emergency personnel who might have otherwise been exposed, contaminated, or had some form of safety risk or threat posed upon them.
  - Coordinate decontamination procedures with the incident commander.
- Knowledge of plans, standards, procedures, and other directions associated with the response to an event:
  - Be able to implement the department or agency emergency response plans as well as local/regional emergency response plans.

- Know how to access local/regional assets to assist with any on-scene resolution or mitigation procedures specific to any potential WMD situation or event.
- Knowledge of plans, standards, procedures, and guidelines with respect to supporting first responders:
  - Coordinate the implementation of any necessary medical monitoring efforts with emergency medical group members and the incident command for those responders entering and leaving non-safety areas.
- Be able to assist in the implementation of rehabilitation assistance to those emergency responders who may have suffered from any frustration or heat-related stress, or other problems arising from protective clothing or that can be controlled or reduced on scene.

6.11.5 Know ICS Performance Procedures

In this step, within this level, it is essential to know the ICS and be able to follow the UCS procedures for integration and implementation methodologies of each system. The following should be incorporated into the overall structure:

- Taking steps to establish the ability to respond:
  - Ensure that skill set and knowledge are available to serve the emergency operations officer for on-scene activities.
  - Be aware of any assets available from the department or agency and from local/regional emergency response organizations, especially regarding handling hazards or threats that may happen on scene specific to a potential WMD situation or event.
  - Know how to obtain the desired assets for on-scene support as necessary, or if needed.
  - Know and follow procedures for working, and coordinating, with other departments or agencies under the UCS to handle specialized hazards or threats on scene specific to potential WMD situations or events.
  - Understand and know how to implement termination procedures at the close of an emergency response incident.
- Be able to ensure that documentation and procedures are adequately documented, reviewed, and signed off on by senior management through the appropriate management or administrative reporting chain:
  - Know how to implement the ICS such that the department or agency has its emergency response plan.
  - Be capable of assisting the incident commander in completing required documentation related to termination procedures, including appropriate measures for cost recovery and management.
- Be able to assist the ICS commander or the entity when reviewing, assessing, and adjusting plan procedures and processes in response to lessons learned:
  - Know how to conduct or assist in conducting critiques of any actions taken before, during, and after the response specific to a potential WMD situation or event.

- Be capable of assisting the incident commander in conducting incident critiques (defined as lessons learned capability, for future situations or events).
- Assist in determining what improvements, if any, would be made for the next emergency response specific to a potential WMD situation or event, especially in areas regarding improvements specific to the tasks defined to those responders on scene and within special operations.
- Know how to coordinate the development of an IAP with the on-scene incident commander that is consistent with the department or agency emergency response plan procedures and practices:
  - Be able to implement IAP, including addressing special on-scene hazards.
  - Recognize coordination efforts with/between other department and agencies that are on scene for gathering any evidence and intelligence data or information.
- Ensure that the ICS commander and key personnel are supported in terms of their ability to achieve situational awareness involving the event and potentially affected areas:
  - Understand the importance of developing and sharing intelligence gathering techniques for on-scene data gathering, including information from any special operations activities.
  - Recognize that any intelligence information gathered should be shared with the on-scene incident commander or incident commander designee, as well as any senior law enforcement leadership that may be on scene.

6.11.6   PLANNING AND MANAGEMENT-LEVEL GUIDELINES

This section addresses training requirements for respondents who may be involved with hazard remediation efforts associated with potential terrorist/criminal use of WMD. Respondents will be involved in planning for and managing the emergency on-site scene, and will help implement the on-scene command post. These individuals might be expected to manage specific tasks while on scene, as well as other allied emergency responders, who will support the ongoing operations to mitigate and control the hazardous agents and materials using any available resources to safely and sufficiently conclude the event. Actions to be taken by respondents should initially be conducted from a safety area. It is expected that respondents will be integrated into the overall command structure that is implemented for the management and supervision of resources and assets being deployed to mitigate and recover from the overall WMD situation or event.

ICS provides a key tool in this regard. What is needed behind the ICS is buy-in from the community of potentially affected entities and not just the lead agencies alone. This community is not just limited to government—it must include entities and other communities from within the private sector given the nature of the event and ownership issues surrounding current infrastructures today.

Consider this: An event may be the result of an incident within a community center—who has the primary responsibility and control? For those who have worked in this domain, the answer is reasonably clear. Where this question becomes important is when those who have a legitimate control over the scene attempt to take over and potentially meet resistance because the community with which they are interacting is unaware of the protocols, and unwilling to cede control over the response of the incident. These problems are the last thing needed when attempting to preserve the safety and security of the affected people.

6.11.7 SUCCESSFULLY COMPLETED AWARENESS, PERFORMANCE, AND MANAGEMENT TRAINING

This section outlines a series of goals and objectives associated with ensuring that awareness, performance, and management training has been completed successfully.

The following should be incorporated into the overall structure:

- Complete training (or have an equivalent training and experience) in and understanding of the guidelines at the awareness and performance levels for Level A training for the function specific to the respondent.
- Know how to implement the department or agency ICS and relevant portions of the department or agency emergency response plan.
- Be capable of implementing local/regional emergency response plans specific to potential WMD situations or events or HAZMAT events.
- Understand the roles of responder personnel within any given emergency response plan.
- Recognize the hazards, risks, and limitations associated with using protective clothing and equipment.
- Be familiar with any assets available for implementing the emergency response plan specific to any potential WMD situation or event.
- Know what additional assets and assistance may be available for assistance with handling WMD or HAZMAT events or situations.
- Understand the importance of implementing appropriate decontamination procedures for any given HAZMAT or WMD situation or event.
- Be able to implement those procedures to protect emergency responders, individuals, public safety personnel, and members of the public, as well as equipment that could be reused.

6.11.8 KNOW ICS MANAGEMENT PROCEDURES

In this step, within this level, knowing the ICS and being able to follow the UCS procedures for integration and implementation methodologies of each system is essential.

The following should be incorporated into the overall structure:

- Know how to manage any one of the five basic functions for operating the department or agency ICS.
- Be capable of assessing needs for additional resources and obtaining those resources from the identified assets.
- Understand the responsibilities and roles of the emergency operations center.

- Be capable of interfacing and coordinating with everyone involved.
- Understand the applications and interfaces of the UCS with the ICS.
- Know best practices and methodologies that are to be used and implemented within the UCS that are on scene specific to a potential WMD or HAZMAT event:
  - This should be extended to include disease, dangerous organisms, and invasive species.
- Be capable of assisting the incident command in the completion of all termination documentation for the situation or event and explaining how specified tasks relate to respondents at the scene.
- Know how to conduct or assist in conducting critiques of any actions to be taken before, during, and after completion of the response specific to the potential WMD situation or event:
  - This should be extended to include disease, dangerous organisms, and invasive species.
- Be capable of developing lesson learned scenarios for future situations/events.
- Define and implement appropriate strategies and tactics that would assist in determining the types and levels of degree of improvements relevant to tasks performed by various responders at the scene, which are or will be needed for the lessons learned documentation.
- Know how to develop a media management plan specific to potential WMD situations or events, or HAZMAT events, in coordination with the on-scene incident commander:
  - This should be extended to include disease, dangerous organisms, and invasive species.
- Be capable of managing responder group activities under the UCS and ICS directives.
- Be capable of assisting the on-scene incident commander or designee on completion or conclusion of the WMD or hazardous situation or event:
  - This should be extended to include disease, dangerous organisms, and invasive species.
- Be capable of advising the incident commander or the management team of the respondents' roles and capabilities, sharing any intelligence data or information gathered, along with any modifications necessary to the department or agency emergency response plans, procedures, and best practices.

6.12 KNOW PROTOCOLS TO SECURE, MITIGATE, AND REMOVE HAZMAT

The containment of HAZMAT is of significant importance, particularly given the fragility of certain environments, the potential impact on the health of those in the area, and the long-term effects on the local population. The following should be included in the overall structure:

- Know how to assess agents or materials used in a potential WMD or HAZMAT event based on the signs and symptoms of any individuals exposed to the area.
- Use appropriate methods in gathering of evidential data or information.
- Follow emergency medical protocols for treating individuals.
- Understand procedures and protocols for defining locations for the command post, staging areas, medical monitoring function areas, and proper isolation boundaries for the different areas at the emergency scene.
- Know how to control entry within, into, and out of these areas.
- Be capable of identifying hazards presented at the scene that will be implemented in the most effective methods, considering alternatives and especially safety concerns of emergency responders at the scene.
- Be familiar with the environmental and public safety requirements for the removal, handling, transportation, and storing of WMD or HAZMAT or agents found at the scene.
- Understand the roles of the responders regarding any evidence gathering efforts, including chain of custody and needs for the secure storage of contaminated and noncontaminated materials gathered at the scene.
- Follow health and safety precautions and procedures for handling such materials.

In July 2007, a crude oil pipeline was ruptured in British Columbia, Canada, and as a result, a number of homes, a highway, and the ecology of Burrard Inlet were affected. This type of event provides a good example of why those working on sites must be trained in the areas that have just been discussed. In these types of scenarios, the preservation of life as well as the environment (and not just in the "green" sense of the word) must be an almost immediate reaction by individuals in the immediate area(s). At the same time, once those have been assured through training, the steps associated with containment and mitigation need to move up on the priority ladder with management. In order to start these as quickly as possible, those working at the scene must be the ones who take appropriate steps—not the first responders called to the scene.[10]

6.13 ADDITIONAL PROTECTIVE MEASURES

This section pertains to the additional measures that are discussed through several doctrines and structures. Basically, these are a repeat of self-protection and protective measures that are to be implemented on scene, with a few additions.

These include the following:

- Recognize the special hazards to human life, local species, and the environment from hazardous materials or dangerous organisms.
- Be able to and capable of assisting in the care for and treatment of individuals who may have suffered exposure.
- Know how to obtain resources for appropriate rescue, transportation, and emergency treatment of contaminated individuals and personnel.

- Follow post-event rehabilitation best practices and procedures for emergency response and other on-scene personnel, including critical incident stress management.
- Be capable of coordinating programs outlined for department or agency personnel if requested, usually by the incident commander or designee in charge.
- Understand the importance of implementing medically prescribed and appropriate prophylactic treatments for those who may have become contaminated with a biological hazard.
- Coordinate any treatments with health officials.
- Understand the importance of the safety officer role in protecting on-scene emergency responders and personnel.
- Be capable of assuming that role if requested, by an incident commander or designee in charge.

6.14   UNDERSTAND THE DEVELOPMENT OF THE IAP

This includes knowing the assets available for controlling situations or events, in coordination with the on-scene incident commander.

- In collaboration with the on-scene incident commander, be able to assist in planning management efforts, thus determining optional goals and objectives to bring the situation or event to successful conclusion.
- Know what assets are available for addressing on-scene hazards.
- Have the necessary communications equipment to request on-site assistance.
- Coordinate activities with the on-scene incident commander.
- Know how to draft an incident mitigation or action plan (referred to as IAP) to address any on-scene incidents, situations, or events, and to obtain assets to control or suppress any such hazards pertinent to any such situation or event.
- Coordinate the development, implementation, and alteration of the plan with the on-scene incident commander.
- Be able to advise the on-scene incident commander as well as other officials regarding site assessment and establishment of any zonal boundaries along with the outer perimeter of respondents and emergency personnel who are on scene, which include an appropriate location for the establishment of a command post.
- Follow procedures and methodologies outlined within the department or agency procedural or policy manuals for assessing any hazard and risk and for protecting the general public as well as any emergency respondents.
- Be capable of identifying any potential targets for what might be considered terrorist attacks.[11]
- Understand and comprehend tactical methods used by individuals who may be classified as terrorists and what they might use within the target area.
- Be capable of developing preplans to mitigate any potential WMD or HAZMAT situation or event involving potential targets.

6.15 KNOW AND FOLLOW PROCEDURES FOR PROTECTING A POTENTIAL CRIME SCENE

Following the event, it is important to be able to gather data that are as complete and accurate as possible. This becomes important when looking at the lessons learned and any potential criminal proceedings that may arise out of the event.

The following should be included in the structure:

- Know appropriate procedures for protecting evidence and minimizing any disturbances of the crime scene to the maximum extent possible, while protecting any individuals at the potential scene.
- Assist any individuals to minimize adverse medical signs and symptoms where possible.
- Understand the importance of coordinating with law enforcement officials to ensure that any department or agency actions do not hinder the gathering of any evidence by law enforcement officers.
- Assist law enforcement officers in identifying and preserving evidence and sharing of intelligence.
- Follow any protocols established that will help in minimizing any disturbances to the potential scene.
- Understand the roles and jurisdictions of any federal or state department or agency pertaining specifically to any potential WMD or HAZMAT situation or event.
- Know how to recognize an incident that may be defined as an act of terrorism.
- Be able to and capable of identifying any evidence that could be useful to the investigation of the potential scene.
- Share intelligence with law enforcement officials and the on-scene incident commander.

6.16 KNOW DEPARTMENT PROTOCOLS FOR MEDICAL RESPONSE PERSONNEL

Knowledge of these protocols is important for ensuring that medical casualties are treated as efficiently and effectively as possible. It is also important to note that these measures also play a role in the protection of the medical response personnel themselves.

The following should be included in the structure:

- Be capable of developing a medical action plan to protect any on-scene emergency responders.
- Coordinate the implementation of the plan with the emergency medical manager and/or on-scene incident commander.
- Know how to implement, in concert with the medical action plan, department or agency procedures for medical monitoring of all respondents and emergency team members involved with, or working with or within, the non-safety areas.

- Ensure that the plan includes the monitoring of baseline vital signs and physical assessments for all personnel either entering or leaving this area.
- Ensure that any signs or symptoms of exposure to potential WMD or HAZMAT agents are included within the medical monitoring and physical assessments of responders who are entering or leaving non-safety areas. This should also be included to be able to identify the potential exposure to disease and dangerous organisms, including invasive species.

6.17 NATIONAL FIRE PREVENTION ASSOCIATION 472

For more definitive guidelines about emergency procedures, the *Standard for Professional Competence of Responders to Hazardous Materials Incidents* (referred to as NFPA 472) identifies the levels of competence required of responders to HAZMAT incidents. It covers the competencies for first responders at the awareness level and the operational level, HAZMAT technicians, incident commanders, HAZMAT branch officers, HAZMAT branch safety officers, and other specialist employees. Guidance is provided for first responders on how to deal with terrorist activities and WMD. NFPA 472 specifically addresses the category of an individual who may be sent to a scene. NFPA 472 defines two categories of such responders: (!) private sector specialist employees B and (2) specialist employees C. Competencies are listed for both categories based on the prerequisite that all such individuals should receive first response awareness training. It should be noted that the distinction may be drawn such that any differences between categories B and C (with respect to additional training for category C specialists, based on the assumption that these personnel) may be required to work in nonsafety areas.[12]

6.18 OSHA HAZARDOUS WASTE OPERATIONS
AND EMERGENCY RESPONSE

The Occupational Safety and Health Administration (OSHA) Hazardous Waste Operations and Emergency Response (HAZWOPER)[13] standard already recognizes that these types of individuals may be called to the scene to assist in the mitigation, control, or other aspects to aid the incident commander, as necessary. HAZWOPER rules include provisions for skilled personnel who have expertise in particular activities that are needed in the response but that cannot be performed promptly by the responding units, such as crane operators or tow truck drivers. These individuals are not expected to be trained emergency responders, nor are they expected to have prior training in accordance with HAZWOPER guidelines. Because it is likely that these individuals may be exposed to the hazards at the emergency response scene, they should receive appropriate on-scene briefing with respect to safety and health protections. Once emergency response operations are concluded and recovery and cleanup operations begin, those workers involved in these activities will not be considered emergency response workers and will be covered by other OSHA requirements. This section addresses only those workers called to the emergency scene to render some assistance to the incident commander, the unified command team, and the response team that is on scene.[14]

Typically, skilled personnel are asked to fulfill a particular task. In doing so, they are often briefed on safety and health hazards that they may encounter, as well as the types of control measures that any given incident commander may want them to follow. Typically, these persons understand the hazards they face in doing their job on a normal day. The briefing is intended to alert them about any extraordinary or unusual hazards that they may face and procedures to help protect them or those around them. Thus no one individual is asked to perform any given job or task in which that person cannot be reasonably protected from on-scene hazards, even though there may be some risks involved.

Specialist employees are those who may have knowledge or expertise specific to particular hazards, equipment, processes, or chemicals that may be present at the emergency incident scene. The incident commander may benefit from their wisdom on the given subject. These personnel are expected to provide technical advice and assistance to the incident commander, and it is assumed that they generally will not be exposed to hazards on the scene. However, certain experts or specialist employees of railroad companies or chemical manufacturers may have been trained to work in Level A suits if necessary. These personnel receive training each year, and must demonstrate their competency in their specialization area.

6.19   SKILLED SUPPORT PERSONNEL

Skilled support personnel may be called upon to perform some functions that are related to a WMD or HAZMAT emergency response, are relied upon within the emergency response plan, and may receive some awareness training. It is suggested that these personnel receive at least the minimum training on the awareness-level guidelines provided to public works agency employees before they have to respond to a WMD incident, situation, or event.[15]

6.20   SPECIALIST EMPLOYEE

Specialist employees may be called upon for a WMD or HAZMAT incident response to provide information and technical advice unique to their particular specialty, or they may be asked to perform specific tasks that fall under their area of expertise, required by the incident commander to be undertaken at the scene. These specialist employees receive annual training in their area of expertise. They are also trained in how to work within an incident command system. Personnel are expected to wear chemical protective clothing, perform unique tasks in the non-safety areas zone, and will typically need additional training beyond the awareness-level guidelines.[16]

6.21   DOT HAZMAT CLASSIFICATIONS

The United Nations and the U.S. DOT have devised a method of classifying HAZMAT based on the chemical and physical properties of the product that is referred to as a hazard class. Each of these classes is divided into specific subsets (e.g., gases that may be poisonous, flammable, or nonflammable). Oxygen and chlorine are gases that have their own individual labels. Each class has a symbol suggesting the primary type of hazard that it poses. DOT has cataloged every known toxic substance in the ERG,[17] compiled by the DOT Research and Special Programs Administration[18] and published by the U.S. Government Printing Office and numerous distributors.[19]

6.21.1   DOT HAZMAT Class 1: Explosives

This is a chemical that causes a sudden, almost instantaneous release of pressures, gas, or heat when subjected to sudden shock, pressure, or extreme temperatures. Explosives usually have thermal and mechanical impact potential.[20]

Explosives may pose other forms of risk, depending on the specific compounds involved. These risks may range from the chemical to the fire hazard.

6.21.2   DOT HAZMAT Class 2: Gases

Gases are grouped into three types: (1) compressed, (2) liquefied, and (3) cryogenic. Gases can be flammable, nonflammable (sometimes called inflammable), or poisonous. Gases have the ability to vaporize, which could cause respiratory issues to human life and cause thermal-related injuries or cause due to exceedingly cold temperatures.[21]

6.21.3   DOT HAZMAT Class 3: Flammable Liquids

This also includes combustible liquids. Flammable liquids are liquid substances with a flashpoint below 10°F (e.g., alcohol or gasoline); combustible liquids are liquid substances with a flashpoint higher than 100°F, but below 200°F (e.g., various oils, such as household heating oil and solvents).[22]

6.21.4   DOT HAZMAT Class 4: Flammable Solids

This also includes solids that are reactive. Flammable solids are likely to cause fires through friction or retained heat from a manufacturing process that may be easy to ignite; reactive solids are solids that are unstable under environmental conditions and can produce or intensify sudden heat or explosive properties when exposed to other chemicals or when they come into contact with water or organic substances (e.g., potassium, sodium, aluminum, or magnesium—all of these solid metals are highly combustible when exposed to water).[23]

6.21.5   DOT HAZMAT Class 5: Oxidizers

This class also includes peroxides. Oxidizers are materials that can be in any form (gas, liquid, or solid state) and have the potential to readily yield oxygen, which supports combustion or explosive scenarios. This can include gases such as oxygen, ozone (which is a gaseous molecule that contains three oxygen atoms

(O_3); ground-level ozone is a product of reactions involving hydrocarbons and nitrogen oxides in the presence of sunlight, and is a potent irritant that can cause lung damage or respiratory problems[24]), or chlorine; liquids such as bromine, hydrogen peroxide, and nitric acid; and solids such as chlorates, iodine, nitrates, and peroxides.[25]

6.21.6 DOT HAZMAT CLASS 6: TOXIC MATERIALS

This also includes infectious substances, which include etiological or infectious organisms (e.g., anthrax, botulism, polio). Toxic materials may be harmful to human life due to inhalation, ingestion, or absorption through external layers of the skin; these substances can be in either liquid or solid form, or may be produced through irritants which are dangerous or harmful fumes when exposed to air or fire (e.g., xylyl bromide).[26]

6.21.7 DOT HAZMAT CLASS 7: RADIOACTIVE MATERIALS

Any material that spontaneously emits ionizing radiation that has specific activity greater than 0.02 µCi per g is considered harmful to human life. Depending on the exposure, it can be fatal or cause serious harm to internal organs or long-term effect, resulting in cancer.[27]

6.21.8 DOT HAZMAT CLASS 8: CORROSIVE MATERIALS

This refers to any liquid or solid material that can damage living tissue, steel, or glass on contact (e.g., sulfuric acid, hydrochloric acid, ammonium hydroxide). Corrosive materials can also be classified as an irritant, as fumes from acids can have debilitating respiratory consequences on humans if inhaled.[28]

6.22 IMPORTANCE OF IMPLEMENTING AN EMERGENCY RESPONSE PLAN

The effectiveness of responses during emergencies depends on the amount of planning and training conducted. During HAZMAT incidents, many additional burdens may be placed on local environments. Stress effects resulting from HAZMAT incidents can cause increases of a plethora of various stress-related symptoms and can produce situations resulting in potentially fatal results, such as cardiac arrest or further contagion to other individuals. When all incidents are compounded, the situation can get out of control—quickly—unless detailed procedures for handling such incidents are available and readily accessible. In addition, simply having these procedures in place may not be enough. Periodic review of the procedures, establishing updates as they are needed, and ensuring that the procedures reflect current environmental conditions are necessary measures to ensure the effectiveness of the utilization of these procedures and planning initiatives.[29]

6.23   AUTHORS' NOTES

Within the incident response realm, the theoretical concept is to identify, report, mitigate, and respond to incidents as quickly as possible. So this question must be asked: Given a limited number of first responders, is there a role for the public's involvement? If critical infrastructure protection has an impact across the whole community, at what point do we engage the citizens as part of the effective response to an event, and to what extent?

This question is fraught with legal and social perils. On one hand, society believes itself to have a right to be protected, but has translated that right into the right to have somebody else come and protect you. Although it is understood that many citizens would be unable to respond effectively and would likely become casualties, should citizens be encouraged to identify what they can do without putting themselves too much into harm's way?

A similar question involves the detection of behavior or situations that can pose a threat to public safety if left unchecked. Consider this situation: Individuals at a processing plant claim to have observed or participated in acts that run contrary to food safety practices. While the focus may be on the management of the plant or the various inspection routines, what does this say about the individual who is willing to participate in those acts but leave them unreported?

Perhaps one illustration of this dilemma comes out of larger organizations. One author has had direct contact with an (anonymous) organization that does not want to provide fire extinguisher training to employees due to the costs associated with that training. The common response is that employees are not firefighters—in the minds of the authors, this becomes a question of due diligence.

NOTES

1. www.ojp.usdoj.gov/odp (alt URL: http://cipbook.infracritical.com/book5/chapter6/ch6ref1.pdf).
2. Ibid.
3. U.S. Department of Justice Office for Domestic Preparedness, *Emergency Response Guidelines*, August 1, 2002; http://www.ojp.usdoj.gov/odp/docs/EmergencyResp GuidelinesRevB.pdf (alt URL: http://cipbook.infracritical.com/book5/chapter6/ch6ref6.pdf).
4. U.S. Department of Justice Office for Domestic Preparedness, *Emergency Response Guidelines*, August 1, 2002; http://www.ojp.usdoj.gov/odp/docs/EmergencyResp GuidelinesRevB.pdf (alt URL: http://cipbook.infracritical.com/book5/chapter6/ch6ref6.pdf).
5. The Whitehouse, Homeland Security Presidential Directive/HSPD-8, December 17, 2003, Section (2) (d), def. "first responder"; http://georgewbush-whitehouse.archives.gov/news/releases/2003/12/20031217-6.html (alt URL: http://cipbook.infracritical.com/book5/chapter6/ch6ref7.pdf).
5a. http://www.publicsafety.gc.ca/prg/em/cbrne-res-strt-eng.aspx.
6. U.S. Department of Transportation Office of Hazardous Materials, *Emergency Response Guidebook*; http://phmsa.dot.gov/hazmat/library/erg, http://www.phmsa.dot.gov/staticfiles/PHMSA/DownloadableFiles/Files/Hazmat/ERG2012.pdf, and http://www.phmsa.dot.gov/staticfiles/PHMSA/DownloadableFiles/Hazmat/

hzmt_lib_erg2012_change_summary_from_2008.pdf (alt URL: http://cipbook.infra-critical.com/book5/chapter6/ch6ref2.pdf, http://cipbook.infracritical.com/book5/chapter6/ch6ref2a.pdf, and http://cipbook.infracritical.com/book5/chapter6/ch6ref2b.pdf).

7. U.S. Department of Transportation Office of Hazardous Materials, *Emergency Response Guidebook*; http://phmsa.dot.gov/hazmat/library/erg, http://www.phmsa.dot.gov/staticfiles/PHMSA/DownloadableFiles/Files/Hazmat/ERG2012.pdf, and http://www.phmsa.dot.gov/staticfiles/PHMSA/DownloadableFiles/Hazmat/hzmt_lib_erg2012_change_summary_from_2008.pdf (alt URL: http://cipbook.infracritical.com/book5/chapter6/ch6ref2.pdf, http://cipbook.infracritical.com/book5/chapter6/ch6ref2a.pdf, and http://cipbook.infracritical.com/book5/chapter6/ch6ref2b.pdf).

8. OSHA requires employers to use personal protective equipment (PPE) to reduce employee exposure to hazards when engineering and administrative controls are not feasible or effective. Employers are required to determine all exposures to hazards in their workplace and determine if PPE should be used to protect their workers. If PPE is to be used to reduce the exposure of employees to hazards, a PPE program should be initialized and maintained. This program should contain identification and evaluation of hazards in the workplace and if use of PPE is an appropriate control measure; if PPE is to be used, how it is selected, maintained, and its use evaluated; training of employees using the PPE; and vigilance of the program to determine its effectiveness in preventing employee injury or illness.

9. U.S. Department of Labor Occupational Safety and Health Administration, Safety and Health Topics: Personal Protective Equipment (PPE), http://www.osha.gov/SLTC/personalprotectiveequipment (alt URL: http://cipbook.infracritical.com/book5/chapter6/ch6ref3.pdf).

10. http://www.canada.com/theprovince/news/story.html?id = 770be975-2f80-4dda-8bb4-a63141964301&k = 97650.

11. Definition of the term *terrorist* is fluid in nature; the term *terrorist* may or may not be someone who enjoys exhibiting any form of terror or mayhem to specified targets, or in some aspects, even general public targets, sites, facilities, or events, resulting in the damage or destruction of life or property. This definition is constantly changing; thus the definition of the term is nonstandard.

12. National Fire Prevention Association, *Professional Competence of Responders to Hazardous Materials Incidents*, NFPA 472, 2002.

13. Occupational Safety and Health Administration, U.S. Department of Labor, HAZWOPER FAQ, http://www.osha.gov/html/faq-hazwoper.html (alt URL: http://cipbook.infracritical.com/book5/chapter6/ch6ref5.pdf).

14. U.S. Department of Justice Office for Domestic Preparedness, *Emergency Response Guidelines*, August 1, 2002; http://www.ojp.usdoj.gov/odp/docs/EmergencyResp GuidelinesRevB.pdf (alt URL: http://cipbook.infracritical.com/book3/chapter6/ch6ref6.pdf).

15. Ibid.

16. Ibid.

17. U.S. Department of Transportation Office of Hazardous Materials, *Emergency Response Guidebook*; http://phmsa.dot.gov/hazmat/library/erg, http://www.phmsa.dot.gov/staticfiles/PHMSA/DownloadableFiles/Files/Hazmat/ERG2012.pdf, and http://www.phmsa.dot.gov/staticfiles/PHMSA/DownloadableFiles/Hazmat/hzmt_lib_erg2012_change_summary_from_2008.pdf (alt URL: http://cipbook.infracritical.com/book5/chapter6/ch6ref2.pdf, http://cipbook.infracritical.com/book5/chapter6/ch6ref2a.pdf, and http://cipbook.infracritical.com/book5/chapter6/ch6ref2b.pdf).

18. Office of Pipeline Safety, Pipeline and Hazardous Materials Administration, U.S. Department of Transportation, PHMSA Research and Development, http://primis. phmsa.dot.gov/matrix/RfpInfo.rdm?rfp = 1&s = 614443CCEA804822B0692455BBA 3651C&c = 1 (alt URL: http://cipbook.infracritical.com/book5/chapter6/ch6ref4.pdf).
19. Federal Emergency Management Agency, *An Orientation to Hazardous Materials for Medical Personnel*, IS-346, September 1997; http://training.fema.gov/EMIweb/IS/ is346.asp (alt URL: http://cipbook.infracritical.com/book5/chapter6/ch6ref8.pdf).
20. Ibid.
21. Ibid.
22. Ibid.
23. Ibid.
24. U.S. Environmental Protection Agency, *Mobile Source Emissions—Past, Present, Future—Definitions*, March 2005.
25. Federal Emergency Management Agency, *An Orientation to Hazardous Materials for Medical Personnel*, IS-346, September 1997; http://training.fema.gov/EMIweb/IS/ is346.asp (alt URL: http://cipbook.infracritical.com/book5/chapter6/ch6ref8.pdf).
26. Ibid.
27. Ibid.
28. Ibid.
29. Ibid.

7 Security Vulnerability Assessment

7.1 INTRODUCTION

This chapter outlines the specifics on security vulnerability assessments (SVAs) for any given critical infrastructure or support organization responsible for a critical infrastructure. It provides a summary of conditions, factors, and states of existence in which it may become necessary to provide levels of countermeasures for remediation efforts of any vulnerability discovered or known. It is one of the more critical chapters in the book, as any professional, specialist, or technician who is responsible for a critical infrastructure, or any aspect of a critical infrastructure, should at the very least have a fundamental understanding of what is involved in securing an organization's or industrial sector's infrastructure.

7.2 WHAT IS A RISK ASSESSMENT?

The term *risk assessment*, whether it pertains to information security or other types of risk, provides decision makers with information necessary in determining and understanding factors that may negatively influence the operations and outcomes of an organization's operational success.[1] Through these assessments, decision makers may be able to make informed judgments concerning the extent of actions needed to reduce risk. As reliance on computer-based systems and electronic data interchanges (e.g., the Internet) has steadily grown, information security risk has joined the ranks of the index of listed and identified risks that both governments and business organizations must manage (and perhaps reduce or remove).

Regardless of the types of risks being considered, most risk assessments generally include the following elements.

7.2.1 IDENTIFY KNOWN, APPARENT, OR EVIDENT THREATS

It should be clear that a threat exploits a vulnerability to cause injury to an asset, leaving the entity suffering some loss. This step outlines those threats that can potentially disrupt, disable, or adversely prevent/inhibit process operations within, throughout, and between critical infrastructures.

Threats may be deliberate, accidental, or natural in origin. This general classification structure is used by those involved in enterprise risk management and enterprise-level security. When looking at the concept of threat, the first stage involves the threat analysis that looks at the various applicable elements of *knowledge, skills, abilities, resources, intent,* and *commitment*. For more technical threats, it may include a detailed analysis of the structure and its ability to replicate, mutate, avoid detection, or cause damage. The second element is the *threat assessment,* which examines the threat, after analysis, and determines whether or not there is a sufficient number of connections to warrant attention.

7.2.2 ESTIMATE THREAT OCCURRENCES

This step looks at the probability of the threat attempting to manifest itself to exploit the vulnerabilities in the system. This will generally involve a combination of historical research (number of occurrences in a period of time) and future projection (based on whether the same factors that allowed the threat to manifest itself persist).

The probability/frequency element of risk is critical when prioritizing later on. Consider two events. The first has an impact that costs the company $100,000. The second has an impact that costs the company $10,000. If the frequency of the lesser impact exceeds 10 times that of the greater impact, then the company actually suffers an increased loss. The assessor needs to ensure that the means of assessing probability aligns with sound practices and is carefully explained.

7.2.3 IDENTIFY AND RANK VALUE, SENSITIVITY, AND CRITICALITY OF OPERATIONS AFFECTED

For those conducting the assessment, it is important to remember the primacy of operations and the need to address legal, regulatory, or other agreements. While some will attempt to render the value to dollars, this does not represent a completely viable approach when looking at critical infrastructure protection (or assurance). That is because of the difficulties associated with internal impacts, external consequences, and the liabilities that can be assigned to an event. A relatively inconsequential act may not affect internal operations to a great extent. If that disruption, however, triggers a cascading failure through critical networks, then the issue changes dynamics. While some companies have attempted to purchase insurance against this kind of scenario, there are some events that will exceed the level of coverage.

7.2.4 ESTIMATE THE LOSSES SHOULD THE THREAT OCCUR

This step is probably the most significant within the risk assessment process cycle in that it assigns a value to the processes, operations, and assets used within, throughout, and produced from or by those processes and operations listed earlier. To many organizations, this step is crucial in that it defines the potential losses or damage that could occur if a threat were to materialize, and this step would include recovery costs to restore service and operations to the organization. Essentially, this step determines (ahead of time if the actual threat were to occur) how much money the organization would need to continue to operate successfully.

The value of assets can be the result of a number of different factors. An asset may be critical to the operations of the facility but largely unregulated. At the same time, a noncritical asset may be subject to significant regulatory controls (linked to significant penalties) that cause it to be considered at the higher value. Also, an asset may have little value to the organization or the regulator but may be part of the irreplaceable cultural heritage to the community. Those conducting asset valuations should be cognizant of the various requirements and sentiments that can result in the organization being impacted through legal, administrative, physical, personnel, technical, operational, intangible (such as brand), or potential losses.

At the same time, the assessor must remain cognizant of the "my darling" principle. That principle basically states that managers and executives can see their organization as being critical even if it is not on its critical path. When conducting this phase of the risk assessment, there is some value in referring to or using an approach that incorporates the business impact analysis of the organization's business continuity program.

7.2.5 BUILD THE THREAT SCENARIO

Keeping the threat scenario both real and well documented is very important. Too often, risk assessments will involve "cooked" scenarios. Because those cooked scenarios cannot be linked back to an identified threat, the organization's operations appear to be reasonably improbable, and they pose significant challenges for the assessor when working with management and others.

When building the threat scenario, one structure that works well involves describing how the *threat causes the impact to the asset within a period of time or under certain conditions.* Following a clear structure when describing the threat scenario allows the reader of the final report to "wrap his or her head" around what is being said, to grow comfortable with the structure, and to align the information being presented in his or her own mind.

This approach can also be used to build a link between traditional corporate threats and the threat profiles that are often used in security and vulnerability analyses (to use a somewhat dated term to describe a host of processes and approaches).

7.2.6 IDENTIFY, ANALYZE, AND ASSESS VULNERABILITIES

The assessment of vulnerability is really a three-part process. The first part is determining the pure risk faced by the organization. This pure risk can be described as the simple relationship between threat, asset, and projected loss. The reason for this is to generate the first prioritized list that can be used by management to look at issues from a purely conceptual view of their operations. It also serves the assessor by identifying a clear start point for the on-site survey that will identify what vulnerabilities are present in the system.

The second part of the vulnerability assessment can be described as the vulnerability analysis. A vulnerability can be described in terms of a deficiency, lack, or incomplete application of something that reduces the impact or probability of an incident. The vulnerability analysis describes what deficiency is exploited by the threat in clinical or near scientific detail; in essence, this analysis describes the mechanics of how the organization is vulnerable.

The third part and final element is the vulnerability assessment. The key difference between the analysis and the assessment is that the analysis focuses on the characteristics of the vulnerability itself, while the assessment answers that most relevant question of "So what?" Consider an example of a maximum security prison. A decision is made not to put a fence around it. Is this a vulnerability? Yes, the vulnerability involves a lack of identification of the perimeter, lack of ability to delay an intruder/escapee, lack of ability to detect a clearly untoward act, and others. The assessment, however, may indicate that the prison is in the high arctic and anything that escapes may be eaten by the local wildlife or die of exposure before it can pose any significant threat—and the vulnerability associated with the lack of fencing is therefore somewhat irrelevant in the grand scheme of things.

There are three elements to align here. The first involves the threat and the *knowledge, skills, abilities, resources, intent*, and *commitment* of that threat. The second is to look at the vulnerability and determine how those characteristics of the threat would affect the *means, opportunity*, or *intent* associated with the vulnerability (all factors that affect probability), as well as the potential impact associated with the event (in terms of nature, extent, containment, etc.). The assessor should arrive at a statement similar to "the threat can, due to its known or inferred training, disrupt the equipment by locating key power or control interfaces and shutting the equipment down manually." Finally, there is the nature of the assessment that answers just how relevant or connected the vulnerability is to operations. That is where probability comes into play.

These three factors can be used to create a roughly prioritized list of risks to the organization.

7.2.7   IDENTIFY ACTIONS TO MITIGATE OR REMOVE THE RISK

This step may include implementation of new organizational policies and procedures as well as forward thinking in technological, physical, and asset control implementations. The goal is to accomplish any one or more of the following:

- Reduce the impact (losses) associated with the event.
- Lower or reduce the probability associated with the event.
- Reduce the means or opportunity that the threat has to exploit the vulnerability.
- Cause the threat to come to its own conclusion that it does not have a realistic chance of success without being apprehended or failing, and therefore suffering negative consequences (such as detention, etc.).

The value of assets can be the result of a number of different factors. An asset may be critical to the operations of the facility but largely unregulated. At the same time, a noncritical asset may be subject to significant regulatory controls (linked to significant penalties) that cause it to be considered at the higher value. Those conducting asset valuations should remain cognizant of the various requirements that can result in the organization being impacted through legal, administrative, physical, personnel, technical, operational, intangible (such as brand), or potential losses.

When looking at the identification of actions to mitigate, the assessor needs to be cognizant of a simple truth: The assessor is there to provide management with the information needed to make sound and appropriate decisions. The assessor is not there to dictate to management, nor is he or she there to manage the operations of the company.

7.2.8 DOCUMENT, DOCUMENT, DOCUMENT

First, the assessor must understand that he or she may be called upon to prove his or her work. This means documentation is necessary from both the perspective of showing work and the ability to manage the significant volume of information that is involved in the assessment process.

Second, documentation will likely be needed as part of the official records associated with work done. While the private sector may have less of a requirement to document all decisions (such as the requirements imposed upon federal departments), it still needs to be able to provide management with the ability to analyze and assess data and information when looking at the underpinnings of recommendations.

Finally, effective processes often result in good, well-thought-out, developed contingency plans when those plans have the appropriate involvement of persons. Without documentation of the results and developing action plans (or courses of action for remediation, removal, or reduction in risk), funding applied toward risk assessments will be wasted.

7.3 METHODS OF ASSESSING RISK

There are various models and methodologies available for assessing risk, the extent of an analysis, the resources expended (which can vary depending on the scope of the assessment), the availability of reliable data of risk factors, and the methods of analysis used. Availability of data used may affect the extent to which risk assessment results may be reliably quantified. Quantitative approaches generally estimate a monetary value/cost associated to a risk and its reduction based on several factors, as follows:

- Identifying the likelihood that a damaging event or occurrence will happen
- Identifying costs resulting from potential losses from the event or occurrence
- Identifying costs necessary for mitigating actions resulting from those losses

The cost of implementing any countermeasures is then compared to the cost of replacing lost assets and information to determine the cost-effectiveness of the countermeasure.[3] When reliable data and costs are not available, the qualitative approach may be taken by defining risk more subjectively in terms of high, medium, and low risks. The definition of the term *high risk* has different meanings between organizations; thus it is subjective to skewed perspectives of the organization conducting the assessment. Qualitative assessments rely on the expertise, experience, and judgment of those conducting the assessment; however, it may be possible to combine both methodologies to form a hybrid quantitative-qualitative approach to any given assessment. Although this may not be practical, or might not apply, this method may be used when other methods fail.

Vulnerabilities are identified and rated from high to low based on their potential impact to the overall operation. Based on the analysis of these threats and vulnerabilities, risks are then identified. Risks with a higher probability of occurring and the potential to have a serious impact or to incur serious damage to the operation are rated as high. Those with a lower probability of occurrence and the potential to have only minimal impact on the operation are rated as low.[4]

7.4   THREAT RISK EQUATIONS

There are two basic equations that can determine the levels of risk. (Both formulae were taken from the American Society of Mechanical Engineers (ASME) presentation.[5])

$$R_{ai} = F_{ai} \times \text{Vulnerability}_{ij} \times \text{Consequences}_{ij}$$

where:

R_{ai} = annual economic risk for a given threat, i

F_{ai} = annual frequency of an adversary attacking a critical asset using a specific type of threat, i

Vulnerability = conditional probability that a specific failure mode, j, will occur, assuming that the assumed potential threat, i, has occurred

Consequences = total measure of consequences of failure for threat, i, failing in mode j

$$R_{ijk} = F_{ai}P_{fij}P_{cijk}C_{cijk}$$

where:

R_{ijk} = economic risk

F_{ai} = annual frequency of an adversary attacking a critical asset using a specific type of threat, i

P_{cijk} = combination of the probability ranges at each node of the event starting at the node, after the node where P_{fij} is defined

P_{fij} = conditional probability of failure mode, j, due to threat i

If F_{ai} is set at 1.0, then the calculated risk is termed a conditional threat risk, such that it may be used to evaluate alternatives and calculate the probability of an occurrence or occurrences that will justify the cost of any countermeasures or mitigation strategies implemented. Conditional threat risks cannot be used to calculate for comparative purposes across diverse assets (or their sectors).

7.5 COMPARISON OF QUANTITATIVE VS. QUALITATIVE RISK ASSESSMENTS

Although quantitative security risk assessments were predominant several years ago, the increasing difficulty of accurately estimating asset values, especially data and information assets, has caused users to question the accuracy of their results. Many risk assessments conducted today are usually conducted, and their tools and utilities used, using the quantitative approach. These tools include optional features (not necessarily required, but which are helpful when demonstrating levels of risk to senior management) that contain such elements as a graphical outage (bar, line, combination charts, and graphs) as well as other graphical representatives to illustrate levels of risk.[6]

One issue that many of these automated reporting tools tend to produce are not-so-meaningful reports to management, primarily because they tend *not* to explain problematic issues and areas identified, nor necessarily identify solutions for these problems—although these tools do permit assessment teams to enhance their output and thus help in the explanation process by providing additional, explanatory text, which is most often not done. Quantitative assessments are being looked upon more favorably once again in that insurance carriers are offering coverage against loss of data—in addition to loss of physical assets and property. Thus having quantitative reports necessitates their method for determining value of data or for performing their own internally conducted risk assessments (meaning that the insurance carriers would bring their own auditor to assess the problematic issue or situation to the customer claiming loss of data and information).

Below is a comparison of ways to measure risk, including the pros and cons of each method.

	Quantitative	Qualitative
Process	Determine cost of assets	Determine information criticality
	Estimate potential asset losses due to risk	Determine impacts to information and service delivery
	Compare to mitigation costs	Perform cost-benefit analysis on mitigation costs vs. potential damage
Advantages	Analysis is easy to follow and decisions are clearly justifiable	Takes operations into account
		Takes subjective issues into account
		Pays more attention to information assets
Disadvantages	Wide margin for error in results	Can reflect personal biases
	Difficult to represent effects on service delivery and information	Dependent entirely on the skills of the assessor (or assessment team)
	Assets as a number	
	Difficult to put cost on subjective assets such as reputation, etc.	

7.6 CHALLENGES ASSOCIATED WITH ASSESSING RISK

Reliably assessing security risks may be more difficult than assessing other forms of risks because data and cost information about threat likelihoods and costs associated with those risk factors may often be limited as these factors are constantly changing. Such changes may be technologically related in that what was once not considered a risk is now deemed a risk as advances in technology have made the obsolete technology vulnerable to attacks. Publicly available information through the Internet or other public forums of data interchange have also made some factors more visible over the years, as information is becoming increasingly available to the general public. Another challenge might be the costs of remediation such that what was once considered possible, because of its low cost associated with its manufacturing, servicing, or availability, now has a higher cost because of economic developments in other geographically separated locations or disruptions in operations, manufacturing, or servicing due to one of those threats previously outlined. Although the cost of manufacturing, operations, or servicing needed to strengthen costs may be known, it is not possible most times to precisely estimate any related indirect costs such as the potential loss of productivity resulting from the newly implemented controls.

7.7 OTHER FACTORS TO CONSIDER WHEN ASSESSING RISK

The lack of reliable information often precludes the ability to precisely determine which risks are most significant as far as comparative factors outlining which controls are most cost-effective are concerned. As a result of these limiting factors, it is important that organizations properly identify and use such methods that will benefit from the use of those risk assessments while avoiding any costly attempts in developing an output that is of questionable nature as far as its reliability and accuracy are concerned.

7.8 WHAT IS AN SVA?

The SVA is a systematic examination of networks to determine the adequacy of security measures, identify security deficiencies, provide data from which to predict the effectiveness of proposed security measures, and confirm the adequacy of such measures after implementation.[8] SVA is another term used for assessing vulnerabilities and threats, and to (1) determine first if there are any that exist within the enterprise, (2) determine the level of risk on the discovery of the vulnerability or threat, (3) determine the level of remediation based on the results, and (4) determine the method by which the results are communicated. The vulnerability assessment is oftentimes referred to as a penetration test (sometimes shortened to "pentest"), in which one or more individuals attempt to penetrate through a given system, environment, or condition. There are many different types of assessments; each one has specific importance as far as its criticality levels are concerned.

7.8.1 NETWORK-BASED VULNERABILITY ASSESSMENT

This test affirms (or reaffirms) the state or condition of the network enterprise and any device connected to, within, and throughout it. In essence, any device connected to the Internet, or internally to the enterprise local area network (LAN) or corporate network, is susceptible to discover and possibly exploit the vulnerabilities of the other connected devices.

7.8.2 COMPUTER-BASED VULNERABILITY ASSESSMENT

This test affirms that systems, not necessarily those connected with or throughout a network, are secured. If this test is being performed, it signifies that the computing device may not be connected to a network; if the device is connected to a network, this may be the control system device that is connected to a network-connected device, and so on. There are several scenarios that can be applied to this condition (sometimes referred to as a host vulnerability assessment).

7.8.3 SOFTWARE-BASED VULNERABILITY ASSESSMENT

This test affirms that whatever application is operating within any given enterprise is secured. This ensures that whatever application or suite of applications being tested does not suffer from buffer overflows, denial of service attacks, etc., and that the application can accommodate any nuance or circumstance.

7.8.4 PHYSICAL-BASED VULNERABILITY ASSESSMENT

This performs functions similar to those of the network-based assessment methodologies, except that its primary function is to breach physical perimeters, doorways, locks, etc., at its given target. This also includes computer-based assessments.

7.8.5 PROTOCOL ASSESSMENT

Oftentimes this is called a documentation assessment or a review assessment, in that this determines if any given target or system environment, or more specifically, its processes within and throughout the enterprise, can account for security incidents, breach attempts, and penetrations. This includes any relevant documentation pertaining to standards, protocols, and procedures (strategic, tactical, and operational) for any given enterprise.

7.9 REASONS FOR HAVING AN SVA

Presidential Decision Directive 63 (PDD-63) directed every department and agency of the federal government to have developed a plan by November 18, 1998, to protect its own critical infrastructure, including, but not limited to, its computer-based and physical-based assets, information of or produced by those assets, etc. Today that requirement has passed into history (replaced by Homeland Security Presidential Decision Directive (HSPD)-7 on December 17, 2003), but the reasons for continuing this kind of practice also have a base in common sense. Before expending significant effort and putting some parts of the organization under additional pressures, it would be well advised that the organization have a clear understanding why those measures are being put in place—or the basis for the regulations. Although the departments or agencies implementing these plans may decide on alternative measures, the overall consideration of these initiatives should include any identification of those critical infrastructures supported and their vulnerabilities, including:

- Identify mission essential communications, information, and other systems
- Identify significant vulnerabilities of organization minimum essential systems
- Identify any external interdependencies
- Assessments to determine vulnerabilities of department or agency minimum essential services to failures by private sector providers of their respective industrial sectors or other infrastructure services

Those who practice in this domain will see that details may have changed but the concepts remain very similar.

7.10   WHAT IS A THREAT?

A threat is any agent (person, activity, or event) with the potential to cause harm to a system or operational environment. All systems, regardless of their type and level of data processed, stored, and used, are subject to harm. The mere existence of the threat does not imply that the system will be harmed; however, the potential for harm can exist. Threats exist simply because the system exists. The probability that its occurrence will impact the system, however, is significantly lowered as a result of the type and degree of protection that is applied.

Threat entries are organized primarily into three distinct main threat categories:

1. Natural disasters
2. Accidental threats
3. Intentional or malicious threats

With accidental and intentional threat categories, threat occurrences or attacks may stem from two sources: (1) inside threats or (2) outside threats. Inside threats and their attacks range from accidental file deletions by administrative staff to deliberate system reconfigurations or modifications of data resulting in impaired, degraded, or terminated operational functionalities.[9] As inside threats relate to individuals who have internal knowledge of the enterprise workings, they pose the most significant threat to security, as opposed to outside threats, which might include hackers who access unauthorized systems through the Internet, former users and employees who still have active access to systems and their environments, or criminal activities for other, more hostile reasons.

Some of the factors to consider when examining this overall set of combinations and permutations are the following:

- With respect to new technology, the level of assurance that the system functions as intended and is free of security-related issues
- With respect to newly integrated technology, the level of testing and training that was performed as part of the integration process
- With respect to the use of the technology, the complexity of the technology both from a technical point of view and in terms of the graphic user interface (GUI), and which has been known affectionately in the IT community as the FUBAR factor
- With respect to the maintenance of the technology, the ability to source, procure, and deal with repairs, replacement, and changes in configuration

The above list is not exhaustive. Those involved should become familiar with the various life cycles and engineering principles.

7.11   WHAT IS VULNERABILITY?

The term *vulnerability* means an inherent weakness in a system or its operating environment that may be exploited to cause harm to the system. These weaknesses may be found in the system design, physical layout of the facility, procedures used, administration of the system, personnel within the system, management, hardware, software, etc. As with threats, vulnerabilities indicate weaknesses or flaws with the potential for exploitation.[10]

Vulnerabilities are evaluated based on the impact after the countermeasure assumptions are applied. The impact of an environment is a rating of the amount of damage that could occur if a particular vulnerability were to be exploited. Impact ratings assigned to the vulnerabilities are qualitatively assigned and are based by assessment teams, as the participants' knowledge of those systems and their processes is being evaluated. The vulnerability of an asset may be modified (in some cases, practically removed) by using countermeasures that can reduce or remove the probability that a particular attack scenario's success is possible. Any consequences of failure resulting from the implementation for a specific attack scenario may be reduced or removed through the use of conventional mitigation strategies.[11]

7.12   COUNTERMEASURES

Countermeasures are active processes, procedures, and system features that serve to detect, deflect, or reduce the probability of a threat or the impact of vulnerability, thereby either reducing or (preferably) removing the system risk.

The term *countermeasure* has synonyms, depending on which community is involved—controls, measures, safeguards, mitigative steps, etc. The challenge here is that the security lexicons are still being resolved and integrated (largely delayed by communities that have not fully accepted the concept of working together in symbiotic relationships rather than authoritarian ones). This delay is compounded by a number of nonpractitioners that occupy policy and regulatory positions that can, if left unchecked, create their own languages pertinent to their regulations.

7.13 VULNERABILITY ASSESSMENT FRAMEWORK

The Vulnerability Assessment Framework (VAF) was designed to assist with whatever an organization required for vulnerability determination, resulting from either prior knowledge issues, or even risks or vulnerability issues recently discovered. The VAF was produced under contract between KPMG Peat Marwick and the Critical Infrastructure Assurance Office (CIAO)[12] (now part of the U.S. Department of Homeland Security), with a review and evaluation process that is based on existing security requirements, standards, and principles. The VAF may be applied across all levels of government—federal, state, or local government—or even private sector industrial organizations and their infrastructures.

The VAF is comprehensive and complete,[13] consisting of a three-tiered set of processes. The VAF enables the implementing organization to:

- Define minimum essential infrastructure (MEI) requirements
- Identify and locate interdependencies and vulnerabilities of the MEI
- Provide a basis and mechanism for development of any remediation plans

The VAF was designed with scalability in mind such that it could be applicable to all levels of any organization or government as well as the broad industrial sectors from the national infrastructures (as outlined from PDD-63 and later HSPD-7).[14]

Although some suggest conducting penetration testing and analysis techniques as an adequate methodological approach for assessing computer-based systems and their potential vulnerabilities, the report recommends a more holistic approach, one that states that although penetration testing and analysis is performed, it is simply a portion of a much larger process, and one that encompasses the embodiment of penetration testing and other methodologies that will produce a more polished assessment of risks and vulnerabilities encountered throughout the assessment process. Identification of those risks and vulnerabilities should be done through root cause analysis (e.g., by asking the questions "What was the primary cause for the vulnerability or risk to occur?" "Why does it exist?" and "How was it that it did not get fixed or patched?") within the assessment process such that through these and perhaps other assessment criteria, established and enabled systemic remediation efforts are effective, efficient, and time affordable—and not time prohibitive such that insufficient time is available to either permanently patch or remediate whatever risk or vulnerability was found or existed at the time of the assessment. In this case, time affordable is productive such that the remediation efforts offered are capable and allowable within the allotted time frame, either outlined or permitted.

7.14 REASONS FOR USING THE VAF

Although there have been historical differences in whatever approaches were used to measure business risk and threats through the assessment of an infrastructure, the importance of flexibility and capabilities of scalability were significant such that those methodologies were necessary in defining the VAF (and its framework). Further, although the framework focuses mostly on computer-based aspects of critical infrastructures, the VAF methodologies defined may also apply to physically based aspects and offer methods that are flexible enough in that, to the extent in which it may be possible to do so, the VAF may be applied in other contexts of requirements of security, risk assessment, and management.[15] The government has implemented a vast range of methodologies and documentation pertaining to these aspects for purposes of this or other related efforts specific to critical infrastructure protection.

In a world of growing dependencies on computer-based solutions, such threats might be construed as being nonconventional in nature, whereby in the case of computer-based and physical-based threats it may not be prudent to suppose that any given organization or entity will know in advance where a threat may arise from. Thus assessments specific to any one infrastructure may or may not be suitable for utilization in other sectors (and their industries). For example, processes and methods used to assess computer-based, network-connected control systems that are interdependent and interconnected with each other within a power generation facility may or may not apply to a petroleum distillation and refinement facility, because the control mechanisms implemented may only specifically apply to the power generation aspect of the energy industrial sector; conversely, the same may hold true when the situation is reversed.

This single, critical aspect seriously complicates how "flat" (the term *flat process* or *flattened process* refers to an aspect of one particular process, such that it may be easily and effectively duplicated within the existing process family, or utilized in other process cycles elsewhere, outside of the scope of the initial process defined) an assessment methodology and its processes may be applied as far as cross-sector utilization is concerned.

The basis of experience for defining the assurance and auditing aspect of the KPMG VAF methodology was taken heavily from several different current process methodologies for measuring information technology (IT) system controls. These include such aspects as the following:

- The April 1998 Control Objectives for Information Technology (COBIT),[16] which is a defined process of the Information Systems Audit and Control Association (ISACA)
- The May 1998 publication of the *Executive Guide for Information Security Management*[17] of the U.S. General Accounting Office (GAO)
- Outlined standards, protocols, and procedures from the GAO's vast library of documentation pertaining to auditing of federal information systems (IS), as outlined within the *Federal Information Systems Control Auditing Manual* (FISCAM)[18]

7.15 FEDERAL INFORMATION SYSTEMS CONTROL AUDITING MANUAL

The FISCAM[19] states that as computer technologies advance, government organizations have become increasingly dependent on computerized IS to carry out their operations that process, maintain, and report essential information. The reliability of these systems is a major concern to auditors of these government organizations. Auditors may need to evaluate the reliability of computer-generated data that support financial statements or are used to analyze specific program costs and outcomes. Additionally, auditors may call on the evaluation of the adequacy of controls in systems to reduce risk of loss due to errors, fraud, or other illegal acts and disasters or other incidents that cause the systems to become unavailable.[20]

The FISCAM describes the computer-related controls that auditors should consider when assessing the integrity, confidentiality, and availability of computerized data. It is an applied guide by GAO primarily for support of statement audits and is available for use by other auditors. It is not an audit standard; its purpose is to:

- Inform auditors about computer-related controls and related audit issues so that they can better plan their work and integrate the work of IS auditors with other aspects of the audit[21]
- Provide guidance to IS auditors regarding the scope of issues that may be considered in review of computer-related controls over integrity, confidentiality, and availability of computerized data associated with those systems[22]

The manual lists specific control techniques and related suggested audit procedures. However, the audit procedures are stated at a strategic level and assume some user expertise about the subject to be effectively performed. As a result, detailed audit steps specific to the organization conducting the audit should be developed by the IS auditor based on the specific software and control techniques used by the audited party after consulting with the auditor about the auditing objectives. Many of the suggested audit procedures start with the word *review*; however, the manual stipulates that the auditor will do more than simply look at the subject to be reviewed. Rather, the auditor will perform a more critical evaluation, whereby the auditor uses professional judgment and experience, undertaking the task with a certain level of skepticism, critical thinking, and creativity.[23]

Although IS audit work, especially control testing, is generally performed by an IS auditor, financial auditors with appropriate training, expertise, and supervision may undertake specific tasks in this area of the audit. This is especially appropriate during financial statement audits where the work of financial auditors and IS auditors must be closely coordinated. Throughout this manual, the term *auditor* should generally be interpreted as either (1) an IS auditor or (2) a financial auditor working in consultation with or under the supervision of an IS auditor.[24]

7.16   GENERAL METHODOLOGIES OF FISCAM AUDITING

A general methodology that should be used to assess computer-related controls involves evaluating:[25]

- General controls at the organization or facility level

- General controls as they are being applied to their environment or the application that is being examined, such as the payroll or financial recording system, or the accounting system
- Application controls, which are controls over input, processing, and output of any data associated with specific applications

7.17   WHAT ARE GENERAL CONTROLS?

The term *general controls* refers to policies and procedures that apply to all or a large segment of an organization's IS, and thus help ensure proper operation. Examples of primary objectives for general controls are to safeguard data, protect computer application programs, prevent system software from unauthorized access, and ensure continued computer operations in case of unexpected interruptions. The effectiveness of general controls is a significant factor in determining the effectiveness of application controls. Without effective general controls, application controls may be rendered ineffective by circumvention or modification. For example, edits designed to preclude users from entering unreasonably large dollar amounts in a payment processing system can be an effective application control. However, this control cannot be relied on if the general controls permit unauthorized program modifications that might allow some payments to be exempt from the edit.[26]

7.18   WHAT ARE APPLICATION CONTROLS?

Application controls are directly related to individual computerized applications. They help ensure that transactions are valid, properly authorized, and completely and accurately processed and reported. Application controls include (1) programmed control techniques, such as automated edits, and (2) manual follow-up of computer-generated reports, such as reviews of reports identifying rejected or unusual items.[27]

Both general and application controls must be effective to help ensure the reliability, appropriate confidentiality, and availability of critical automated information.

7.19   CAVEATS WITH USING AN SVA

Considering that an assessment may find faults at the infrastructure level, or processes that surround or work within the infrastructure, assessors need to determine if the senior or executive management is aware of any of the security risks; as such, if those within management are cognizant of such risks, they are usually interested in taking preventative measures in understanding and managing those risks or threats found resulting from the assessments performed.[28] Having an interest at those levels within management ensures that the necessary precautions are (or will be) taken considerably more seriously at lower organizational levels, and ensures that security specialists have the necessary resources needed for implementing an effective countermeasure initiative. In a perfect world, this may be the case; however, in the real world it is not always the case. Within a government office, department, or agency, senior or executive-level management might find obstacles or factors that would be inhibitive of their ability to effectively implement or execute management directives toward their remediation. Such factors (which are not limited to any one specific factor) include:

- Political motivation (or upheaval; depending on the circumstances, how much funding is involved, and who is affected by the outcome resulting from the assessment)
- Government funding (what one manager or executive may find useful or important, another may not, again, probably based on political motivations, funding, or all of the above)
- Motivation or influence from industrial private sectors
- Influences from other offices, departments, or agencies, either similar to or indirectly influenced by the targeted organization

The political undertows within an organization tend to be more subversive within private sector industries rather than government organizations, because private sector organizations may or may not necessarily have reporting and accountability responsibilities, aside from the reporting of the financial health of a corporation (as required for publicly traded companies with the Sarbanes-Oxley Act of 2002),[29] which are necessarily required. Many large corporations have a "don't ask, don't tell" approach, in that if there is no acknowledgment of a security problem (or even worse, a security breach), then there is no problem. Having an SVA will shed light on most cracks and crevices of any organization, and if there are holes or leaks, it will find something.

7.20   HOW THE SVA IS USED

As a minimum, the overall recommendation is that first-discovery vulnerability assessment processes should consist of a broadened, organization-wide assessment of the organization's MEI, and the organization's relationship to, and in connection with (if applicable), national-level MEI standards. Once the area of scope and MEI(s) are defined, the assessment team can then target specific functions outlined within the SVA, focusing on core processes that are considered key components of a critical infrastructure.[30]

7.21   AUDIENCE OF AN SVA

The initial audiences for any given assessment consist mainly of organizations that will be directly affected by whatever remediation efforts are practiced resulting from the outcome of the assessment. Its implementation with an assessment team should be formed, which includes members of management or those who are directly impacted by the assessment. The team will consist of an internal auditing group (if one exists; if no internal auditing group exists, then an external auditing group may be required), the chief information officer (CIO) or members of senior or executive management who report to the CIO, someone who is familiar with the audit process and oversees output produced throughout the assessment process, and individuals responsible for information and data security, physical security, and personnel security where applicable.[31]

7.22   INITIAL SVA PLAN

The initial plan is designed to be used by security professionals and auditors (internal or external, depending on the size of scope, and whether internal auditors are involved), and will serve as a common language for facilitating communications, levels of expectations, and cooperation among the various groups. This plan will aid and guide team members in effectively working together as a team, while understanding the tasks to be accomplished, and achieving the common goal of minimizing any discovered or known vulnerabilities that may diminish the organization's ability to achieve operational success.[32]

If the organization is already conducting vulnerability assessments, or has conducted one recently, the assessment team should examine the processes currently in use against the VAF process and determine if any process gaps exist. The sole intention of the VAF process is to use, if available, existing data gathering and analysis techniques in the identification and documentation of discovered or known vulnerabilities within an infrastructure; additionally, these intentions are not meant to lay blame on any one particular group or organization. Such efforts are merely to reduce the amount of time spent in the data gathering step of the assessment; that is, it is a time- and cost-saving measure.

7.23   NECESSARY STEPS OF AN SVA

The assessment team generally determines the level of detail to which it should be applied for any given enterprise environment and the analysis required to assess the MEI and its vulnerabilities. Each step of the VAF is outlined in a manner similar to what is shown below.

> *Goals and objectives.* This provides the basis or reason(s) for having the assessment performed. This step outlines why an assessment is needed.
> *Critical success factors (CSFs).* Factors, principles, and elements performed within and throughout the assessment that will determine if the assessment was successful. This step outlines the how and determines the success (or lack thereof) of an assessment.
> *Anticipated or expected outcomes.* This step identifies the anticipated or expected outcome(s) from its performance and what should be expected. This step outlines what an assessment should expect given the scenario.
> *Activities performed.* This step outlines the where and when within an assessment; it outlines the detailed and summarized aspects of the assessment throughout its performance.

7.24   CRITICAL SUCCESS FACTORS

CSFs are objectives and factors vital to the operational success of the assessment. The fact that an assessment is initiated, and no vulnerabilities, risks, or threats are found, may (or may not) signify if the assessment was considered successful or not.[33] Some CSF aspects that might be necessary to take into consideration are:

- VAF must apply to infrastructure vulnerabilities in both computer-based and physical-based areas.
- VAF must be scalable; that is, the assessment process must be capable of being applied to larger, more sophisticated organizations, and then converge upon the small organization with little or no experience with infrastructure vulnerability issues.
- VAF must be flexible, allowing individuals to give corresponding emphasis to certain areas depending on how important they are to the targeted organization.
- VAF should be capable of addressing multiple audiences; much depends on whether the information is leaving the organization, and whether or not it is government related. Consequently, many private sector industrial infrastructures may define their assessments based on previously defined assessments conducted by the government.
- VAF should incorporate a delivery mechanism that is readily acceptable to all involved parties, and not one that would require government regulation or involvement.
- VAF may be implemented by the auditing group, both within the context of a traditional business risk assessment and through the growing accountancy requirements that are necessary in assessing risk and adequacy of controls over any given system and its processes.
- VAF must be flexible enough to draw on information and materials from other sources, for levels of understanding, levels of expertise, and updated applied information, either at the current organization or at other similar organizations within the industry.
- VAF must be an integral part of long-term investment strategies of the organization; remediation costs might be more manageable if part of an information and comprehensive investment strategy.
- The VAF process must be repeatable; that is, similar tests conducted must be exercised again to ensure consistency with similar results, especially if there are comparative analysis reports being produced between current and previously performed assessments.
- Senior or executive management of the assessed organization must understand and accept the reasons for the assessments to ensure that the VAF process is successful.
- VAF is not synonymous with penetration testing; penetration testing is one aspect of the overall assessment process cycle, and should not be considered a "surefire" method for identifying and classifying vulnerabilities or threats.

7.25   VAF METHODOLOGY

The VAF consists of an almost cascading style of analysis such that information is isolated within each major step before proceeding to the next step, thus ensuring better accuracy. Each step consists of a series of activities, which are outlined within each section. Using these outlined steps, the assessment team will compile a list of vulnerabilities for the organization to evaluate and determine appropriate measures and countermeasures. Next steps include determining the order in which vulnerabilities might be addressed, resources applied in remediation, and the level of investment necessary to meet assessment objectives.

> *Step 1: Establish the organization MEI.* The assessment team defines the MEI requirements for the organization. The focus is on specific infrastructure components supporting essential processes that are critical in achieving the organization's operational success.[34]
>
> *Step 2: Gather data to identify MEI vulnerabilities.* The VAF evaluation will review actions, devices, procedures, techniques, and other measures that can potentially place the organization at risk. The outcome will be the identification and reporting of flaws and omissions in control structures (e.g., vulnerabilities) that may affect the integrity, confidentiality, accountability, or even availability of utilized resources that are essential in achieving the organization's operational success.[35] This represents the intelligence gathering phase of the assessment, in which assessment team members attempt to gather as much data as possible about the organization, determine what information is available to the general public and what information is available within the organization, and determine whether any exposed information offered to potential intruders has provided an adequate view of the operational environment of the target facility, location, or enterprise.[36]
>
> *Step 3: Analyze, classify, and prioritize vulnerabilities.* The assessment team will define, analyze, and classify any discovered or known vulnerabilities identified in step 2, as well as any external dependencies from step 1, thus prioritizing either minimization or remediation efforts. This step will move processes from the vulnerability assessment phase into the first steps of the remediation process, with estimated costs necessary for remediation.[37] This step conducts active reconnaissance through the utilization of whatever tools and utilities are necessary in succeeding within the vulnerability assessment. The end result generates a partial list of services, facilities, and operations that are vulnerable.[38]
>
> *Step 4: Privileged escalation.* The assessment team determines if the assessment will become problematic; this step simulates privileged escalation as a preventative measure to determine to what extent the vulnerability will extend without causing degradation of services or operational services failures. This step is considered optional.

7.26   INITIAL STEPS OF THE VAF

Throughout the process, the assessment team will gather information through a number of data gathering activities, which include the following:

Facilitated sessions. Also called discovery sessions, this is similar to the interview process, targeted toward a group of individuals, and specifically directed for defined input from group members.

On-site surveys. This method is passive in that through observation while at the facility being assessed, the observer is gathering information about process flow (or lack thereof), observed methods of attack, etc.

Interviews. In this step, the team interrogates personnel and staff members of the facility being assessed. Usually interviews are conducted in one-on-one situations.

Documentation reviews. The team reviews documented procedures, protocols, and processes outlined, and makes comparative notes against what is stated vs. what is actually being performed. Any variation in process flow is usually checked again.

Validation activities. Also called process reviews, these include procedural checks and system and processing tests and simulations. This step determines if buffer overflows or application (or environmental) failure is possible; if this step demonstrates that a process can fail, a course of action for its remediation is recommended.

7.27   VAF STEP 1: ESTABLISH THE ORGANIZATION MEI

The objective of this step is to define the MEI. The two levels of MEI are (1) national-level MEI and (2) organizational-level MEI:

1. National-level MEI is defined as the framework of critical organizations, personnel, systems, and facilities that provide a flow of goods and services that are absolutely essential to the economic operational success, as well as national security of the United States. This definition of MEI is at a national level such that any interruption, slowdown, or shutdown of that infrastructure would have a cataclysmic effect on other infrastructures that may be dependent on the denied infrastructure. An example might be airline traffic control such that any severe effect at any metropolitan hub would have a detrimental effect nationwide, thus causing delays throughout the United States.

2. Organizational-level MEI is defined as the framework of critical organizations, personnel, systems, and facilities that provide inputs and outputs necessary to support core processes essential in accomplishing an organization's operations, as they may relate to national security, national economic security, or continuity of government services. The functions factor in the operational success of each component that may make up the infrastructure, such as one aspect of one organization that is part of an infrastructure

(e.g., computer components of the electrical power grid) relies on one or more components to regulate power flow to itself. IT services provided by those private sector industries represent one aspect of the MEI; henceforth, it is at an organizational level, and may be strategic or tactical in nature depending on the circumstances.

In most cases, the MEI is intended to be the core component of an organization's mission-critical elements (MCEs); oftentimes, businesses will refer to key computer servers and systems that represent revenue stream and collection services as mission critical. This would be a prime example of that factorization. Essentially, the organization would cease to function if that element was inhibited or prevented from operating. Another example would be airline scheduling systems. Without these systems, ticketing agents would have to schedule passengers, their tickets, and the airplanes departing with those passengers manually—something that would severely cripple the airline(s) affected. Most organizations have several key critical elements defined that are essential to that organization's continued operational success. The MCEs are the resources that are necessary in addressing each and every mission within or throughout the organization, regardless of its relevance to the core processes outlined.[39]

The assessment team must determine the scope of the assessment in order to decide whether a national-level MEI, organizational-level MEI, or both, need to be defined. Once the scope has been defined, the MEI will allow the assessment team to target the next steps within the VAF methodology process, focusing on appropriate core processes that are considered components of the critical infrastructure.[40]

7.27.1 Strategic-Level MEI

This area consists of the following:[41]

- Mission statements and high-level organization plans, goals, and attributes
- Organizational structure—essentially, who reports to whom
- Governance—what is affected by which ordinance, public law, or act

Critical components make up the fabric of any given critical infrastructure; without this key item, part, or service, the infrastructure would grind to a halt.

7.27.2 Tactical-Level MEI

This is also referred to as resource elements and is an area consisting of the following:

- System-specific functions that represent either individual or systematic functionalities of a given infrastructure. Essentially, what aspect or system does this element perform?
- Facility-specific functions that represent functionalities of a given facility supporting a critical infrastructure (slightly more detailed, and is specific to facility issues).

- Personnel-specific functions that represent roles and functions of personnel supporting the critical infrastructure. This includes classification of those who are critical within the organization, which may include both management and non-management personnel and staff members.
- Process-specific functions that represent the actual process of the control system of any given critical infrastructure (e.g., electrical power flow regulation vs. electrical power generation—both represent two distinctly different processes).

7.27.3   Resource Elements Comprising an MEI

Once the strategic-level MEI is defined, the tactical-level MEI or resource elements are examined. Essential resource elements include the following factors:[42]

People. This includes the staff members, management, and executives needed to plan, organize, acquire, deliver, support, and monitor mission critically related services, IS, and their facilities. This also includes groups and individuals who are external to the immediate organization involved, such as contractors or supporting vendors of critical equipment, software, or services provided that are required as part of the fulfillment process applied toward the organization's operational success.

Technology. All equipment, hardware and software, connectivity, countermeasures, or safeguards that are utilized in support of the core processes.

Applications. All application systems, internal or external, utilized in support of the core processes.

Data. All data (electronic and written form) and information required to support core processes; this includes numbers, characters, images, or other methods of recording, in a form that may be assessed by human intervention or (especially) input mechanisms for computer devices that are stored and processed there, or transmitted on some form of digital communications channel (e.g., the Internet or private area network).

Facilities. All facilities that are required to support the core processes, including the resources to house and support IT resources, as well as other resource elements defined earlier.

7.27.4   Defining Team Composition

Within any organization, formation of a team framework is necessary for determining sizing, communications, and capabilities of each team member. It is recommended that *at least* two experts form a group, and the group should consist of the following types of individuals.

Project/team leader. Skilled in auditing (or perhaps forensics) methodologies.

Personnel safety, training, awareness, and education. Skilled in performing background investigations, training and awareness issues, dealing with personnel security issues. This person may be the project/team leader.

Information security. If government affiliated, this individual should be familiar with security protocols pertaining to government security (especially military-grade security and classification); if nongovernment affiliated, this individual should be familiar with the various security standards and guidelines for private sector industries, which include ISO 17799, COBIT, Sarbanes-Oxley, the Health Insurance Portability and Accountability Act (HIPAA), etc., and is also skilled in auditing or forensics management, project development life cycle, business continuity, and security administration.

For larger organizations requiring a more in-depth and detailed evaluation, it is recommended that at least five experts form the group, and the group should consist of the following types of individuals.

Project/team leader. Skilled in auditing (or perhaps forensics) methodologies.

Personnel safety, training, awareness, and education. Skilled in performing background investigations, training and awareness issues, and dealing with personnel security issues.

Information security. If government affiliated, this individual should be familiar with security protocols pertaining to government security (especially military-grade security and classification); if nongovernment affiliated, this individual should be familiar with the various security standards and guidelines for private sector industries, which include ISO 17799, COBIT, Sarbanes-Oxley, HIPAA, etc., and is also skilled in auditing or forensics management, project development life cycle, business continuity, and security administration.

Telecommunications and networks. Skilled in WAN and LAN network design and architecture, as well as public branch exchange (PBX) systems.

Physical security. Skilled in on-site assessment of perimeters, doors, entrances/exits, as well as surveillance systems.

7.27.5 IDENTIFYING THREAT AWARENESS

This includes any awareness by management staff of any threats or inherent risks that exist against their strategic mission(s) and goals, which may cause individuals, groups, or entire organizations to take appropriate actions that may threaten their implementation and continued operations. This level of awareness for any vulnerabilities identified is outlined within VAF step 2. When considering threats in any environment for intentional acts, consideration should be given to defining potential threat sources and their motivations.[43]

7.27.6 POTENTIAL THREAT SOURCES

Some sources that might be considered a threat to an environment might include one of the following:[44]

- Nations (hostile or otherwise)
- Intelligence services or economic competition
- Sub- or transnational groups (e.g., terrorist factions or organized crime groups)
- Nontraditional threats (e.g., weapons of mass destruction or information warfare)
- Malicious computer code (intentionally transferred or otherwise)
- Threats to personal privacy
- Environmental (e.g., debris, smoke, water, heat, electrical)
- Unwitting or unknowing third party (bystander)
- Disgruntled employee, contractor, vendor, or service personnel
- Hackers, crackers, whackers, or vandals
- Criminal (e.g., fraud, theft)

7.27.7   POTENTIAL THREAT MOTIVATION

For each of the entities listed as potential threat sources, the motivation that leads them to become a threat must be identified. These motivations may include any one or more of the following (list not exhaustive):[45]

- Economic gain
- Revenge
- Political objectives (power)
- Extortion
- Competitive advantage (may tie in with economic gain)
- Invasion of privacy (power)
- To meet a challenge or dare

7.28   VAF STEP 2: GATHER DATA TO IDENTIFY MEI VULNERABILITIES

The objective of this step is to identify the vulnerabilities within the organization relating specifically to the MEI identified throughout VAF step 1. The VAF process defined will be much broader in its approach than some of the more traditional methods used to produce a comprehensive vulnerability identification framework. Although penetration testing may have its place within the traditional methodologies used elsewhere, several documents state that penetration testing may be inadequate or inappropriate for performing infrastructure vulnerability assessments. Reviews of root causes of infrastructure vulnerabilities may be necessary before any meaningful efforts to minimize those vulnerabilities may be undertaken.[46]

The criteria used to identify those vulnerabilities are categorized into three distinct groups:[47]

Areas of control. Collectively, controls consist of policies, procedures, and best practices, along with organization structures and framework design to provide reasonable assurances that organizational success will be achieved, and that undesirable events or situations are detected quickly and corrected. These control areas are expanded from GAO's FISCAM definitions of control areas, and thus may be incorporated into infrastructure vulnerability issues.

MEI resource elements. These are broad categories of resources, all or a portion of which constitutes the minimal essential infrastructure necessary for an organization to conduct its operations. These resource elements are similar to those outlined in the COBIT framework developed by ISACA, and have been expanded to incorporate physical infrastructure vulnerability areas as well.

Areas of potential compromise. These are also broad areas representing categories where losses that can occur will impact both the organization's MEI and its ability to conduct its operations.

7.28.1 AREAS OF CONTROL

Entity-wide security. Planning and management that provide a framework and continuing cycle of activity for managing risk, developing security policies, assigning responsibilities, and monitoring an organization's security controls.

Access controls. Procedures and controls that limit or detect MEI resource elements, thereby protecting those resources against loss of integrity, confidentiality, accountability, and availability.

Segregation of duties. Policies, procedures, and organizational structure established such that no one individual can control key aspects of any part of the organization's operations and thereby conduct unauthorized actions or gain unauthorized access to MEI resource elements.

Continuity of service and operations. Controls ensuring that, when unexpected events occur, organizational MEI services and operations continue without interruption or are promptly resumed, and critical or sensitive data are protected through adequate contingency and business recovery plans and exercises.

Change control and life cycle management. Procedures and controls that prevent unauthorized operations or modifications of operations from being implemented.

System controls. Controls that limit and monitor access to operations, as well as to areas that (1) control other aspects of operations and (2) secure those environments supported by the operations systems.

7.28.2 AREAS OF POTENTIAL COMPROMISE

If vulnerabilities are identified and reviewed against the areas of control and the MEI resource elements, this would conclude that controls are not in place to ensure the following factors:

Integrity. This represents the accuracy, completeness, and reliability of transmission data, the reception of information, and its validity in accordance with business values and expectations. It is also the adequacy and reliability of processes assuring authorized access to and the safety of systems, and their facilities.

Confidentiality. This represents the protection of sensitive information from unauthorized disclosure and sensitive facilities from physical, technical, or electronic penetration or exploitation.

Availability. This represents the ability to have access to MEI resource elements as necessary, both presently and for future use. Essentially, this concerns the safeguarding of those resources and associated capabilities.

Accountability. This represents an explicit assignment of responsibilities for ownership or the overseeing of a process, a system, and its input and outputs. Accountability may be assigned at any level within a given organization to include executives, management, staff, system, information, or facilities owners, providers, and users of the MEI resource elements. These assignments are reviewed for effectiveness and appropriateness within the areas of control.

7.28.3 AREAS OF CONCERN USING THE FRAMEWORK

It is essential that the security program planning and management organization provides a framework and continuing cycle of activities for managing any risks, developing security policies, assigning responsibilities, and monitoring the adequacies of the organization's controls.[48]

The critical elements in developing and implementing an organization-wide security program involve factors that are essential to several internal control components, including the control environment. These critical elements ensure that the effectiveness of the organizational overall internal controls is intact. The relevant factors, which include supportive attitudes and actions expressed and conveyed by senior management, ongoing assessments of risk, and monitoring of related policies, along with effective communications between management and staff, are crucial. All internal control components should be present and functioning effectively to ensure that those internal controls are effective and operational. As such, the control environment defines and sets the precedence for the rest of the organization. Specific control techniques, which include methodologies such as penetration testing, cannot be relied on to be effective on an ongoing basis unless supported by strong control environments. For this reason, the auditor conducting the investigation should be aware of any (and all) control environmental factors throughout the audit, and adjust the audit procedures accordingly.[49]

7.28.4 CONTROL OBJECTIVES USED IN THE FRAMEWORK

Some of the objectives are more apparent than others, but almost all have equally significant importance to the success of the audit investigation conducted. The objectives are as follows.

7.28.4.1 Risk Management

Risk assessments should consider data sensitivity and the need for integrity and the range of risks that an organization's MEI resource elements may be subjected to, including those risks posed by authorized internal and external use, not to mention those outside of the organization attempting unauthorized access. Such analysis draws on reviews conducted on systems, networks, and operations of existing security controls of those systems, as well as reviews and tests conducted on controls for other resource elements.

Organization-wide security program plan. Entities should have a written, documented plan that clearly describes the organization's security program, policies, and procedures. At the very least, the plan and any related policy should cover all MEI resource elements, outlining duties and responsibilities for overseeing security and the organization's resources.

Security management structure. Senior management should establish a structure to implement a security program throughout the organization. The structure generally consists of a core of personnel who are designated as security resources. This staff will then serve a crucial role in developing, communicating, and monitoring compliance with security policies, reporting activities periodically to management. The security resources also provide roles in evaluating the effectiveness of security controls for daily operations, which include program managers who rely on those systems, administrators, and their user base.

Security personnel policies. Policies relating to personnel action, such as hiring and terminating staff members and employee expertise, are important factors for security staff. If personnel policies are not adequate, an organization runs the risk of (1) hiring unqualified or untrustworthy individuals; (2) providing terminated employees with opportunities for sabotage or operational impairment, disablement, or rendering the organization inoperative; (3) failing to detect continuing unauthorized employee actions; (4) lowered employee morale; and (5) allowing staff expertise to decline.

Outsourcing. A rather sensitive area of discussion due to social impacts resulting from downsizing, but nonetheless necessary. Vendor management controls involve the definition of procedures or services to be provided, adherence to agreements and service levels, and qualifications of personnel.

Electronic commerce (or e-commerce). Electronic commerce controls involve the management of contractual standards for transactional security and minimum standards requirements for authentication using certificate authorities.

Interdependencies. Important considerations in managing organization-wide security are the resulting risks to organizational entities from interdependencies of forces internal and external to the organization. A good example of internal and external interdependencies might be a labor strike from outsourced service providers or contractual difficulties by service providers—in either circumstance, neither situation is controllable, as it is beyond the control of the organization.

7.28.5   DATA CLASSIFICATION

Resource owners should determine the level of protection that is most appropriate for the resources that are their responsibility. These determinations should flow directly from the results of the risk assessments that identify threats, vulnerabilities, and possible negative effects that could result from disclosure of confidential or sensitive data or failing to protect the integrity of data supporting mission-critical environments.[50]

All resource classifications should be reviewed and approved by senior management, maintained on file, and periodically reviewed to ensure that they reflect current conditions. Implementing adequate access controls involves determining the level and type of protection, what is appropriate for resources, and who needs access to those resources. Resource owners typically perform and assign these tasks.

Policies specifying classification categories and criteria assist resource owners in classifying their resources according to the need for protective controls. The Computer Security Act of 1987 requires federal government departments and agencies to identify systems that process sensitive data. The term *sensitive data* is defined as "any information, the loss, misuse, or unauthorized access to or modification of which could adversely affect the national interest or the conduct of federal programs, or the privacy to which individuals are entitled under section 552a of title 5, United States Code (the Privacy Act), but which has not been specifically authorized under criteria established by an Executive Order or an Act of Congress to be kept secret in the interest of national defense or foreign policy.50a." OMB Circular A-130, under Appendix III, directs federal agencies to assume that all major systems contain some sensitive information that needs to be protected, but focus extra security controls on a limited number of systems considered high risk.[51]

7.29   VAF STEP 3: ANALYZE, CLASSIFY, AND PRIORITIZE VULNERABILITIES

The major objective of this step is to define and analyze the vulnerabilities identified within the VAF process, most notably step 2 and the MEI external dependencies outlined from step 1, thereby enabling the first order of prioritization for purposes of remediation and minimization of any threats. This step will move the process from the vulnerability assessment phase into the first steps of the remediation phase, with accompanying funding and resource estimates and timelines.[52] For areas of potential compromise involving aspects of integrity, confidentiality, or availability, the assessment team will assign a color-coded value to indicate the impact if the vulnerability were executed and exploited. Color coding graphically demonstrates overall just how vulnerable an operational system is in terms of its levels of exposures and risks to those threats. Most assessment color-code mechanisms weigh the risks and their threats using red (extremely risky), yellow (moderately risky), and green (not risky at all) colors; these threat matrices vary from organization to organization.[53]

7.30 AUTHORS' NOTES

There are many varying methodologies that one can use to perform SVAs, usually tailored or based specifically for their respective industrial sector. For instance, the U.S. federal government has defined and made available a guideline methodology that it recommends for the energy sector through the Energy Sector ISAC, which in many ways is similar to the SVA methodology tool that has been explained in this chapter.[54]

Similarly, the U.S. Department of Homeland Security's Office of Domestic Preparedness has a more generic vulnerability assessment methodology criteria for general non-specific-based vulnerability assessments.[55] The important aspects about vulnerability assessments are (1) what defines risk, (2) how to measure for risk, and (3) how to remediate (if possible) for risk.[56]

NOTES

1. U.S. General Accounting Office, *Information Security Risk Assessment: Practices of Leading Organizations*, GAO/AIMD-00-33, Washington, DC, November 1999; http://www.gao.gov/special.pubs/ai00033.pdf (alt URL: http://cipbook.infracritical.com/book5/chapter7/ch7ref1.pdf).
2. ASME Critical Assets Protection Initiative, ASME Homeland Security, *Risk Analysis and Management for Critical Assets Protection (RAMCAP) Methodology Document*, PS&S Interagency Working Group, September 17, 2004.
3. *ITSC UI Security Risk Assessment Guidebook*, September 2001.
4. Ibid.
5. ASME Critical Assets Protection Initiative, ASME Homeland Security, *Risk Analysis and Management for Critical Assets Protection (RAMCAP) Methodology Document*, PS&S Interagency Working Group, September 17, 2004.
6. *ITSC UI Security Risk Assessment Guidebook*, September 2001.
7. Ibid.
8. http://www.bitpipe.com/tlist/Vulnerability-Assessments.html.
9. *ITSC UI Security Risk Assessment Guidebook*, September 2001.
10. Ibid.
11. ASME Critical Assets Protection Initiative, ASME Homeland Security, *Risk Analysis and Management for Critical Assets Protection (RAMCAP) Methodology Document*, PS&S Interagency Working Group, September 17, 2004.
12. U.S. Critical Infrastructure Assurance Office, *Vulnerability Assessment Framework 1.1*, Washington, DC, October 1998; http://www.defenselink.mil/policy/sections/policy_offices/hd/assets/downloads/dcip/Studies/Other/CIAOCriticalInfrastructureVulnerabilityOct98.pdf (alt URL: http://cipbook.infracritical.com/book5/chapter7/ch7ref2.pdf).
13. Ibid.
14. President Bill Clinton Presidential Decision Directive No. 63, *Critical Infrastructure Protection*; http://www.fas.org/irp/offdocs/pdd/pdd-63.htm (alt URL: http://cipbook.infracritical.com/book5/chapter7/ch7ref5.pdf).
15. U.S. Critical Infrastructure Assurance Office, *Vulnerability Assessment Framework 1.1*, Washington, DC, October 1998; http://www.defenselink.mil/policy/sections/policy_offices/hd/assets/downloads/dcip/Studies/Other/CIAOCriticalInfrastructureVulnerabilityOct98.pdf (alt URL: http://cipbook.infracritical.com/book5/chapter7/ch7ref2.pdf).
16. http://www.isaca.org/cobit.htm.

17. U.S. General Accounting Office, *2010 Census: Basic Design Has Potential, but Remaining Challenges Need Prompt Resolution*, GAO/-05-9, Washington, DC, January 2005; http://www.gao.gov/new.items/d059.pdf (alt URL: http://cipbook.infracritical.com/book5/chapter7/ch7ref4.pdf).

18. U.S. General Accounting Office, *Federal Information Systems Controls and Auditing Manual: Financial Statement Audits*, Volume I, GAO/AIMD-12.19.6, Washington, DC, January 1999, has been replaced by the document contained within the U.S. General Accounting Office, *Federal Information Systems Controls and Auditing Manual*, GAO-09-232G, Washington, DC, February 2009 (document changes effective February 2, 2009); http://www.gao.gov/new.items/d09232g.pdf (alt URL: http://cipbook.infracritical.com/book5/chapter7/ch7ref3.pdf) and ref URL: http://www.gao.gov/products/GAO-09-232G (alt URL: http://cipbook.infracritical.com/book5/chapter7/ch7ref3a.pdf).

19. Ibid.

20. Ibid.

21. Ibid.

22. Ibid.

23. Ibid.

24. Ibid.

25. Ibid.

26. Ibid.

27. Ibid.

28. U.S. Critical Infrastructure Assurance Office, *Vulnerability Assessment Framework 1.1*, Washington,DC,October1998;http://www.defenselink.mil/policy/sections/policy_offices/hd/assets/downloads/dcip/Studies/Other/CIAOCriticalInfrastructureVulnerabilityOct98.pdf (alt URL: http://cipbook.infracritical.com/book5/chapter7/ch7ref2.pdf).

29. U.S. Securities and Exchange Commission, Division of Corporation Finance, *Sarbanes-Oxley Act of 2002—Frequently Asked Questions*; http://www.sec.gov/divisions/corpfin/faqs/soxact2002.htm (alt URL: http://cipbook.infracritical.com/book5/chapter7/ch7ref8.pdf).

30. U.S. General Accounting Office, *Federal Information Systems Controls and Auditing Manual*, GAO-09-232G, Washington, DC, February 2009 (document changes effective on February 2, 2009); http://www.gao.gov/new.items/d09232g.pdf (alt URL: http://cipbook.infracritical.com/book5/chapter7/ch7ref3.pdf) and ref URL: http://www.gao.gov/products/GAO-09-232G (alt URL: http://cipbook.infracritical.com/book5/chapter7/ch7ref3a.pdf).

31. Ibid.

32. Ibid.

33. U.S. Critical Infrastructure Assurance Office, *Vulnerability Assessment Framework 1.1*, Washington,DC,October1998;http://www.defenselink.mil/policy/sections/policy_offices/hd/assets/downloads/dcip/Studies/Other/CIAOCriticalInfrastructureVulnerabilityOct98.pdf (alt URL: http://cipbook.infracritical.com/book5/chapter7/ch7ref2.pdf).

34. Ibid.

35. Ibid.

36. State of North Carolina, *Information Security Vulnerability Assessment*, Preliminary Statewide Assessment, Office of the State Auditor, December 2002; http://www.ncauditor.net/EPSWeb/Reports/InfoSystems/ISA-2002-1000.pdf (alt URL: http://cipbook.infracritical.com/book5/chapter7/ch7ref12.pdf).

37. U.S. Critical Infrastructure Assurance Office, *Vulnerability Assessment Framework 1.1*, Washington,DC,October1998;http://www.defenselink.mil/policy/sections/policy_offices/hd/assets/downloads/dcip/Studies/Other/CIAOCriticalInfrastructureVulnerabilityOct98.pdf (alt URL: http://cipbook.infracritical.com/book5/chapter7/ch7ref2.pdf).

38. State of North Carolina, *Information Security Vulnerability Assessment*, Preliminary Statewide Assessment, Office of the State Auditor, December 2002; http://www.ncauditor.net/EPSWeb/Reports/InfoSystems/ISA-2002-1000.pdf (alt URL: http://cipbook. infracritical.com/book5/chapter7/ch7ref12.pdf).

39. U.S. Critical Infrastructure Assurance Office, *Vulnerability Assessment Framework 1.1*, Washington,DC,October1998;http://www.defenselink.mil/policy/sections/policy_offices/ hd/assets/downloads/dcip/Studies/Other/CIAOCriticalInfrastructureVulnerabilityOct98. pdf (alt URL: http://cipbook.infracritical.com/book5/chapter7/ch7ref2.pdf).

40. Ibid.

41. Ibid.

42. Ibid.

43. Ibid.

44. Ibid.

45. Ibid.

46. Ibid.

47. This document has been updated with a revision (February 2006) with the same title: *Guide for Developing Security Plans for Information Technology Systems*, NIST Special Publication 800-18, National Institute of Standards and Technology, Washington, DC, 1998; URL to the old document: http://cipbook.infracritical.com/ book5/chapter7/ch7ref7.pdf; URL to the current SP800-18-Revision-1 document: http://csrc.nist.gov/publications/nistpubs/800-18-Rev1/sp800-18-Rev1-final.pdf   (alt URL: http://cipbook.infracritical.com/book5/chapter7/ch7ref7a.pdf).

48. U.S. Critical Infrastructure Assurance Office, *Vulnerability Assessment Framework 1.1*, Washington,DC,October1998;http://www.defenselink.mil/policy/sections/policy_offices/ hd/assets/downloads/dcip/Studies/Other/CIAOCriticalInfrastructureVulnerabilityOct98. pdf (alt URL: http://cipbook.infracritical.com/book5/chapter7/ch7ref2.pdf).

49. Ibid.

50. U.S. Critical Infrastructure Assurance Office, *Practices for Securing Critical Information Assets*, Washington, DC, 2000; http://www.infragard.net/library/pdfs/securing_critical_ assets.pdf (alt URL: http://cipbook.infracritical.com/book5/chapter7/ch7ref6.pdf).

50a. http://csrc.nist.gov/publications/nistbul/csl92-11.txt (alt URL: http://cipbook.infracritical.com/book5/chapter7/ch7ref13.pdf).

51. U.S. Critical Infrastructure Assurance Office, *Vulnerability Assessment Framework 1.1*, Washington,DC,October1998;http://www.defenselink.mil/policy/sections/policy_offices/ hd/assets/downloads/dcip/Studies/Other/CIAOCriticalInfrastructureVulnerabilityOct98. pdf (alt URL: http://cipbook.infracritical.com/book5/chapter7/ch7ref2.pdf).

52. Ibid.

53. Ibid.

54. U.S. Department of Energy, Office of Energy Assurance, *Vulnerability Assessment Methodology, Electric Power Infrastructure*, September 30, 2002; http://www.esisac. com/publicdocs/assessment_methods/VA.pdf (alt URL: http://cipbook.infracritical. com/book5/chapter7/ch7ref9.pdf).

55. U.S. Department of Homeland Security, Office of Domestic Preparedness, *Vulnerability Assessment Methodologies Report*, July 2003; http://www.ojp.usdoj.gov/odp/docs/vam-report.pdf (alt URL: http://cipbook.infracritical.com/book5/chapter7/ch7ref10.pdf).

56. National Oceanic and Atmospheric Administration, Coastal Services Center, *Vulnerability Assessment Techniques and Applications*; http://www.csc.noaa.gov/vata/ case_pdf.html (alt URL: http://cipbook.infracritical.com/book5/chapter7/ch7ref11.pdf).

8 Regulations

8.1 INTRODUCTION

This chapter examines the role of regulation within the critical infrastructure protection (CIP) and critical infrastructure assurance (CIA) domains. It is an overview of the major relationships between international, national, and industrial standards, along with several emerging issues.

8.2 THE ROLE OF OVERSIGHT

The term *oversight* is of particular importance to the CIP and CIA domains. This is because these domains involve three very particular sets of demands:

- The public demand for a service or good that is necessary to preserve their safety, security, or economic well-being
- The corporate demand for the ability to generate a reasonable return on investment (ROI)
- The government accountability for ensuring that an appropriate balance can exist between the two above competing demands

Consider the following examples.

A meat processing plant handles a significant amount of the raw beef production in the regional economy. The corporation, in order to generate wealth, attempts to reduce costs and increase the amount of production in some combination of number of units and time spent per unit. As a result, it strives to spend the minimum amount of time and effort per unit of production (efficiency) in reaching the point at which it can sell its product. At the same time, the public wants an absolute assurance that the food product it is eating is safe for consumption. The government's role in terms of oversight is to ensure that each side is aware of any limitations. These are communicated through either laws or regulations or both, that are associated with the production and processing of the finished meat products.

One can also see this in other infrastructure sectors, such as the transportation sector. On one hand, the public would like to be able to drive as fast as it wants to on major highways, to reduce the amount of time spent getting to what they want to be doing next. But at the same time, drivers want assurances that they are driving on reasonably safe highways. In this context, the government's role involves licensing, laws, regulations, and other measures (including maintenance of the roadway) while at the same time trying to maintain that balance between the conflicting priorities described above.

Where this becomes problematic is when it is no longer recognized that each party (the public, the corporations, and the government) has a role to play. It is not the role of government, for example, to manage businesses, and it is not the role of business to assume the role of government. Finally, it is not the role of the public to attempt to do either. Each party has its own role to play, which can be defined as follows:

- The role of the public is to conduct itself in line with laws, regulations, and corporate policies (when at work) and to take measures that are considered to be reasonable in protecting itself (such as cooking certain foods, etc.).
- The role of the corporation is to conduct itself in line with certain constraints and restraints (laws, regulations, and risk management) and to exercise due care in its operations when it comes to dealing with the public (such as not selling unsafe automobiles, etc.).
- The role of the government includes two key accountabilities. The first and most important is the protection of its population and its own national integrity. For example, allowing a manufacturing process that can be reasonably expected to kill a number of workers per year might be considered a failure of government to exercise appropriate control—particularly if you are a family member of the killed worker. The corollary, however, is that the government is also required to exercise due care in its decision making so as not to inappropriately affect business or the personal lives of its populations.

What happens when these factors become misaligned? The answer is fairly simple in that the system is like a wine glass, which, being subjected to sound, will at first begin to vibrate, then resonate, and if conditions meet a certain set of criteria, ultimately shatter. As we work through this chapter, the various ways that this vibration, resonance, and destruction come about will be examined.

8.3   THE EFFECT OF GLOBALIZATION

Perhaps the largest impact of globalization comes from how oversight activities have changed. As long as private sector entities were required to adhere to the laws of the nation in which they were registered, the situation could be argued as being relatively controllable. If the company failed to adhere to the written law or, at the least, to maintain the intent of that law, then the overseeing body (often the state) could step in and demand changes be made.

Today, globalization takes on three major forms:

- Companies registering in other countries, often due to issues associated with taxation and regulation
- Companies outsourcing certain parts of their operations in order to realize benefits associated with lowered costs
- Outside companies competing more aggressively to take over part of the operations of a company or establish market share in a new market

We see clear examples of the first instance in the transportation sector, specifically within the maritime sector. Shipping companies often register their ships under what is called a "flag of convenience." What this basically involves is that a country offers a company the opportunity to register its ships to that country's flag, usually for a small fee and as long as it establishes a branch office. Because the United Nations Convention on the Law of the Sea[1] indicates that it is the flag to which the ship is registered that is responsible for the administration of law on board the vessel, this allows companies to register their ships where they perceive the ability to increase their profits due to less regulation or less tax burden.[2]

While this may be an accepted business practice, it can also be looked upon as an imbalance where the company has found a way to sidestep its own nation's controls and operate under what may be considered more agreeable terms. For example, if Country A taxes ship operations to 10% and Country B taxes those same operations to a 5% level, that difference then becomes part of the company's ROI. This also applies to the costs that can be incurred through compliance within regulatory regimes including safety, security, and environmental or pollution control.

A second example can be seen in situations where companies have decided to move part or all of their production operations offshore to realize cost savings. These cost savings can be linked to things like labor costs, cost of infrastructure, utility costs, and raw material costs, but can also include costs associated with oversight regimes in their host country. In these cases, the offshoring movement can again be linked to a cost reduction (and its obvious link to competitiveness) effort, and the company's desire to increase its overall ROI.

While this may not be an overt attempt to bypass the oversight associated with government regimes, those factors often play at least a participatory role. For example, labor costs must also factor in costs associated with the maintenance of safety programs and their systems. Where one regime's safety program costs significantly more than that of another regime, the other costs associated with labor must logically decrease if the total costs associated with labor are to remain the same. Given that these other costs also tend to increase, then the natural bias shifts toward those places where the overall costs are lower.

The third instance can be seen in terms of the natural competition within the marketplace. Consider the energy sector, for example. There is a logical argument to be made that a nation should maintain at least some of its capacity to bring its own natural energy resources to their end usable state. Otherwise, it faces a strategic vulnerability in that the lack of processing capability can result in the loss of a key resource necessary to sustain the supply of fuels or lubricants. In order to gain control over market share, companies attempt to either develop or acquire companies that represent that part of the market, and consequently to be able to increase their influence in environments that can generate profits.

This last factor can extend, under the right conditions, to a state of competition between nation-states. Consider the premise that a nation that controls the critical infrastructure of another nation, its ability to generate wealth through export and the exploitation of resources, and can influence public policy can be seen as having achieved strategic advantage over that nation. In this case, international competition may shift somewhat from the limited conflicts we have seen to the attempts to gain control over specific sectors that would lead to the ability to identify, assess, establish, maintain, and adjust potential avenues of advantage—specifically energy, telecommunications, transportation, and government.

8.4   CONVENTIONS, LAWS, AND REGULATIONS

If the role of the nation-state is being eroded through international and transnational business, then there is a difficult choice to be made. Does the government restrict businesses from operating at this level, risking its ability to compete internationally or losing the business as it shifts offshore? Does a different mechanism come into play that serves to elevate the interest of the state in such a way that the overall balance is maintained? National bodies seeking to cooperate may do so through a number of mechanisms, and the convention is one of the most common of these.

We see this in the level of influence of various international bodies that have overseen international operations—notably in sectors such as banking, transportation, and emergency services. These organizations can be put under increasing pressure as their level of involvement increases at both tactical/operational levels that may require immediate decisions and at strategic levels where they are asked to provide an increasing level of input into how certain issues are addressed.

This is largely due to a failure to maintain an appropriate scope of activities and level of participation at this level. These bodies are generally formed in order to ensure compatibility and coherence between the various participants in the sector. Should certain participants become more complacent, they can put themselves in a situation where their government's policy objectives are not heard and the decisions made by consensus actually impose directions on the sovereign state.

These decisions, *conventions,* can be described in terms of sets of rules that are expressly recognized by consenting states. In this context, enforcement is based on a combination of community involvement and sanctions being linked to either agreed-upon penalties, limitation of operations, or in extreme cases, exclusion from the community of signatory states.

The convention system provides a relatively consistent framework from which all countries operate. This has been particularly evident in the aviation safety and security domains, international shipping and human rights law, as well as a host of similar agreements. In each of these cases, the basic requirements are communicated to the world as being the minimum standards or the desirable standards to achieve if membership within that community is to be maintained.

This is where the sovereignty of nations comes into play and has an impact on measures associated with the convention. Where the convention was agreed to, there are many circumstances where it must be ratified through the appropriate legislative bodies. At the same time, the measures put forward in the convention may actually become minimum requirements (baselines) if the country's legislative bodies determine that they wish to impose more significant or broader measures. At this point, the convention becomes the minimum set of requirements and the legislation put in place becomes the higher set of requirements.

The legislation that is put into place does not necessarily reflect the exact requirements of the convention involved. It often acts as an enabling mechanism that allows a senior government official to establish requirements to be met in response to the nation's requirements under the convention. These requirements, supported by legislation, are often referred to as regulatory requirements.

8.5 GUIDANCE AND BEST PRACTICES

While the nations have their legislation and regulations, the holder of the convention will often promulgate guidance and best practices associated with meeting the requirements of the convention. These may be done through a committee or working group that has a specific interest in the topic.

There is a difference between the intent of legislation and regulation and its written word. The intent of legislation is something that is fixed (like a snapshot) in time and is best described in terms of being a goal. It is often aspirational in nature. For example, the intent of legislation may be to reduce the amount of crime on the streets or it may be to deter persons from attempting to disrupt certain core services. In any case, it needs to be clear that the legislation and regulations are put in place for a specific reason and that reason becomes its intent.

The written word of legislation and regulation is continuously being interpreted and reinterpreted, not necessarily in line with the intent of the legislation. Regulation is not necessarily a cooperative effort—it has an element of intrusion and enforcement built into it. As a result, it is constantly under examination by the private sector, special interest groups, and even individuals to see whether or not the legislation or regulation can be used to advantage.

Legislation and regulation may require a level of clarification. Guidance, in this case, serves to provide a greater level of clarity with respect to what the legislation or regulation intended. Guidance will generally involve a description of the intent that is at the foundation of the requirement, a reference to the specific guidance itself, and ultimately further information regarding what is needed to meet the intent.

Guidance, however, does not constitute law. It clarifies the written requirements and ensures that the interpretation of the written requirements remains in line with the overall intent. It can also serve to educate those falling under the legislation by providing a level of instruction or explanation. Unless that guidance is passed through the legislative process, it is not considered law.

While guidance may not be included in the same administrative category as law, it still has a level of weight. This comes from the fact that the guidance is related back to the intent associated with the legislation or regulation. Consider the following chain of events:

- A need is identified, and a convention is established, to address that international need.
- A convention is ratified by a number of signatory states.
- Each signatory state passes requirements defined within the convention into law.
- Regulations or similar requirements are established in order to specifically define the requirements.

- Individuals seek to interpret the regulations—either in order to meet the requirements or to find ways to bypass the regulations.
- It is observed that there are a number of entities that are failing to meet the requirements.
- It is determined that this failure is due to some apparent lack of understanding.
- Further information is provided that describes the goal and specific nature of the requirement, often in terms of guidance.

Therefore guidance plays an important role in the defining or refining of the intent of something that is not clear. By doing so, it helps to offset misinterpretation of the written word. This can be looked at in the context of *mens rea*,[3] one of the foundational elements of criminal law. There may be an argument that where the intent is defined and further refined through guidance, an individual that chooses to interpret it another way may find himself or herself to be in difficult legal territory and may need to consult with legal experts.

Best practices, as compared to a guidance, are little more than an example. The specific measures are in response to a decision to ensure that risk does not reach unacceptable or inappropriate levels. This risk is based on a range of factors (impact, probability, asset value, and vulnerability). What the best practices do is provide an example of how to meet a specific goal (such as keeping a ship from being hijacked, a network from being compromised, and so on) given certain circumstances and conditions. It should be clear that best practices do not necessarily translate across all environments.

8.6 PRESCRIPTIVE VS. PERFORMANCE BASED

The need for flexibility has led to two different kinds of requirements being set:

- Prescriptive regulations
- Performance-based regulations

The term *prescriptive* can be described in terms of what is supposed to happen. For example, a door may need to be fitted with a very specific sort of lock, be constructed a certain way, and need to be checked at certain clearly defined intervals to ensure that it is undamaged and locked. The key factor is that prescriptive regulations are often highly measurable—such as fencing at a certain height and of certain design, etc.

Prescriptive regulations are often argued as being superior because they are clear and allow little room for interpretation. For instance, if requirements call for a six-foot fence, then one simply has to measure the fence, determine that it meets or exceeds the six-foot height criteria, and check off that that requirement had been met. For those organizations that are regulated, the use of prescriptive requirements also allows them to make a much more clear and defensible *business impact assessment* statement—the design of the fence (and hence its cost to install) being known. These assessments, and those that are similar, are often used in the consultative processes associated with the drafting of measures and regulations as the foundation for seeking funds through contribution programs or similar mechanisms.

Prescriptive regulations also lend themselves to the inspection process. This is again because the nature of the requirements is empirical (measurable and repeatable). An inspector can present himself or herself at the location being inspected with a list of items to be checked, can check the items against clearly defined criteria, and can issue an indication almost immediately as to whether the location being inspected was compliant with the requirements. In short, it is a basic process of verification.

Performance-based regulation, on the other hand, uses the concept of goals and objectives as opposed to specific, empirical measures. These goals include things such as preventing unauthorized entry, deterring specific events, responding effectively to situations, or taking reasonable steps to accomplish certain goals. This lies in the realm of risk management in that it defines the acceptable thresholds of risk and the approaches to be taken in managing that risk.

This is not the realm of inspection, but rather the realm of auditing and testing. The inspection process may be used to verify if plan measures have been put in place, but those plans must take into account the need to adjust measures in such a way that the measures align appropriately with the goal and the operational and threat environments. In other words, if the threat to the facility changes, then the system must be able to adapt to meet that new threat.

8.7 IMPACT ON CRIMINAL, ADMINISTRATIVE, AND CIVIL LAW

The difference between *prescriptive* and *performance-based* systems is profound when entering into the realm of enforcement and the law. This is because there are layers of complexity that must be addressed.

First, legal issues are handled through the criminal courts. The mechanics of these courts are fairly straightforward and relatively well known to persons involved. There is the stating of the charge, the requirement to prove that an individual is guilty beyond a reasonable doubt, and the assignment of a sentence that falls within the range allowed by the legislation and that is consistent and commensurate with past actions. In the realm of critical infrastructure protection and critical infrastructure assurance, however, the use of criminal charges is not common. In fact, the majority of the CIP and CIA-related issues will be handled through other means.

This alternate means falls within the realm of administrative law. In this case, the power is held by the various federal bodies (departments, agencies, etc.) and stems from their ability to set regulations under enabling legislation. In this area of law, one finds the "rules" within structures similar to those of the United States and the "regulations" for systems similar to those of Canada.

The difference between the criminal court and the administrative tribunal also includes the burden needed to be met in order for the regulator to receive a favorable outcome. In a criminal court one's guilt has to be proven beyond a reasonable doubt. In the case of the administrative tribunal, the burden is based more along the lines of a preponderance of evidence.

Civil law deals with disputes between individuals and organizations—such as tort (injury), contracts, property disputes, and similar kinds of issues. Within the realm of CIP and CIA, civil law can create a significant challenge. For example, an organization that causes damage to one individual's property may be responsible for a few thousand dollars damage. If that organization is responsible for damages that span thousands of properties and may have been involved in a loss of life, then the consequences associated with the event would be several orders of magnitude higher.

When the first edition of this work was written, a significant number of companies followed the practice of attempting to cover their liabilities through insurance coverage. Since that time, it has become more and more widely accepted that insurance coverage can be at best a partial coverage. This is for the following reasons:

- *Limitation on the level of coverage.* Particularly the fact that the consequences of an event are likely to outstrip any insurance coverage unless very significantly underwritten.
- *Exclusions.* Eliminating coverage for certain kinds of acts, property, or types of damage.

Civil proceedings are the mechanism that would set the level of damages—individually or as part of a class action. The question would be whether or not either of the two insurance limitations would apply and, as a result, how exposed the company would be to losses.

In the context of civil proceedings, the burden lies with being able to demonstrate whether or not the organization took all reasonable steps to prevent harm. This again falls into a more subjective category involving tests like the reasonable person test, which essentially assesses whether or not a person with similar background and experience would come to the same conclusion under the same circumstances, or perform the same steps. It may also include determining whether or not a duty of care existed and whether or not the standard of care had been breached. In both cases, the tests are reasonably subjective in nature.

8.8   POTENTIAL ABUSES OF AUTHORITY AND CREDIBILITY

Individuals often assume that when they are charged with any kind of offense, they have the option of going to court. One of the challenges associated with the increase in regulatory regimes is that it is becoming increasingly possible for an individual to be sanctioned, usually in terms of a fine, without having the opportunity to appear before a court—only an appointed adjudicator. This is of significant concern in that the burden of proof placed on the system is far lower in these administrative tribunals than they are in the various court systems.

These systems function as a part of the executive branch of government. As noted by Justice William Vancise,[4] these tribunals were created to bypass problems experienced in the courts, including the following:

- The formality and reliance on procedures
- Retention of counsel and costs associated with that
- Unable to reach expeditious decisions under the adversarial model
- Unable to meet the demands associated with a high volume of cases
- Lacking expertise in some public policy matters[5]

When looking at this list, one might be forgiven for asking whether or not these tribunals fall into line with the intention of the judicial branch in terms of protecting individuals against abuses of process, although this should be tempered by the knowledge that these are risks to be guarded against and not necessarily the situation in all cases.

8.9   GOVERNMENT VS. INDUSTRY SELF-REGULATION

While the potential for administrative tribunals to cause unfair situations certainly exists, it is not the only issue that should be watched closely. The other movement is toward industry self-regulation—often due to factors such as a lack of government resources, a lack of technical knowledge, or simply as a result of pressure placed on government bodies.

In the concept of industry self-regulation, the various private sector participants come together under a common body that is then delegated to act in terms of center of expertise, regulatory body, and auditor/evaluator. The delegation from the state is needed so as to maintain the link between the state's accountability and responsibility to the population it intends to protect as well as setting a framework around the activities of the body.

This body is then expected to set structures that see its membership meeting the requirements of the overall balance. This may include operational constraints, the requirement to adhere to a code of conduct, or other challenges. It requires that each participant in the body places a limit on its own self-interest, and a check is applied to ensure that this limit remains in force.

The challenge with industry self-regulation lies in the accountability and the level of trust that can be placed in organizations that are intended to generate wealth. Will those organizations apply the necessary level of effort and commitment toward setting down appropriate conduct and constraints, establishing various monitoring and enforcement regimes, or even maintaining the ability to follow up on apparent failings in the system?

Several other factors come into play when looking at self-regulation. Self-regulation, like regulation, is not something that just happens. These factors include the following:

- There are costs involved. Industry participants will often require third parties to perform the various oversight roles in order to ensure that proprietary information and trade secrets are appropriately protected from competition.
- Gathering the necessary intelligence and data can also be costly. Government regulatory bodies often have access to the information from other departments without having to incur significant costs.

These are two of the major challenges associated with this form of regulatory oversight, and while they are relatively empirical in nature, they cannot be looked at outside of the potential influences in terms of public confidence and the issues associated with conflicts of interest or vested interests.

8.10   KNOWLEDGE GAPS ARISING FROM PERFORMANCE-BASED REGULATION

Combined with the above challenges, performance-based regulations can lead to the creation of a knowledge gap, particularly if any one of the parties fails to maintain its knowledge base. The performance-based system relies heavily upon the assessment that all reasonable steps have been taken to achieve some goal or maintain some objective.

In order to assess the outcome of the various steps, the inspector has to possess an adequate understanding of the technical details surrounding the security control and the skills necessary to assess it appropriately. In cases where the inspector does not possess that knowledge, then a potential problem arises with respect to maintaining the ability to enforce regulations.

Should the inspector demand that an enforcement action be taken, the ability to enforce the regulation at the tribunal level could also be challenged. This again casts back to the reasonable person test. If the security controls are designed by individuals that possess advanced education and training, including relevant professional designations or certifications, the inspector could be challenged on a lack of knowledge if he or she does not possess an adequate level of demonstrable understanding of the control.

This is of particular concern in periods of fiscal restraint. While much of the CIP and CIA domains are evolving rapidly, organizations are often tempted to cut back on training and professional development costs as a means of protecting their budgets. This essentially trades short-term gain for long-term pain—similar to a lack of exercise.

8.11   PREDICTABILITY IN PRESCRIPTIVE SYSTEMS: A SYSTEMIC VULNERABILITY

The use of prescriptive regulations and regimes built on best practices also creates additional vulnerabilities within the system. These regimes are often published to assist those who fall under them gain access to information that helps them remain compliant. This assumes that only those persons that we want to have access to that information will download it and no others—wishful thinking.

When prescriptive regulations and checklist-driven inspections begin to overtake effective risk management, there are two things that will occur over time. The first is that the probability of undetected risks creeping into the overall system will gradually increase. The second is that somebody will gain access to the information and use it to engineer his or her way into the overall facility—using the information as a road map through the protective measures. Neither of these conditions is particularly acceptable given that the goal is to secure and assure critical infrastructure and services.

8.12   AUTHORS' NOTES

The concept of regulation needs to be approached carefully and in accordance with an understanding of the various risks involved. It needs to establish the necessary balance between the priorities of public safety, economic performance, and credible oversight in order to function appropriately. While this chapter has provided a brief overview of some of the challenges that are currently emerging, this is one area where there will certainly be more opportunity for work by those in the public administration and legal communities.

NOTES

1. United Nations Law of the Sea Treaty; http://www.unlawoftheseatreaty.org.
2. United Nations Convention on the Law of the Sea, Agreement Relating to the Implementation of Part XI of the Convention; http://www.un.org/Depts/los/convention_agreements/texts/unclos/closindx.htm.
3. The term *mens rea* is Latin, meaning "guilty mind." This term is used within criminal law, as it is viewed as one of the elements considered for a crime.
4. http://www.cba.org/cba/cle/pdf/Vancise_bio.pdf.
5. http://www.ombudsman.sk.ca/uploads/.../sk-law-review-for-web-en.pdf.

9 Information Sharing and Analysis Centers

9.1 INTRODUCTION

This chapter outlines all Information Sharing and Analysis Centers (ISACs) established throughout the United States for various critical infrastructure sectors. Not all sectors have ISAC organizations, and therefore may be conglomerated or associated with other sectors' ISAC organizations.*

Added to this chapter are some of the challenges that have arisen within the ISAC context. It is the contention of the authors that these challenges are a significant hurdle that needs to be crossed in order for critical infrastructure to be truly protected. To accomplish this, a fundamental change in perspective is necessary in how we look at and share information, perhaps even at how the private and public sectors interact in this respect.

9.2 WHAT IS A CRITICAL INFRASTRUCTURE ASSET?

A *critical infrastructure asset*[1] is an asset, both physical and logical, that is so vital that its disruption, infiltration, incapacitation, destruction, or misuse would have a debilitating impact on the health, safety, welfare, or economic security of citizens and businesses. Critical infrastructures shall include human, physical, and cyber assets.[2] An example might be a business master file (BMF) identified within the Internal Revenue Service (IRS),[3] which is labeled as an IRS-critical infrastructure asset; all tax data and related information pertaining to individual business income taxpayers are posted to the BMF so that the file reflects a continuously updated and current record of each taxpayer's account. All settlements with taxpayers are effected through computer processing of the BMF account, and the data therein are used for accounting records, for issuance of refund checks, bills, or notices, answering inquiries, classifying returns for audit, preparing reports, and other matters concerned with the processing and enforcement activities of the IRS.[4]

It is important to distinguish between the term *critical infrastructure* and, in this sense, what may be described as an infrastructure that is critical or vital to the performance of tasks or abilities of an entity to meet its obligations. Critical infrastructure is limited to infrastructure that directly supports the safety, security, and economic well-being of the population. Essentially, one (critical infrastructure) is about importance to an entire society, whereas the latter (an infrastructure that is

---

* At the time of writing this book, there were additional ISAC organizations found or established. Not all ISAC organizations may be listed within this book, and as such, may be revised for future releases.

vital) is important only to that organization, and not necessarily to an entire society. It is equally important to understand that the key resources and interdependencies associated with an entity's ability to deliver a service may actually have an impact (directly or indirectly) on a critical infrastructure or the ability of that infrastructure to support society.

9.3   WHAT IS AN ISAC?

An ISAC provides several services that are key specific to whatever sector (as outlined within Presidential Decision Directive (PDD)-63 and Homeland Security Presidential Decision Directive (HSPD)-7) is specified—that is, an ISAC fulfills the following functions:

- It provides a 24/7 early threat and detection warning system, and incident reporting and response processes.
- It provides a "members area" that ensures the protection of member, proprietary, and sensitive information, specific to one or more sectors and the companies that they represent.
- It provides an open forum community to all pertinent members within the sector being serviced (usually limited only to membership).
- It provides tailored/customized alerting mechanisms based on membership physical and IT-based profiles.
- It promotes information sharing among members; membership decides and determines methods of dissemination.
- It collects information reports from various sources, which include educational institutions, government, law enforcement (along with public safety), and vendors supporting the sector; information is consolidated and vetted based on the criteria established by the membership.
- Information that is facilitated and distributed is sanitized of any classified or proprietary information for general distribution and dissemination to the membership.

9.4   ADVANTAGES OF BELONGING TO AN ISAC

An ISAC is a one-stop clearinghouse for information relating to information technology (IT) threats, physical threats, risks, vulnerabilities, and their solutions. The member company (individual or agency) will better understand the threats and vulnerabilities for that sector to take any appropriate action, when and where necessary. Members may submit information anonymously and receive near-real-time updates, receiving information, patches, and updates from the 24/7 incident response center(s) from sector experts.

9.5   ACCESS TO ISAC INFORMATION

Access to industry-specific sources of information includes:

- U.S. and foreign government information (not necessarily publicly released or available through public communications channels)
- National and international Computer Emergency Response Team (CERT) information (not necessarily publicly available through public communications channels)
- Law enforcement/public safety agencies, departments, and related information
- Hardware and software vendors and manufacturing information
- Independent research and analysis information from sector experts
- Geospatial analysis of threats to membership assets within the sector

The concept of having access to ISAC information has been a significant challenge. On one hand, certain entities cannot legitimately share information given any legal constraints that may have been placed on them. On the other hand, certain other entities may be unwilling to share information given a lack of confidence that information regarding their vulnerabilities would be kept from their competitors, regulators, or the public in general.

9.6 EXPANDED ISAC SERVICES

Expanded membership services allow for the immediate availability of additional services and products at discounted prices, which include:

- Network vulnerability assessments and information obtained from those assessments (recent and historical information is often available)
- On-site incident reporting and response support mechanisms
- Intrusion investigation and IT/data forensics capabilities (where applicable)
- Remote monitoring of intrusion attempts for either physical or IT-related intrusions, or both
- Risk management, mitigation, and its analysis, along with any and all data produced from the investigation process

9.7 SURFACE TRANSPORTATION ISAC

At the request of the U.S. Department of Transportation (DOT), the Surface Transportation ISAC (ST-ISAC) was formed, which includes the Public Transportation ISAC (referred to as an ISAC within an ISAC), taking advantage of the overarching capabilities of the ST-ISAC to realize economies of scale. The ST-ISAC provides a secure physical and IT-related security capability for owners, operators, and users of the transportation infrastructure(s). Security and threat information is collected from worldwide resources, analyzed, and distributed to members to help protect vital systems from any potential attack (physical or IT related). The ST-ISAC is owned by the EWA Information and Infrastructure Technologies, Inc. (EWA/IIT; www.ewa-iit.com) and co-owned by the Association of American Railroads (AAR; www.aar.org) and the American Public Transportation Association (APTA; www.apta.com).[5]

The ST-ISAC is a natural extension of the railroad industry's *Terrorism Risk Analysis and Security Management Plan*[6] and will work in conjunction with the DOT's Transportation Information Operations Center, which will rely on industry resources, receiving information from the AAR/Railinc ST-ISAC, for physical and cyber-related information and to serve as a link with industry.[7]

9.8 SUPPLY CHAIN ISAC

The supply chain ISAC (SC-ISAC) collects, analyzes, and disseminates security intelligence across the supply chain industry. At the heart of SC-ISAC is SC Investigate, a Web-based application for the collection, analysis, and dissemination of information relating to cargo theft, counterfeit products, illegal diversion, and organizations behind smuggling operations.[8]

SC-ISAC was launched in June 2006 with the announcement of its sponsorship by the International Cargo Security Council at its annual conference in Nashville, Tennesee. SC-ISAC was unanimously voted into the ISAC Council in September 2006.[9]

9.9 PUBLIC TRANSIT ISAC

Through the APTA Executive Committee's Security Task Force, the transit industry identified a nationwide need for sharing security intelligence information. In January 2003, the APTA was designated as the sector coordinator by the DOT in the creation of the Public Transit ISAC (PT-ISAC) to further promote security for the public transportation industry. As the designated sector coordinator, APTA serves as the primary contact to organize and bring the public transportation community together to work cooperatively on physical and IT-related security issues. The PT-ISAC collects, analyzes, and distributes critical security and threat-related information from government and private information resources, and is an ISAC within an ISAC, signifying that it has taken advantage of the already-existing support structure mechanisms currently supported by the ST-ISAC, which is sponsored and coordinated by AAR. The PT-ISAC has specialists with security clearances working at government-cleared facilities with secured communications. The advantages of being part of the ST-ISAC are that the viability of reporting and support is greatly increased and enhanced, and economies of scale are more easily realized.[10] Best security practices and plans to eliminate threats, attacks, vulnerabilities, and countermeasures are drawn on to protect the sector's cyber and physical infrastructures.[11]

The PT-ISAC collects, analyzes, and distributes critical cyber and physical security and threat information from various sources, such as law enforcement, government operations centers, the intelligence community, the U.S. military, academia, and IT vendors on a 24/7 basis. The PT-ISAC has government-experienced analysts with top secret and higher clearances working in government-cleared facilities with secure communications focusing on transit-specific information requirements.[12]

There was no cost to the organization during the initial two years of service. Through a two-year grant from the Federal Transit Administration (FTA),[13] APTA has retained a private sector contractor, EWA/IIT. EWA/IIT, which employs counterterrorism and intelligence community experts, currently operates both the Surface Transportation and Water ISACs.[14]

9.10 AMERICAN PUBLIC TRANSPORTATION ASSOCIATION

APTA is a nonprofit international association of more than 1,500 public and private member organizations, including transit systems and commuter rail operators; planning, design, construction, and finance firms; product and service providers; academic institutions; transit associations; and state departments of transportation. APTA members service the public interest by providing safe, efficient, and economical transit services and products. Roughly 90% of all public transportation systems within the United States and Canada are served by APTA members.[15]

9.11 ASSOCIATION OF AMERICAN RAILROADS

AAR members include the major freight railroads in the United States, Canada, and Mexico, as well as Amtrak. Based in Washington, D.C., the AAR is committed to keeping the railroads of North America safe, fast, efficient, clean, and technologically advanced, which includes involvement in programs to improve efficiency, safety, and servicing capabilities of the railroad industry. Two subsidiaries of AAR, the Transportation Technology Center, Inc. (TTCI) and Railinc, ensure that railroads remain up-to-date in terms of transportation and information technologies.[16]

9.12 TRANSPORTATION TECHNOLOGY CENTER, INC.

The TTCI is one of two wholly owned subsidiaries of AAR. Located in Pueblo, Colorado, TTCI provides intermodal research and test center information used in both passenger and freight operations. TTCI focuses on programs that will enhance railroad safety, reliability, and productivity, and operates a 24/7 training facility for emergency response personnel responding to transportation accidents involving hazardous materials (HAZMAT). The facilities that may conduct any testing are owned by the Federal Railroad Administration but are operated by TTCI.[17]

9.13 RAILINC

Railinc is an owned subsidiary of AAR. Located in Cary, North Carolina, Railinc is the leading provider of IT and related services to North America's railroads. It has extensive databases that include information such as all rail freight inventories within North America. It also supports one of the world's largest electronic data interchange (EDI) networks, over which approximately 5.8 million messages and transactions are transmitted and processed daily. Railinc also operates a Web-based service in which rail customers can track shipments, receive estimated time of arrival information, order equipment, discover shipping options, and find out pricing information.[18]

9.14   WATER ISAC

More than 170,000 public water systems provide water for more than 250 million people in the United States. The Safe Drinking Water Act (SDWA)[19] defines *public water system* as "a system for the provision to the public of water for human consumption through pipes or other constructed conveyances, if such system has at least 15 service connections or regularly serves at least 25 individuals ... and includes collection, treatment, storage, and distribution facilities used primarily in connection with the system."[20] The Environmental Protection Agency (EPA) regulations recognize two primary types of such systems: (1) "community water systems," which provide drinking water to the same people year-round, and (2) "non-community water systems," which serve people on a less than year-round basis at such places as schools, factories, or gas stations.[21]

There are approximately 16,000 municipal sewage treatment works, servicing 73% of the U.S. population. Privately owned treatment systems, including septic tanks, serve the remaining population. The Federal Water Pollution Control Act[22] (also known as the Clean Water Act)[23] defines treatment works as "any devices and systems used in the storage, treatment, recycling, and reclamation of municipal sewage or industrial wastes of a liquid nature including intercepting sewers, outfall sewers, sewage collection systems and any works that will be an integral part of the treatment process."[24]

Physical threats to drinking water systems include chemical, biological, and radiological contaminants, and disruption of flow through explosions or other destructive actions. In recent years, much attention has been focused on threats to drinking water systems, particularly in regards to water storage reservoirs. Similar to sewage treatment plants, drinking water facilities may have stockpiles of chemicals that could create fire, explosion, or other hazards. Cyber threats are an increasing concern, given the automated, remote control nature of most drinking water treatment and distribution systems. Systems are also dependent on other critical infrastructure systems, such as energy, telecommunications, and transportation. For example, a water treatment plant that depends on daily deliveries by truck of aluminum sulfate, chlorine, or other chemicals needs an emergency operations plan in case such deliveries are interrupted.

Waste water treatment facilities have received increasing attention after the September 11, 2001, attacks. Like drinking water plants, they face physical and cyber threats and the vulnerability of dependence on other critical infrastructures. Particular attention has also focused on the large volume of liquid chlorine, sulfur dioxide, and other toxic chemicals that may be stored or in use at sewage and waste remediation facilities, and the potential for an explosion to create a toxic cloud that could threaten employees and communities. Some research has been conducted with respect to alternative treatment systems and chemicals (such as chlorine bleach or sodium hypochlorite in lieu of liquid chlorine). As such, the importance of establishing the Water ISAC provides a communications continuity between all water districts, organizations, and affiliates.

The Water ISAC provides America's drinking water and waste water system managers with a forum for sharing and discussing sensitive information through secure electronic bulletin boards. It is a repository for water security data, a resource for education on water security topics, a contact point for resources beyond the world of utilities, and a secure library tailored to the needs of the water sector. The Water ISAC offers a secure database, expert analysis, information gathering, and rapid distribution of reports and government alerts about threats to America's drinking water and waste water utilities. It is the most comprehensive and readily available resource about water system vulnerabilities, incidents, and solutions, and provides subscribers with Internet access to exhaustive research for improving the security of their utilities, planning for emergencies, and responding to physical and environmental threats of any type. A board of managers, composed of appointed water utility managers representing several national drinking water and waste water organizations, governs the Water ISAC.[25]

9.15 ASSOCIATION OF STATE DRINKING WATER ADMINISTRATORS

The Association of State Drinking Water Administrators (ASDWA) is a professional association serving state drinking water programs. Formed in 1984 to address a growing need for state administrators to have national representation, ASDWA has become a respected voice for state agents with Congress, the EPA, and other professional organizations. ASDWA's principal activities include:

- Representing states' SDWA implementation issues
- Keeping Congress informed on key issues related to drinking water, including appropriations, new legislation, contaminants of concern, and program efficiency and effectiveness
- Informing states about federal and state activities and initiatives through regular communications channels, which include newsletters, annual conferences, annual membership meetings, electronic mail, periodical mailings, and facsimiles
- Providing technical training opportunities to state agencies and water departments

ASDWA is governed by a board of directors consisting of a state program administrator from each of the 10 federal regions, the president, the president-elect (who may also represent a region), and the past president. The ASDWA executive director serves on the board as an ex officio member, with staff personnel located in Washington, D.C., managing the daily activities of the association.[26]

9.16 WATER ENVIRONMENT RESEARCH FOUNDATION

The Water Environment Research Foundation (WERF) is a subscriber-based organization consisting of utilities and municipalities, environmental engineering and consulting firms, government agencies, equipment manufacturers, and industrial organizations, all with a common interest in promoting research and development in water quality science and technology. WERF personnel consist of volunteers of environmental professionals who work with subscribers and staff to help select, fund, and coordinate hundreds of research projects specific to water. Investigations from WERF-related research projects include individuals and organizations from municipal agencies, academia, government laboratories, and various industrial and consulting firms specific to the research and development of water collection and treatment systems, watersheds and ecosystems, human and environmental health, and storm water collection and dispersal. WERF helps its subscribers improve the water environment and protect human health by providing sound, reliable science and innovative, effective, cost-saving technologies for improved management of water resources.[27] It provides information related to advancing science and technology to address water quality issues as they impact water resources, the atmosphere, the lands, and quality of life.[28]

9.17 ASSOCIATION OF METROPOLITAN WATER AGENCIES

The Association of Metropolitan Water Agencies' (AMWA) primary objective is to be the unified and definitive voice for the largest publicly owned drinking water systems on regulatory, legislative, and security issues. To this end, the association works with Congress and federal agencies to ensure safe and cost-effective federal drinking water laws and regulations, and to develop federal-local partnerships to protect water systems and consumers against acts of terrorism. AMWA provides collection and exchange of management, scientific, and technical information to support competitive utility operations, effective utility leadership, safe and secure water supplies, and effective public communication on drinking water quality.[29]

9.18 ASSOCIATION OF METROPOLITAN SEWAGE AGENCIES

The Association of Metropolitan Sewage Agencies (AMSA) represents the interests of the country's waste water treatment agencies, true environmental practitioners that serve the majority of the sewer population in the United States, and collectively treatment and reclamation of more than 18 billion gallons of waste water daily. AMSA maintains key roles in the development of environmental legislation, and works closely with federal regulatory agencies in the implementation of environmental programs. AMSA is a dynamic national organization involved in all facets of water quality protection. Viewed as a key stakeholder in both the legislative and regulatory arenas, AMSA has built credible, collaborative relationships with members of Congress, presidential administrations, and the EPA. Recent years have reflected heightened involvement in a broadening array of environmental laws and regulations that include the entire scope of ecosystem issues encompassed under the umbrella of watershed management, among them nonpoint source pollution control and the protection of air quality and endangered species.[30]

9.19 NATIONAL ASSOCIATION OF WATER COMPANIES

The National Association of Water Companies (NAWC) is the only national trade association that exclusively represents the private and investor-owned water utility industry. Its members provide safe, reliable drinking water to 22 million Americans across the country. The NAWC seeks to strengthen America's investor-owned drinking water supply industry by affording its members the means to develop responses to federal legislative and state regulatory initiatives having broad impacts on the industry. The association's relations with federal legislators and agency directors, as well as with public service commissions and staff, improve its members' effectiveness in addressing common concerns of the industry; concerns range from federal legislation and water quality regulations to state regulatory decisions having broad implications. NAWC will continue to pursue:[31]

- Favorable amendments to the SDWA
- Favorable tax legislation
- Involvement in state regulatory decisions that may set national precedents
- Education of public utility companies concerning economic realities for investor-owned utilities
- Sharing of information, through NAWC, its affiliates, and any information provided through publication

9.20 AMERICAN WATER WORKS ASSOCIATION

The American Water Works Association (AWWA) is a powerful advocate for meeting public health needs of water quality and supply. AWWA serves as the voice of the drinking water community, building and bridging gaps with regulators, legislators, and special interest groups, as well as the general public in its stead as a vital resource to its subscriber-based membership, the water profession, and the public.[32]

9.21 AWWA RESEARCH FOUNDATION

The AWWA Research Foundation's (AWWARF) mission is the advancement of the science of water to improve the quality of life. AWWARF personnel serve as a coordinating group for various research functions. The research agendas are developed using the consultation from subscriber-based membership, drinking water community experts, working professionals, and technical advisor groups. With its member base, hundreds of suggestions are examined to identify high-priority projects that are crucial to the drinking water community. The final research agenda is then approved by a board of trustees, upon which information is disseminated to its member base.[33]

9.22 FINANCIAL SERVICES ISAC

The Financial Services ISAC (FS-ISAC), under the auspices of the president's Commission on Critical Infrastructure Protection (CIP), is a private partnership of major banks, brokerages, insurance companies, and utilities and is managed by a board of managers elected by the FS-ISAC membership,[34] and is exclusively for, and designed by, professionals in the banking, securities, and insurance industries. No federal government agency, regulator, or law enforcement agency may access the FS-ISAC incident database. The mission of the FS-ISAC is to disseminate trusted and timely information to increase sectorwide knowledge about physical and IT-related security operating risks faced by and within the financial services sector. The FS-ISAC has access to a secure database, analytic tools, and information gathering and distribution facilities designed to allow authorized people to submit either anonymous or attributed reports about cyber and physical security threats, vulnerabilities, incidents, and recommended solutions. Members have access to information and analysis provided by other members and obtained from other sources, such as federal law enforcement agencies, technology providers, and security associations.[35]

Through the FS-ISAC, some of the nation's leading experts in the financial services sector share and assess threat intelligence provided by its membership and by the National Infrastructure Protection Center (NIPC), an arm of the Department of Homeland Security (DHS), and other public and commercial sources, and assist the NIPC to prepare warnings of threats against the financial services infrastructure. Through the FS-ISAC, the financial service companies pass and receive incident information to and from the federal agencies that are responsible for seeking patterns that may indicate pending threats. The secure FS-ISAC Web site offers security information on the latest physical and cyber vulnerabilities, threats, and incidents related to the banking and finance industries. Physical security, such as regional intelligence, travel advisories, benchmarking, and best practices, is also addressed. In December 2003, the FS-ISAC began devoting a $2 million award from the U.S. Department of the Treasury to programs designed to enhance security awareness for all financial institutions, including providing members with secure collaboration, additional feeds for threats and vulnerabilities, confirmation of alerts, and new analytical capabilities.[36]

Science Applications International Corporation (SAIC) is the service provider for the FS-ISAC.[37]

9.23   SCIENCE APPLICATIONS INTERNATIONAL CORPORATION

SAIC is the nation's largest employee-owned research and engineering company, providing IT, systems integration, and e-solutions to commercial and government customers. SAIC engineers and scientists work to solve complex technical problems in national and homeland security, energy, the environment, space, telecommunications, healthcare, transportation, and logistics.[38]

9.24   ELECTRICITY SECTOR ISAC

The North American Electric Reliability Council (NERC)[39] is the Electricity Sector ISAC (ES-ISAC) that essentially performs the same functions that have been required of NERC for physical sabotage and terrorism, and it coordinates all activities between the NIPC[40] and the Critical Infrastructure Protection Advisory

Group (CIPAG).[41] NERC created CIPAG to evaluate sharing cyber and physical incident data affecting the bulk electric systems throughout North America. This advisory group, which reports to NERC's board of trustees, has regional reliability council and industry sector representation as well as participation by the Critical Infrastructure Assurance Office (CIAO) in the Department of Commerce (which is now part of the DHS),[42] U.S. Department of Energy (DOE), NIPC (also assimilated into the DHS),[43] and the Federal Energy Regulatory Commission (FERC).[44] CIPAG activities are conducted so as to reduce the vulnerability of the North American bulk electric system to the effects of physical and cyber terrorism. The advisory group's activities include developing recommendations and practices related to monitoring, detection, protection, restoration, training, and exercises.[45]

For electricity sector segments to be represented within any given CIP development process, participants must include dedicated personnel from the electricity sector who represent physical, cyber, and operations security. NERC is recognized as a representative organization of the electricity sector for this coordination function, as demonstrated by NERC's performance as project coordinator for the electricity sector for the year 2000 transition.[46] The security committees and communities associated with industry organizations (American Public Power Association, Canadian Electricity Association, Edison Electric Institute, and National Rural Electric Cooperative Association) provide the expertise for physical security in the electricity sector to complement NERC's existing operational and cyber security expertise.

The advisory group relies on small self-directed working teams, which appeared to be an effective method for developing detailed processes, and practices by subject matter experts, concluded with peer review in forum environments.[47]

After CIPAG established its relationship with the Sector Liaison, the U.S. DOE, the advisory group, and representatives of the DOE met with the NIPC.[48] From this meeting there emerged a close security working relationship that resulted in the development of the electricity sector's NIPC Indications, Analysis, and Warning Program (IAWP).[49,50]

The IAWP provides several reporting mechanisms that enable reliable and secure communications between electricity sector entities and the NIPC; the IAWP operating procedures contain several event criteria and thresholds with report timing for nine physical/operational and six cyber/social engineering event types. The events to be reported include those occurrences to an electricity sector entity that are either of known malicious intent or of unknown origin. Events include such things as the loss of a key element of an electric power system or telecommunications critical to system operations, announced threats, intelligence gathering (surveillance), and computer system intrusion detection (each event type contains specificity as to level of actual or potential impact on operations of the reporting electric entity).[51] The IAWP evolved from this work, and was implemented in July 2000; the initial emphasis was on reporting mechanisms established by NERC reliability coordinators and utility control areas. Individual electric utilities, marketers, and other electricity supply and delivery entities have been encouraged to participate by submitting incident data and receiving various types of NIPC warnings and related materials.[52]

With board approval, NERC announced the ES-ISAC in October 2000. This function has grown in capability and support since then, and is staffed by NERC personnel who consult with subject matter experts throughout the electricity sector.[53]

The CIPAG provides oversight to the ES-ISAC with regular reviews at each meeting.[54]

Essentially, the CIPAG oversees just about everything, with several security and CIP reliability groups reporting or communicating with it, and with the ES-ISAC collecting, analyzing, and disseminating critical information to ES-ISAC participants.[55]

The mission of the ES-ISAC is to disseminate and establish communications channels with an ISAC to communicate with its members, its government partners, and other ISACs about threat indications, vulnerabilities, and protective strategies.[56] ISACs work together to better understand cross-industry dependencies and to account for them in emergency response planning. All entities within the electricity sector are participants with the ES-ISAC.[57]

The ES-ISAC and CIPAG coordinate with many organizations, including:[58]

American Gas Association
American Petroleum Institute
American Public Power Association
Canadian Electricity Association
CIAO (now part of DHS)
Department of Defense
Department of Energy (including several national laboratories)
Department of the Interior
Edison Electric Institute
Electricity Consumers Council
Electric Power Supply Association
Federal Energy Regulatory Commission
National Infrastructure Protection Center (now part of DHS)
National Rural Electric Cooperative Association
Nuclear Energy Institute
Nuclear Regulatory Commission
Oil and Gas Sector Partnership for Critical Infrastructure
Rural Utility Services

The ES-ISAC is funded as part of the NERC budget, which is approved by an independent board of trustees. The participants do not receive any fees from any electricity sector entities.[59]

9.25   EMERGENCY MANAGEMENT AND RESPONSE ISAC

The mission of the Emergency Management and Response ISAC (EMR-ISAC) is to promote CIP and the deterrence or mitigation of all-hazards attacks by providing timely and consequential information to the Emergency Services Sector (ESS) of the nation. In October 2000, the U.S. Fire Administration (now part of the Federal Emergency Management Agency, which is part of the DHS; www.usfa.fema.gov) established the EMR-ISAC to develop and manage the CIP program in support of federal government initiatives. On the local level, community leaders, including emergency response organizations, have the responsibility to determine which infrastructures must be protected from attacks by people, nature, or HAZMAT accidents. The EMR-ISAC performs the following major tasks to accomplish this mission and assist community and agency leadership:[60]

- Conducts daily research for current CIP issues
- Facilitates CIP information sharing between the DHS and ESS
- Publishes weekly INFOGRAM newsletters and periodic CIP bulletins
- Disseminates CIP notices "for official use only" (FOUO)
- Develops instructional materials for CIP implementation or training needs
- Provides technical CIP assistance to the ESS leadership

Primarily, the EMR-ISAC offers no-cost CIP consultation services to ESS leaders by a variety of convenient methods. To assist the implementation of CIP, the EMR-ISAC also published a *CIP Process Job Aid and Homeland Security Advisory System Guide*, which is posted on the USFA Web site. Additionally, the EMR-ISAC offers quick and user-friendly CIP portals on the disasterhelp.gov Web site (www. disasterhelp.gov). By using the Internet-based, nonsecure portals, registered and verified users of disasterhelp.gov will receive the following:

INFOGRAM newsletters containing four very short articles about the protection of the critical infrastructures of communities and their emergency responders, issued weekly[61]

CIP bulletins containing timely, consequential homeland security information affecting the CIP of emergency response agencies, published as needed[62]

Furthermore, the EMR-ISAC disseminates DHS CIP information (FOUO) to the ESS key leaders through the secure portals of disasterhelp.gov. These CIP (FOUO) notices contain emergent, actionable information regarding threats and vulnerabilities to support effective advanced preparedness, protection, and mitigation activities.[63] To receive electronic CIP (FOUO) notifications, senior emergency managers, fire, EMS, police department chief and deputy chief officers, and fire marshals must subscribe to receive the INFOGRAM newsletters and complete the online application process.[64] Only senior leadership positions will receive CIP (FOUO) notices after their identity has been validated.[65]

9.26 INFORMATION TECHNOLOGY ISAC

CSC helped found the Information Technology ISAC (IT-ISAC) in January 2001 in response to PDD-63. PDD-63 called for increased cooperation and partnership between the federal government and the private sector to address critical cyber and physical infrastructure vulnerabilities. IT-ISAC and other ISACs formed in other industries became even more important following the events of September 11, 2001, and again with the formation of the DHS. IT-ISAC is a coalition of leading IT companies that provides members with real-time and historical information about urgent alerts, security news, vulnerabilities, viruses, and other threats, thus providing a comprehensive picture of current Internet threats. It provides a forum for information sharing, joint analysis, and incident response coordination with the other sector ISACs and the federal government to protect critical infrastructure.[66]

9.27   NATIONAL COORDINATING CENTER FOR TELECOMMUNICATIONS

In January 2000, the national coordinator for Security, Infrastructure Protection, and Counterterrorism designated the National Coordinating Center for Telecommunications (NCC) ISAC as the ISAC for telecommunications. On March 1, 2000, the NCC-ISAC commenced operations. The initial NCC-ISAC membership is based on NCC membership, which is evolving to reflect a broader base of technologies comprising the telecommunications infrastructure. NCC-ISAC will support the mission assigned by Executive Order 12472 and the national CIP goals of government and industry. The NCC-ISAC will facilitate voluntary collaboration and information sharing among its participants, gathering information on vulnerabilities, threats, intrusions, and anomalies from the telecommunications industry, government, and other sources. The NCC-ISAC will analyze the data with the goal of averting or mitigating impact on the telecommunications infrastructure.[67] Additionally, data will be used to establish baseline statistics and patterns and maintained to provide a library of historical data. Results are sanitized and disseminated in accordance with sharing agreements established for that purpose by the NCC-ISAC participants. In October 1999, the Network Reliability and Interoperability Council (NRIC) IV recommended a voluntary outage reporting trial by commercial mobile radio, satellite, cable, data networking, and Internet service providers. Participants are to alert the NCC of outages likely to have significant public impact.[68]

9.28   COMMUNICATIONS RESOURCE INFORMATION SHARING

Many federal departments and agencies possess telecommunications assets, services, and capabilities that could be made available to other federal departments and agencies during emergency situations. The National Communications System (NCS) Communications Resource Information Sharing (CRIS) initiative established an information source that identifies transportable communications equipment, over-the-counter services, and fixed communications networks of the federal government, which could be used on a shared basis with other federal organizations to support national security and emergency preparedness (NS/EP) requirements. NCS Directive 3-9, CRIS Initiative, approved by the Executive Office of the President in February 1996, established the program. CRIS further implements Executive Order 12472, *Assignment of National Security and Emergency Preparedness Telecommunications Functions*,[69] dated April 3, 1984. Participation in the CRIS initiative is open to all NCS member organizations and their affiliates on a voluntary basis. Identification of telecommunications resources for use in CRIS is also on a voluntary basis, and the sharing of such resources is not to interfere with the organization's mission. There are 26 federal and industrial organizations that currently contribute resources to CRIS. Telecommunications resources identified for use in CRIS consist of agency points of contact, associated communications resources, and supporting information. CRIS resources are listed as source data in NCSH 3-9-1, CRIS Directory, which is processed and maintained as an NCS Issuance System document. Guidance and direction for the CRIS initiative is the responsibility of the NCS CRIS Working Group. Made up of representatives from the NCS member organizations, the CRIS Working Group is a formally established standing committee under the NCS Council of Representatives (COR). The NCS Committee of Principals, in accordance with NCS Issuance System procedures, establishes a policy for the CRIS initiative. Day-to-day administration of CRIS is provided by the Chief Operations Division (N3) and NCS.[70]

9.29 GOVERNMENT EMERGENCY TELECOMMUNICATIONS SERVICE

The Government Emergency Telecommunications Service (GETS) is a White House-directed emergency phone service provided by the NCS in the Information Analysis and Infrastructure Protection Division of the DHS. GETS supports federal, state, local, and tribal government, industry, and nongovernmental organization personnel performing their NS/EP objectives.

GETS provides emergency access and priority processing in the local and long-distance segments of the public switched telephone network (PSTN). It is intended for use in an emergency or crisis situation when the PSTN is congested and the probability of completing a call over normal or other alternate telecommunication means has significantly decreased. GETS is necessary because of the increasing reliance on telecommunications. The economic viability and technical feasibility of such advances as nationwide fiber optic networks, high-speed digital switching, and intelligent features have revolutionized the way we communicate. This growth has been accompanied by an increased vulnerability to network congestion and system failures.

Although backup systems are in place, disruptions in service can still occur. Recent events have shown that natural disasters, power outages, fiber cable cuts, and software problems can cripple the telephone services of entire regions. Additionally, congestion in the PSTN, such as the well-documented Mother's Day phenomenon, can prevent access to circuits. However, during times of emergency, crisis, or war, personnel with NS/EP missions need to know that their calls will go through. GETS addresses this need.

Using enhancements based on existing commercial technology, GETS allows the NS/EP community to communicate over existing PSTN paths with a high likelihood of call completion during the most severe conditions of high-traffic congestion and disruption. The result is a cost-effective, easy-to-use emergency telephone service that is accessed through a simple dialing plan and personal identification number (PIN) card verification methodology. It is maintained in a constant state of readiness as a means to overcome network outages through such methods as enhanced routing and priority treatment.

To provide guidance to financial organizations seeking sponsorship for NCS services, the Financial and Banking Information Infrastructure Committee (FBIIC)[71,72] developed policies on the sponsorship of priority telecommunications access for private sector entities through the NCS. The goal of the policies was twofold: (1) to make financial organizations aware of NCS programs and (2) to provide a consistent set of guidance regarding qualification criteria and the appropriate process for interested organizations.[73]

As a first step, on July 22, 2002, the FBIIC established a policy and process to sponsor qualifying financial sector institutions for GETS. GETS was designed to help assure communication between key public and private sector personnel during times of crisis.[74]

On December 11, 2002, the FBIIC established a policy and process to sponsor qualifying financial sector organizations for the NCS Telecommunications Service Priority (TSP) program.[75] The TSP program was developed to ensure priority treatment for the nation's most important telecommunications services.[76]

On July 22, 2002, the GETS policy was updated to include the NCS Wireless Priority Services (WPS). Both GETS and WPS are designed to help assure communication between key public and private sector personnel during times of crisis.[77] GETS uses these major types of networks:[78]

- The local networks provided by local exchange carriers (LECs) and wireless providers, such as cellular carriers and personal communications services (PCS)
- The major long-distance networks provided by interexchange carriers (IXCs), which include AT&T, MCI Nextel, and Sprint (now owned by Verizon), including their international services
- Government-leased networks such as the Federal Technology Service and the Defense Switched Network

GETS is accessed through a universal access number using common telephone equipment such as a standard desk set, facsimile, modem, or wireless phone. A prompt will direct the entry of your PIN and the telephone number. Once authenticated as made by a valid user, the call is identified as an NS/EP call, receiving priority treatment.[79]

There are five broad categories that serve as guidelines for determining who may qualify as a GETS user:[80]

1. National security leadership
2. National security posture and U.S. population attack warning
3. Public health, safety, and maintenance of law and order
4. Public welfare and maintenance of national economic posture
5. Disaster recovery

The FBIIC agencies have determined that to qualify for GETS sponsorship, organizations must support the performance of NS/EP functions necessary to maintain the national economic posture during any national or regional emergency. In particular, the FBIIC agencies view maintenance of the national economic posture as the minimization of systemic disruption to the financial system directly related to the operation of critical financial markets and related essential services and systems.[81]

Essential services and systems are those that have no easily accessible substitute and are necessary to support one of three critical NS/EP functions in key financial markets and payment mechanisms: necessary crisis response and coordination activities, resumption and maintenance of economic activity, and the orderly completion of outstanding financial transactions and necessary offsetting transactions. Essential services and systems include:[82]

- Critical funds transfer systems (wholesale/large-value payment systems)
- Securities and derivatives clearing and settlement systems
- Supporting communication systems and service providers
- Key financial market trading systems and exchanges

Private sector financial organizations and their service providers may qualify for GETS sponsorship if they play a significant role in one or more financial markets or essential services or systems. In determining whether an individual organization plays a significant role, the appropriate FBIIC member agency may consider whether the organization:[83]

- Is a registered securities or futures exchange, self-regulatory organization, registered securities clearing agency/depository, or futures clearinghouse, and their critical service providers and utilities
- Acts as a market utility for effecting payments or clearance and settlement of transactions
- Processes a large aggregate value of daily payments
- Provides critical services or systems to financial institutions
- Has a national or large regional presence in one or more product lines
- Demonstrates other facts or circumstances that suggest facilitating the organization's access to the GETS priority service in times of national emergency would serve to maintain the national economic posture

The FBIIC agencies may contact those organizations that clearly qualify under these criteria and inform them of the availability of GETS sponsorship.[84,85]

9.30 TELECOMMUNICATIONS SERVICE PRIORITY

The TSP program provides NS/EP users' priority authorization of telecommunications services that are vital to coordinating and responding to crises. Telecommunications services are defined as the transmission, emission, or reception of intelligence of any nature, by wire, cable, satellite, fiber optics, laser, radio, visual, or other electronic, electric, electromagnetic, or acoustically coupled means, or any combination thereof. As a result of hurricanes, floods, earthquakes, and other natural or man-made disasters, telecommunications service vendors may become overwhelmed with requests for new telecommunications services and requirements to restore existing telecommunications services. The TSP program provides service vendors with a Federal Communications Commission (FCC) mandate for prioritizing service requests by identifying those services critical to NS/EP. A telecommunications service with a TSP assignment is assured of receiving full attention by the service vendor before a service that is not TSP. The procedures identified here are applicable to the manager, National Communications System; NCS member organizations; and other federal executive entities participating in the TSP program. All other telecommunications service users (e.g., state, local, foreign governments, or private industry) who request and obtain a TSP assignment agree to its application by their use of the TSP program.[86] The TSP system replaced the restoration priority system effective September 1990.[87]

9.31 SHARED RESOURCES HIGH FREQUENCY RADIO PROGRAM

The NCS, in its role of planning and preparing for NS/EP, has undertaken a number of initiatives to provide communications to support all hazardous situations. One of these initiatives, developed through the combined efforts of the 23 NCS member organizations, is the Shared Resources (SHARES) High Frequency (HF) Radio Program. The purpose of SHARES is to provide a single, interagency emergency message handling system by bringing together existing HF radio resources of federal, state, and industry organizations when normal communications are destroyed or unavailable for the transmission of NS/EP information. SHARES further implements Executive Order 12472 (*Assignment of National Security and Emergency Preparedness Telecommunications Functions*),[88] dated April 3, 1984.

As of July 2004, more than 1,000 HF radio stations, representing 93 federal, state, and industry entities, are resource contributors to the SHARES HF Radio Program. SHARES stations are located in every state and at 20 overseas locations. Roughly 194 emergency planning and response personnel also participate in SHARES. More than 90 HF frequencies have been authorized for use in SHARES. A SHARES Bulletin is published periodically to keep members updated on program activities.

SHARES provides the federal community a forum for addressing issues affecting HF radio interoperability. The SHARES HF Interoperability Working Group (IWG), established as a permanent standing committee under the NCS COR, is responsible for providing guidance and direction for the SHARES radio network, and for fostering the interoperability of federal HF radio systems through the examination of regulatory, procedural, and technical issues.[89]

The SHARES HF IWG currently consists of 91 members and 105 participating entities vice organizations. Overall support for the SHARES HF Radio Program is the responsibility of the manager, National Communications System. The chief, Operations Division, Office of the Manager, NCS, is responsible for administering the SHARES program. The manager, National Coordinating Center for Telecommunications, is responsible for the day-to-day operations of SHARES.[90]

9.32   NETWORK RELIABILITY AND INTEROPERABILITY COUNCIL

In October 1999, the NRIC IV recommended a voluntary outage reporting trial by commercial mobile radio, satellite, cable, data networking, and Internet service providers. Trial participants were alerted to contact the NCC of any outages likely to have a significant public impact.[91]

9.33   NATIONAL SECURITY TELECOMMUNICATIONS ADVISORY COMMITTEE

President Ronald Reagan created the National Security Telecommunications Advisory Committee (NSTAC) by Executive Order 12382 in September 1982. Since then, the NSTAC has served four presidents.[92]

Composed of up to 30 industry chief executives representing the major communications and network service providers and IT, finance, and aerospace companies, the NSTAC provides industry-based advice and expertise to the president on issues and problems related to implementing NS/EP communications policy. Since its inception, the NSTAC has addressed a wide range of policy and technical issues regarding communications, information systems, information assurance, CIP, and other NS/EP communications concerns.

NS/EP communications enable the government to make an immediate and coordinated response to all emergencies, whether caused by a natural disaster such as a hurricane, an act of domestic terrorism such as the Oklahoma City bombing and the September 11 attacks, a man-made disaster, or a cyber attack.

NS/EP communications allow the president of the United States and other senior administration officials to be continually accessible, even under stressed conditions. The impact of today's dynamic technological and regulatory environment is profound: New technologies and the increasingly competitive marketplace combine to bring both new opportunities and new vulnerabilities to the information infrastructure.

The NSTAC is strongly positioned to offer advice to the president on how to:

- Leverage this dynamic environment to enrich NS/EP communications capabilities and ensure that new architectures fulfill requirements to support NS/EP operations
- Avoid introducing vulnerabilities into the information infrastructure that could adversely affect NS/EP communications services

For over two decades, industry chief executives from communications and IT companies have offered their expertise to give the president NSTAC's independent, private sector, nonpartisan, provider-based perspective. By virtue of its mandate to address NS/EP communications issues, the NSTAC's partnership with government through the NCS is unique in two ways—direct industry involvement, with both the defense agencies and the civil agencies comprising the NCS; and regular, sustained interaction between industry and the NCS member departments and agencies through the NCC-ISAC, and the Network Security Information Exchange (NSIE) process.[93] The NSTAC's perspective and its experiences with a broad range of federal departments and agencies make the NSTAC a key strategic resource for the president and his national security team in their efforts to protect our nation's critical infrastructures in today's dynamic environment. The NSTAC's current work plan includes initiatives that intersect with several programs set forth in the National Plan for Information Systems Protection, that is, information sharing, the security and reliability of converged networks, and research and development issues related to converged networks. NS/EP communications services were, 30 years ago, provided by a communications infrastructure based on a discrete, monolithic, domestic, terrestrial, circuit-switched voice network, supported primarily by mechanical controls.[94]

Today's communications infrastructure is composed of interdependent, diverse, circuit, and packet-switched networks using terrestrial, satellite, and wireless transmissions systems to support voice, data, image, and video communications, supported primarily by software-based controls. Globalization introduces another element of diversity and interdependence, as domestic service providers establish joint ventures or merge with foreign service providers.[95] Communications networks and information systems have inextricably converged into an information infrastructure in which neither communications nor information processing can fully function without the other. This growth and convergence have offered capabilities and applications that have profoundly changed how both the public and private sectors conduct business, increasing their dependence on the technologies comprising the information infrastructure.[96]

Although it is critical to the government, the information infrastructure is owned and operated by the private sector. Consequently, the government is unable to fully address NS/EP communications issues associated with the information infrastructure without a government-industry partnership, such as that offered by NSTAC.[97]

As the strategic and technological environments have changed, NSTAC's work has kept pace with these changes and has evolved from an initial emphasis on NS/EP communications to a broader scope that encompasses the information infrastructure. Today, NSTAC offers advice to the president on policy issues affecting not only the government's ability to leverage the information infrastructure to better support NS/EP operations, but also the government's ability to protect the information infrastructure itself from threats and vulnerabilities that might ultimately jeopardize the country's national and economic security.[98]

The NSTAC has addressed numerous issues in the past 18 years. Three accomplishments best illustrate NSTAC's capabilities to address NS/EP communications issues in today's environment: the establishment of the NCC and its ISAC, the implementation of the government and NSTAC NSIE process, and the examination of the NS/EP implications of Internet technologies and the vulnerabilities of converged networks. These accomplishments are briefly described below. The NCC was established in 1984 as a result of an NSTAC recommendation to develop a joint government-industry national coordinating mechanism to respond to the federal government's NS/EP communications service requirements. The NCC's mission is to assist in the initiation, coordination, restoration, and reconstitution of NS/EP communications services or facilities. Currently, 13 NSTAC member companies are represented in the NCC.[99]

The NSTAC was instrumental in expanding the NCC's responsibilities, to include functioning as an ISAC for the telecommunications infrastructure. Established in January 2000, the NCC-ISAC was the second ISAC to be formed following the promulgation of PDD-63 and the first ISAC with both industry and government membership.[100] The NCC-ISAC gathers information about vulnerabilities, threats, intrusions, and anomalies from telecommunications industry, government, and other sources, and then analyzes the data with the goal of averting or mitigating the effects on the communications infrastructure.[101] Results are sanitized and disseminated in accordance with sharing agreements established by the NCC-ISAC participants. In 1991, the NSTAC, working with the NCS, recommended establishing a government-industry partnership to reduce the vulnerability of the nation's telecommunications systems to electronic intrusion.[102] The NSIE process was established as a forum in which government and industry could share information in a trusted and confidential environment.[103] The NSIE process continues to function today, demonstrating that industry and government will share sensitive security information if they find value in doing so.[104]

In 1998, PDD-63 called for the establishment of similar information exchange forums to reduce vulnerabilities in all critical infrastructures.[105] In 1999, the NSTAC identified the need for the government to consider how the convergence of traditional circuit switched telecommunications systems with the Internet might affect the government's existing priority communications systems. The NSTAC also recommended that the government determine how it could obtain priority services in the next-generation packet-based networks.[106]

## 9.34	WIRELESS PRIORITY SERVICES

In the early 1990s, the Office of the Manager, National Communication System (OMNCS)[107,108] initiated efforts to develop and implement a nationwide cellular priority access capability in support of NS/EP telecommunications and pursued a number of activities to improve cellular call completion during times of network congestion. Subsequently, as a result of a petition filed by the NCS in October 1995, the FCC released a Second Report and Order (R&O; FCC-00-242, July 13, 2000) on wireless priority access service (PAS). The R&O offers federal liability relief for NS/EP wireless carriers if the service is implemented in accordance with uniform operating procedures. The FCC made PAS voluntary, found it to be in the public interest, and defined five priority levels for NS/EP wireless calls. WPS, the NCS program implementation of the FCC PAS, is the wireless complement to the wireline GETS.[109]

GETS uses the PSTN to provide enhanced wireline priority service to qualified NS/EP personnel. WPS users are authorized and encouraged to use GETS to improve their probability of completing their NS/EP call during periods of wireless and wireline network congestion. Wireless network congestion was widespread on September 11, 2001. With wireless traffic demand estimated at up to 10 times normal in the affected areas and double nationwide, the need for WPS became a critical and urgent national requirement.[110]

Reacting to the events of September 11, 2001, the National Security Council issued the following guidance to the NCS:

- NCS will move forward on implementing an immediate solution (target: within 60 days) using channel reservation capabilities from one vendor for the Washington, D.C., area, and based on lessons learned in Washington, D.C., the NCS will make a recommendation on whether to expand the immediate solution to other metropolitan areas.
- In parallel, the NCS will proceed with deploying a priority access queuing system for wireless nationwide (target: within one year).

This triggered the development of two WPS efforts to overcome the wireless priority access problem.

- Immediate solution: A solution using commercially available and readily implemented technology for limited geographic areas.
- Nationwide solution: This solution is aimed toward the development of a long-term, nationally available solution.

With White House guidance in October 2001, the NCS began immediate acquisition of service for the Washington metropolitan area and recommended and proceeded with services for New York City as well. The NCS entered into subcontracts with the immediate WPS service providers, T-Mobile (previously VoiceStream) and Globalstar.[111]

The NCS provided Globalstar satellite phones to quickly field the immediate WPS in the Salt Lake City area during the Olympics for more than 600 users. Globalstar increased satellite capacity and redirected Utah calls directly to a U.S.-based earth station. Globalstar also increased landline trunking at the earth station for GETS calls. T-Mobile uses Global System for Mobile Communications (GSM) technology and has capitalized on an existing GSM feature called Enhanced Multilevel Precedence and Preemption.

During congestion, this feature allows the emergency call to queue for the next available radio channel, without preempting any calls in progress.

This immediate capability required an FCC waiver for T-Mobile because it did not initially conform to the R&O requirement to invoke the priority service on a call-by-call basis. This means that all calls using authorized immediate WPS phones receive priority service when the radio channels are congested. T-Mobile's implementation of the immediate solution became operational during May 2002 in Washington and New York. By November 2002, T-Mobile supported 2,084 WPS users in Washington and 725 in New York, for a total of 2,809 WPS cellular users. Globalstar also supported 906 customers.

Due to the requirement for nationwide WPS coverage, multiple carriers and multiple access technologies are needed. WPS is based on the two digital access technologies most widely available in the United States, GSM (i.e., AT&T Wireless, Cingular, Nextel (Sprint), and T-Mobile) and code division multiple access (CDMA) (i.e., Sprint PCS and Verizon Wireless). Nationwide WPS is provided in two major phases: initial operating capability (IOC) and full operating capability (FOC).

IOC is a GSM-based solution only, consisting of priority radio channel access at call origination. IOC began on December 31, 2002, and it satisfied the requirements of the FCC Second R&O for invocation of the service on a call-by-call basis by dialing the WPS prefix (*272) at the start of each NS/EP WPS call. FOC provides a full, end-to-end capability, beginning with the NS/EP wireless caller, through the wireless networks, through the IXC or LEC wired line networks, and to the wireless or wired line called party.

T-Mobile began deploying WPS FOC in December 2003. AT&T Wireless and Cingular began deploying WPS FOC in July 2004. Nextel (now part of Sprint) also deployed WPS in July 2004, and upgraded to FOC in April 2005.

As of December 2004, there were more than 11,000 WPS users. It is the objective of NCS to provide the WPS capability to an estimated NS/EP wireless user population of 200,000 GSM users and 90,000 CDMA users.

Congestion occurs when the network becomes overloaded and is unable to respond to additional requests for service. The PSTN has hundreds of millions of customers, all of whom may try to make a call at the same time. However, it can only accommodate a much smaller percentage of these potential calls simultaneously. When that design threshold is exceeded, congestion occurs. In some cases, this is first recognized by a user being unable to complete calls (slow busy tone), followed by the user's inability to even access the network (fast/rapid busy tone), which can be further followed by the complete loss of dial tone. This can occur as a result of a natural or man-made disaster when the network is being heavily used and needed the most. WPS and GETS are designed to mitigate this situation by providing users with NS/EP missions a higher probability of completion for their emergency calls.

The nationwide WPS capability is based on wireless standards with Industry Requirements (IR) documents defining specific WPS requirements. The active and cooperative participation of all stakeholders, including major wireless equipment vendors and service providers, successfully produced these IR documents. Definitions of the FOC requirements were initiated in the fall of 2002 to allow the switch vendors to include WPS capabilities in the next software development cycle.

The NCS has also taken steps to ensure that the use of the nation's cellular telecommunication networks by NS/EP personnel does not hinder public use during emergency events. The FCC issued guidelines for NS/EP use of wireless networks, and only NS/EP leadership and key personnel will be approved to use WPS. For those critical individuals who require the priority service, WPS will be a powerful new emergency communications asset and an important national resource.[112]

WPS works also with SAFECOM. SAFECOM[113] is managed by the DHS Science and Technology Directorate's Office for Interoperability and Compatibility. Its mission is to serve as the umbrella program within the federal government to help local, state, tribal, and federal public safety agencies improve public safety response through more effective and efficient interoperable wireless communications, allowing public safety agencies to talk across disciplines and jurisdictions via radio communications systems, exchanging voice and data with one another on demand, in real time, when needed, as authorized.[114]

SAFECOM is the first national program designed by public safety for public safety. As a public safety-driven program, SAFECOM works with existing federal communications initiatives and key public safety stakeholders to address the need to develop better technologies and processes for the cross-jurisdictional and cross-disciplinary coordination of existing systems and future networks. SAFECOM harnesses diverse federal resources in service of the public safety community.[115]

9.35   ALERTING AND COORDINATION NETWORK

The Alerting and Coordination Network (ACN) is an emergency voice communications network for communications service providers.[116]

The network supports NS/EP communications restoration coordination when the public switched network (PSN) is inoperable or congested. It is engineered to provide a reliable and survivable network capability, and has no logical dependency on the PSN. As a result, if the PSN is congested, the ACN will not be affected. ACN members include all of the major telecommunications companies in the United States as well as some federal agencies. Currently, the ACN connects 32 users and the NCC-ISAC. The ACN is one of a number of initiatives sponsored by the NCS in its role of planning and preparing for NS/EP communications within the DHS.

The ACN is operational 24/7 to support the NCC-ISAC during normal and emergency operations. The ACN is an emergency communications (voice) network connecting the communications service providers' network operations and emergency operation centers to support restoration coordination, transmission of telecommunications requirements and priorities, and incident reporting when the PSN is inoperable or congested.[117]

One challenge that the ACN concept was intended to assist in was ensuring that emergency operations centers (EOCs) remained able to communicate. There is an emerging challenge here as the lines of communication, when looking at the combination of EOCs, back up sites and other coordination points, are able to maintain the high volume of communication that is likely to flow. At the same time, ensuring the necessary coordination through shared rules will be similarly challenging.

9.36   ENERGY ISAC

The Energy ISAC is exclusively for, and designed by, professionals in the energy industries. No federal government agency, regulator, or law enforcement agency can access the Energy ISAC. Other critical industries, such as finance and telecommunications, have ISACs in place. The threats and vulnerabilities to the energy industry are increasing. The events of September 11, 2001, introduced heightened physical security measures. The energy infrastructure also depends on IT and telecommunications security. Critical systems include supervisory control and data acquisition (SCADA), trading, Internet-based transactions, and e-commerce. The Energy ISAC is the one-stop clearinghouse for information on threats, vulnerabilities, solutions, and best practices. Members can submit information anonymously and receive near-real-time updates.[118]

At the time of writing, it would appear that the Energy ISAC has been discontinued. There are no specific dates as to when the ISAC operations ceased, nor do there appear to be any news releases or discussions from any source, public or private, as to its final operations.

However, in lieu of the Energy ISAC, a privately funded organization called the Energy Sector Security Consortium (ENERGYSEC), which is funded through the

National Energy Sector Cybersecurity Organization (NESCO),[165] appears to be filling the void left behind from the Energy ISAC.[119]

9.37 ENERGY SECTOR SECURITY CONSORTIUM

ENERGYSEC is an outgrowth of Energy Security Northwest (E-Sec NW), an informal association of energy sector security professionals formed in the Pacific Northwest sometime in 2004. In 2007, E-Sec NW received a National Cybersecurity Leadership Award from the SANS Institute. Current participation includes over 150 industry professionals representing more than 60 energy companies throughout North America. ENERGYSEC is currently funded by the National Energy Sector Cybersecurity Organization (NESCO).[165]

Attendance at ENERGYSEC's annual summit averages 150 participants, including representatives from FERC, NERC, regional reliability organizations, state regulatory commissions, and numerous energy companies.

ENERGYSEC provides Internet-based communication channels that support collaboration between energy industry professionals. These technologies will now be available nationally. ENERGYSEC also organizes a variety of summits and meetings focused on cyber and physical security, and regulatory compliance. These events will also be expanded nationally.[120]

9.38 CHEMICAL SECTOR ISAC

In 2002, the Chemical Transportation Emergency Center (CHEMTREC®), in conjunction with the former NIPC, created the Chemical Sector ISAC (CHEM-ISAC). The purpose of the CHEM-ISAC was to provide a means for security-related information to move between the multiagency NIPC and the chemical sector. In March 2004, the NIPC was dissolved and the DHS assumed its responsibilities. The CHEM-ISAC now receives information from several divisions within DHS, including the Information Analysis and Infrastructure Protection Division. The goal of the CHEM-ISAC is to enable the chemical sector to receive fast and cost-effective access to sensitive information about cyber, physical, and contamination issues. It accomplishes this by providing a venue for DHS to disseminate assessments, advisories, and alerts to the private sector when such incidents are deemed to have possible serious national security, economic, or social consequences. Since 9/11, CHEMTREC and other elements of the American Chemistry Council (ACC) have worked closely with the DHS and the Federal Bureau of Investigation (FBI) to provide information to help federal law enforcement and intelligence agencies better understand the potential threats that might be of concern to the business of chemistry and to provide actionable and timely threat information to industry. This relationship led ACC and CHEMTREC to establish the CHEM-ISAC. A primary goal of the CHEM-ISAC is to enable DHS to disseminate timely and actionable assessment, advisories, and alerts to appropriate government and private sector entities when such incidents are deemed to have possible serious national security, economic, or social consequences. The CHEM-ISAC is intended for those companies or other organizations involved in the production, storage, transportation, and delivery of chemicals.[121]

Participation by the chemical industry is intended to be inclusive to maximize the value and utility of the ISAC. The CHEM-ISAC utilizes CHEMTREC, the chemical industry's 24-hour emergency communication center, as the communication link between the DHS and CHEM-ISAC participants. When CHEMTREC receives information from the DHS, that information is immediately transmitted, on an around-the-clock basis, to CHEM-ISAC participants using electronic mail and a secure Web site. The CHEM-ISAC includes the following key elements:

- A 24-hour electronic communication network to provide chemical facilities and chemical transportation systems with timely, accurate, and actionable warning for both physical and IT-related threats
- An electronic communication system that will allow for voluntary and secure electronic reporting to DNS of any malicious, unexplained, or suspicious incidents involving chemical facilities or chemicals in commerce to allow federal intelligence and law enforcement agencies to identify and analyze incidents[122]

9.39 CHEMICAL TRANSPORTATION EMERGENCY CENTER (CHEMTREC®)

CHEMTREC is a 24-hour emergency communications center operated as a public service by the ACC. Since its creation in 1971, CHEMTREC has provided critical emergency communications services to emergency first responders and to shippers of HAZMAT.[123]

9.40 HEALTHCARE SERVICES ISAC

The Healthcare ISAC never left its developmental stages. The initial advisory council, established in 2003, had consisted of representatives from nearly all aspects of the healthcare infrastructure: research and academic, healthcare providers, and pharmaceutical companies, along with several industry associations. The intent was originally to develop similar analytical and alert capabilities found in other ISAC organizations. The organization never became fully operational.[124,125]

9.41 HIGHWAY ISAC

The Highway ISAC is operated by the American Trucking Associations (ATA), in partnership with the state and national trucking associations and conferences of the ATA Federation, numerous other national highway transportation organizations in the HighwayWatch® Coalition in cooperation with the DHS, for the benefit of the entire highway transportation sector. The web site contains public bulletins and advisories, and both national and specific alerts for the highway sector and industry subsectors.[126]

Transportation professionals can observe things such as trucks parked under bridges, routes that make no sense, abandoned rigs, frontline participants who do not really know their business, shipping practices that make no sense, or any of a thousand items that an experienced professional is well suited to discern. Currently operated by the ATA in cooperation with the Transportation Security Administration and supported by the HighwayWatch Coalition and Antiterrorism Working Group and the NIPC of the DHS, the Highway ISAC benefits the entire transportation industry. Its mission is to serve as an alert system, leveraging the Internet and other communication channels to provide the transportation industry with incident, threat, and vulnerability information. By compiling industry and government intelligence in one location, the Highway ISAC assists both the private and public sectors in creating security measures, planning for emergencies, and protecting our nation's citizens and infrastructure.[127]

9.42   CARGO THEFT INFORMATION PROCESSING SYSTEM

The Cargo Theft Information Processing System was developed in response to the need for a national cargo theft database. The system was designed as a result of a partnership between law enforcement authorities and the transportation industry to turn the tide on escalating crime. With cargo theft information ascertained, development of a comprehensive assessment of the problem to begin a counterattack may be formulated.[128]

9.43   AMERICAN TRUCKING ASSOCIATIONS

The mission of ATA is to serve and represent the interests of the trucking industry with one united voice; to positively influence federal and state governmental actions; to advance the trucking industry's image, efficiency, competitiveness, and profitability; to provide educational programs and industry research; to promote highway and driver safety; and to strive for a healthy business environment.[129]

9.44   HIGHWAYWATCH®

HighwayWatch is the roadway sector's national safety and security program that utilizes the skills, experiences, and "road smarts" of America's transportation workers to help protect the nation's critical infrastructure and the transportation of goods, services, and people. HighwayWatch participants are transportation infrastructure workers, commercial and public truck and bus drivers, and other highway sector professionals, and are specially trained to recognize potential safety and security threats and avoid becoming a target of terrorists. The HighwayWatch effort seeks to prevent terrorists from using large vehicles or hazardous cargoes as weapons. HighwayWatch training provides HighwayWatch participants with observational tools and the opportunity to exercise their expert understanding of the transportation environment to report safety and security concerns rapidly and accurately to the authorities. In addition to matters of homeland security, stranded vehicles or accidents, unsafe road conditions, and other safety-related situations are reported, thus eliciting the appropriate emergency responders. HighwayWatch reports are combined with other information sources and shared with both federal agencies and the roadway transportation sector by the Highway ISAC. After completing the HighwayWatch training, transportation professionals use cellular telephones and other telecommunications equipment to contact emergency personnel through a special HighwayWatch hotline, providing emergency responders with precise location and incident information. A trained operator at the HighwayWatch call center verifies the highway professional's identity (each participant has a unique HighwayWatch ID number) and location, and then routes the call to the appropriate law enforcement authorities in that area.

The HighwayWatch call center correlates the location information and routes the call to the appropriate response agency in that area or to the appropriate state or regional emergency dispatch center. Additionally, HighwayWatch training instructs all participants to use 911 for life-threatening emergencies.[130]

9.45   FOOD AND AGRICULTURE ISAC

On February 9, 2002, a public-private sector partnership known as the Food and Agriculture ISAC was created. The objectives of the Food and Agriculture ISAC include:

- Making the food industry a difficult and undesirable target for terrorist attacks
- Bringing the industry's talents together to deal with preventing terrorism and deliberately malicious attacks
- Providing a rapid means of communicating and disseminating information relevant to those tasks
- Providing, in the event of an attack, a means for a coordinated industry-wide response to limit the effect and enable the food system to recover as rapidly as possible
- Working directly with the NIPC and the FBI's Weapons of Mass Destruction Unit to identify credible threats and craft specific warning messages for the food industry
- Facilitating the development of, and serve as a central repository for, best practice recommendations and countermeasures for preventing and recovering from malicious attacks. These would include bioterrorism attacks, attacks on physical assets, and cyber attacks on the industry's computer or financial networks

The Food Marketing Institute (FMI), located in Washington, D.C., coordinated this voluntary industry network. For information on FMI, see the institute's Web site, www.fmi.org. Because the food supply is a critical national resource, the Food Industry ISAC is supported by FMI at no additional charge to those food industry companies that participate.[131]

The Food and Agriculture Sector abandoned its information sharing model sometime early in 2008. The Food and Agriculture Sector was the first infrastructure sector to form an ISAC, and was established before the DHS came into existence. However, the FMI, the former owner and sponsor for the ISAC, suspended, and eventually disbanded, all ISAC activities because it had not received any terrorism-based threat information; essentially, either no one had any information to share or no one wanted to share. Nonetheless, FMI disconnected service for the ISAC sometime in 2008.[132,133]

However, another similar service, called FoodSHIELD,[134] was established by the U.S. Department of Agriculture (USDA), along with the University of Minnesota's DHS-funded National Center for Food Protection and Defense (NCFPD). As even this effort is facing loss of funding, DHS may integrate the use of its Homeland Security Information Network Food and Agriculture (HSIN-FA), which is an Internet-connected, Web-based information portal.

9.46 FOODSHIELD

FoodSHIELD is a Web-based platform designed to create a community between the various laboratories and regulatory agencies that make up our nation's food and agricultural sectors. Through secure, integrated resources such as detailed agency profiles, departments of agriculture and health, as well as laboratories, have the ability to communicate and coordinate with their peers in other states.[135]

FoodSHIELD got its start with the creation of LabDIR as a result of the National Food Safety System (NFSS)[136,137] Laboratory Operations and Coordination Workgroup vision of transforming a paper-based directory into a Web-based directory designed for easy access. Discussions with the Food and Drug Administration (FDA), USDA, Association of Public Health Laboratories, and American Association of Veterinary Laboratory Diagnostics identified the need for a searchable Web-based directory across the full spectrum of farm-to-table laboratories as well as clinical laboratories that respond to outbreaks and food safety concerns.[138]

It was later decided to develop an expanded prototype of this comprehensive laboratory directory to model concepts and features being requested by diverse groups and officials responsible for emergency response encompassing the entire food and agricultural farm-to-fork continuum.

Hence, FoodSHIELD came into existence as a comprehensive infrastructure supporting the protection and defense of our food and agricultural resources as a whole—including the scientific and technological diversities of the laboratory community.

Initial funding for FoodSHIELD was provided by grants from the USDA and NCFPD,[139–141] a Homeland Security Center of Excellence. FoodSHIELD start-up development has occurred under a USDA Cooperative State Research, Education, and Extension Service (CSREES)[142–145] grant to NCFPD and University of Minnesota researchers.

Also through USDA, the Food Emergency Response Network (FERN) provided additional funds, which FoodSHIELD uses to host the FERN Web site.

FoodSHIELD is also supported through its partnership with the Association of Food and Drug Officials. The DHS agreed to continue funding FoodSHIELD through NCFPD after the USDA CSREES grant expired in fiscal year 2009.[146]

Work began in September 1998 when the FDA hosted a meeting of food safety officials from federal agencies and agencies in all 50 states. This meeting produced a broad consensus on the need to integrate food safety activities at all levels of government. Workgroups were formed with federal, state, and local officials from health, agriculture, and environmental agencies. Under the guidance of a diverse, multilevel, multiagency coordinating committee, the workgroups were tasked with generating ideas for action that would promote an integrated food safety system.

In 1999, the workgroups developed numerous innovative ideas and provided invaluable assistance on a number of federal projects consistent with the federal agencies' FY 1999 plans, authorities, and appropriations. The development of guidelines for coordinating multistate foodborne outbreaks and traceback investigations and the development of standards for sampling, testing methods, and data exchange for *E. coli* 0157:H7 are two examples of such projects (http://cipbook.infracritical.com/book5/chapter9/ch9ref18.pdf).

NCFPD is one of six academic Centers of Excellence for multidisciplinary research and innovative educational programs aimed at improving the nation's ability to prevent and respond to acts of terrorism (www.foodshield.org/about/funding.cfm; alt URL: http://cipbook.infracritical.com/book5/chapter9/ch9ref19.pdf).

CSREES anticipates that $190 million will be available for the Agriculture and Food Research Initiative to support six priority areas: (1) plant health and production and plant products; (2) animal health and production and animal products; (3) food safety, nutrition, and health; (4) renewable energy, natural resources, and environment; (5) agriculture systems and technology; and (6) agriculture economics and rural communities.

The Request for Applications was expected to be released early in 2009 on the CSREES and Grants.gov Web sites (http://foodshield.typepad.com/foodshield_announcements; alt URL: http//cipbook.infracritical.com/chapter9/ch9ref26.pdf).

9.47   FOOD MARKETING INSTITUTE

As the representative of one of the largest single business categories in the world, the FMI will:

- Provide its retail and wholesale membership with a forum to work effectively with the government, suppliers, employees, and customers and their communities
- Promote the principles of free enterprise to ensure a vigorous, competitive, economically healthy food industry
- Program its efforts and energies in five primary areas: (1) research and development, (2) education, (3) public information and its dissemination, (4) government relations, and (5) industrial relations

By pursuing these activities, the FMI will provide leadership and support for the role of the grocery retailer and wholesaler as a purchasing agent for our consumers.[147]

9.48   MULTISTATE ISAC

Recognizing the need for collaboration, a multistate ISAC (MS-ISAC) was established in January 2003. The MS-ISAC began with the Northeast states and quickly expanded. Currently, there are 49 states and the District of Columbia participating. The goal is to have this MS-ISAC include all 50 states, which would provide a valuable centrally coordinated mechanism for sharing important security intelligence and information between the states. The MS-ISAC can serve as a critical point of contact between the state and the federal government. A primary goal of the MS-ISAC is to eliminate duplicative efforts. The MS-ISAC member states meet monthly by teleconference to discuss issues and share information relating to each state's cyber security readiness and resilience.

The MS-ISAC has moved quickly since its inception and has been recognized by the DHS for its proactive role in bringing the states together. It is only through collaboration and communication that we can be successful in helping to protect and secure the critical infrastructure that supports all of our citizens and businesses.[148]

9.49   ISAC COUNCIL

The mission of the ISAC Council is to advance the physical and cyber security of the critical infrastructures of North America by establishing and maintaining a framework for valuable interaction between and among the ISACs and with the government.[149]

9.50   WORLDWIDE ISAC

The Worldwide ISAC (WW-ISAC) offers a confidential venue for sharing security vulnerabilities and solutions. It facilitates trust among its participants. Members benefit from the WW-ISAC organization's means of mitigating cyber security risks.[150]

9.51   REAL ESTATE ISAC

The Real Estate ISAC (RE-ISAC), a not-for-profit organization formed by the Real Estate Roundtable, was announced in February 2003. The organization represents both coordinated and elevated response efforts toward security-related issues. RE-ISAC is a public-private partnership between the U.S. real estate industry and federal homeland security officials.[151]

Principally, RE-ISAC serves three roles:

1. Disseminate information from the federal government, including terrorist alerts and advisories, to real estate industry participants, and bring government officials and building owners and operators together to assess and evaluate the information so it becomes more useful and actionable for real estate. With the latest validated intelligence, building owners and operators are better prepared to develop and activate their own counterterrorism activities, including steps to protect people and property.

2. Facilitate the industry's reporting to government authorities of credible threats to real estate assets and enable analysis of the information to detect patterns or trends, and to develop potentially coordinated action steps.

3. Bring private and public sector experts together to share useful information, and discuss and develop best practices and solutions on subsector-specific issues (such as matters affecting retail or office property owners) or cross-sector issues (such as risk assessment, asset fortification/hardening, building security, and emergency response planning).[152]

9.52   THE REAL ESTATE ROUNDTABLE

The Real Estate Roundtable is the organization that brings together leaders of the nation's top publicly and privately held real estate ownership, development, lending, and management firms with the leaders of major national real estate trade associations to jointly address key national policy issues relating to real estate and the overall economy.[153]

9.53   RESEARCH AND EDUCATIONAL NETWORKING ISAC

The Research and Educational Networking ISAC supports higher education and the research community by providing advanced security services to national supporting networks, and supports efforts to protect the national cyber infrastructure by participating in the formal sector ISAC infrastructure.[154]

9.54   BIOTECHNOLOGY AND PHARMACEUTICAL ISAC

The Biotechnology and Pharmaceutical ISAC (BioPharma ISAC) was being established to enhance the security of its members and the nation's critical infrastructure by developing and sharing information on cyber and physical security threats, vulnerabilities, countermeasures, and best practices in the biotechnology and pharmaceutical industry sector.[155]

This ISAC has also disappeared, but no further information appears to be available as to when the ISAC was discontinued. However, Internet domain squatter and scam artist Pharmacy Express has purchased the former BioPharma ISAC Internet domain to provide, offer, and sell (what appears to be) illegal pharmaceutical drugs, with the main Web page displaying male and female performance-enhancing drugs.[156,157]

9.55   MARITIME ISAC

The Maritime ISAC (M-ISAC) was originally established specifically to collect, analyze, and disseminate maritime threat information in coordination with the federal government intelligence and security agencies. By its charter, the M-ISAC was supposed to work in close cooperation with U.S. and international port and shipping industries. M-ISAC was originally intended to serve as the principal means by which the maritime industry communicates security and intelligence concerns with appropriate government agencies. Industry representatives are drawn from strategic seaports and multinational shipping companies. Such information sharing has been made essential in light of the International Ship and Port Facility Security Code, which was adopted by the International Maritime Organization, an arm of the

United Nations. M-ISAC is a not-for-profit Florida corporation and is sponsored by the Maritime Security Council (MSC).[158]

For reasons not stated, the port and maritime sector never really created its own ISAC. Therefore the U.S. Coast Guard (USCG) took the leadership role, in which sometime in February 2003, the USCG signed a memorandum of understanding with the National Response Center as well as the FBI's NIPC, now part of the DHS Information Analysis and Infrastructure Protectorate. The USCG is responsible for the collection of reports of any suspicious activities or behavior within the maritime environments throughout the United States (and its ports), and for the distribution of any threat-related information.[159]

For threat information relating to the port and maritime sector, the DHS sends a copy of threat-related information to the USCG Headquarters, located in Washington, D.C., where it is further distributed to the Coast Guard captains of the port as well as other command staff. The captains of the port, as the federal maritime security coordinators (defined within the Maritime Transportation Security Act of 2002), distribute threat-related information to their responsible security committee members, other stakeholders for their representative ports, and their affiliates. Currently, the USCG distributes threat-related information to approximately 50 national maritime-affiliated associations and their organizations.[160]

Other maritime affiliated organizations now include:[161]

- The meta-association responsible for various trade associations
- The Marine Transportation System National Advisory Council (MTSNAC)
- Various harbor operations or harbor safety committees
- Various area maritime security committees
- Various maritime associations or maritime exchanges
- The MSC

9.56 MARITIME SECURITY COUNCIL

In addition to being the principal clearinghouse for the exchange of information between its carrier members, the MSC also acts as a liaison with regulators and governments, offering vital intelligence on crimes at sea and information to U.S. Customs to assist with its antidrug efforts. As a consequence of this role, the MSC assisted in the development of the Sea Carrier Initiative and Super Carrier Programs and actively participates in international activities with the U.S. Drug Control Program, World Customs Organization, and the Baltic and International Maritime Council. Because of its successful assistance to the government, the MSC was the proud recipient of the U.S. vice president's National Performance Review (or Hammer Award), and has been a maritime security advisor to the White House, National Security Council, U.S. Customs, U.S. DOT, and the USCG. In 2000, the MSC was appointed as the technical advisor to the U.S. State Department's Overseas Security Advisory Council on maritime security issues. The MSC is also an advisor to the International Criminal Police Organization, the international police organization.[162]

9.57 MARINE TRANSPORTATION SYSTEM NATIONAL ADVISORY COUNCIL

The Marine Transportation System (MTS) consists of waterways, ports, and intermodal land-based connections that allow for the various modes of transportation moving both people and goods to, from, and on the water. The MTSNAC is a chartered, nonfederal body whose sole purpose is to advise the Secretary of Transportation on matters pertaining to MTS issues. Its membership is composed of leadership members from more than 30 commercial transportation firms, trade associations, state and local public entities, recreational boating interests, academics, and environmental groups. MTSNAC exists to assist policy and decision makers, and also provides general public information that will help the public understand security-related issues, thus permitting greater flexibility and participation pertaining to the development of possible solutions to their issues.[163] Member organizations affiliated with and supporting the MTSNAC include:[164]

American Association of Port Authorities
American Great Lakes Ports Association
American Maritime Congress
American Trucking Associations
Association of Metropolitan Planning Organization
Boat Owners Association of the United States
Coastwise Coalition
Gulf of Mexico States Partnership, Inc.
I-95 Corridor Coalition
Intermodal Association of North America
International Longshore and Warehouse Union
International Longshoreman's Association
Lake Carriers' Association
Maritime Information Services of North America
Maritime Security Council
National Association of Counties
National Association of Waterfront Employers
National Governor's Association
National Industrial Transportation League
National Waterways Conference
Pacific Maritime Association
Propeller Club of the United States
Shipbuilders Council of America
Society of Naval Architects and Marine Engineers
U.S. Chamber of Commerce
U.S. Maritime Alliance, Ltd.
The Waterfront Coalition
World Shipping Council

9.58 AUTHORS' NOTES

Although some ISACs have flourished and others appear to be floundering somewhat, there is another aspect of the ISAC structure that appears through the World Wide Web. Over the past number of years, various blogs, mailing lists, and other kinds of Internet-related tools have enabled communities to come together to exchange ideas.

Although such efforts are noble, they also have some level of risk. The Internet is still a relatively anonymous place, and individuals can misrepresent themselves in attempts to gain access to the groups. At the same time, individuals who maintain these lists do not always have formal access to the means of conducting checks. As a result, most communities have acknowledged that these lists are a good place to meet, share general ideas, and then develop lines of communications outside of them, where participants may be able to share more sensitive topics.

At the same time, such lists provide a valuable education tool for the public at large. Being able to identify and access capable personnel in the field can prove significantly beneficial to students or researchers—something that would have posed significant challenges before the advent of this tool.

Concurrent to these tools, there is an influx of intelligence and similar organizations that have entered the marketplace. Although these groups often boast ex-military or civilian intelligence personnel, they may come at a cost—sometimes a significant one. Although these services have received some criticism, the more capable of them help address a significant gap in the lack of a clear mechanism by which credible threat information can be communicated into the public domain.

NOTES

1. http://cip.gmu.edu/clib/350_CyberSecurity-ProtectingNYSsCriticalInfrastructur.htm (alt URL: http://cipbook.infracritical.com/book5/chapter9/ch9ref1.pdf).
2. Ibid.
3. Internal Revenue Service, *Privacy Impact Assessment—Business Master File (BMF)*; http://www.irs.gov/privacy/article/0,,id = 130752,00.html (alt URL: http://cipbook. infracritical.com/book5/chapter9/ch9ref2.pdf).
4. Ibid.
5. http://www.surfacetransportationisac.org (alt URL: http://cipbook.infracritical.com/book5/chapter9/ch9ref3.pdf).
6. The *Terrorism Risk Analysis and Security Management Plan* represents a security task force composed of railroad representatives with expertise in such areas as operations, legal issues, railroad police activities, hazardous materials transportation, and information technology; outside consultants with expertise in intelligence and counterterrorism were retained to provide advice on best practices.
7. U.S. Department of Transportation Applauds Association of American Railroads' Initiative to Create a Center to Enhance Security; http://www.dot.gov/affairs/dot4502. htm (alt URL: http://cipbook.infracritical.com/book5/chapter9/ch9ref4.pdf).
8. http://secure.sc-investigate.net/SC-ISAC/ISACFAQ.aspx (alt URL: http://cipbook. infracritical.com/book5/chapter9/ch9ref10.pdf).
9. http://secure.sc-investigate.net/SC-ISAC/ISACFAQ.aspx (alt URL: http://cipbook. infracritical.com/book5/chapter9/ch9ref10.pdf).
10. http://www.surfacetransportationisac.org/APTA.asp (alt URL: http://cipbook.infracritical.com/book5/chapter9/ch9ref5.pdf).

11. U.S. DOT, *State Safety Oversight Newsletter*, Issue 12, Summer 2004; http://transit-safety.volpe.dot.gov/Safety/sso/archive/newsletters/Issue12/PDF/Issue12.pdf (alt URL: http://cipbook.infracritical.com/book5/chapter9/ch9ref6.pdf).
12. Ibid.
13. http://www.fta.dot.gov (alt URL: http://cipbook.infracritical.com/book5/chapter9/ch9ref7.pdf).
14. U.S. DOT, *State Safety Oversight Newsletter*, Issue 12, Summer 2004; http://transit-safety.volpe.dot.gov/Safety/sso/archive/newsletters/Issue12/PDF/Issue12.pdf (alt URL: http://cipbook.infracritical.com/book5/chapter9/ch9ref6.pdf).
15. http://www.apta.com.
16. http://www.aar.org.
17. http://www.ttci.aar.com/.
18. http://www.railinc.com.
19. http://www.epa.gov/safewater/sdwa/index.html (alt URL: http://cipbook.infracritical.com/book5/chapter9/ch9ref8.pdf), http://www.epa.gov/safewater/sdwa/basicinformation.html (alt URL: http://cipbook.infracritical.com/book5/chapter9/ch9ref8a.pdf), and http://www.epa.gov/safewater/sdwa/laws_statutes.html (alt URL: http://cipbook.infracritical.com/book5/chapter9/ch9ref8b.pdf).
20. U.S. Environmental Protection Agency, *Information for the Public on Preparing Capacity Development Strategies*, EPA 8916-R-98-009, July 1998.
21. http://bulk.resource.org/gpo.gov/record/2001/2001_H10188.pdf (alt URL: http://cipbook.infracritical.com/book5/chapter9/ch9ref9.pdf).
22. Growing public awareness and concern for controlling water pollution led to the enactment of the Federal Water Pollution Control Act Amendments of 1972. As amended in 1977, this law became commonly known as the Clean Water Act. The act established the basic structure for regulating discharges of pollutants into the waters of the United States. http://www.epa.gov/region5/water/cwa.htm.
23. http://www.epa.gov/lawsregs/laws/cwa.html and http://epw.senate.gov/water.pdf (alt URL: http://cipbook.infracritical.com/book5/chapter9/ch9ref29.pdf and http://cipbook.infracritical.com/book5/chapter9/ch9ref30.pdf).
24. Ibid.
25. http://www.waterisac.org.
26. http://www.asdwa.org.
27. http://www.werf.org.
28. http://www.cdc.gov/nceh/ehhe/water/links.htm (alt URL: http://cipbook.infracritical.com/book5/chapter9/ch9ref31.pdf).
29. http://www.amwa.net.
30. http://www.amsa-cleanwater.org.
31. http://www.nawc.org.
32. http://www.awwa.org.
33. http://www.awwarf.org.
34. The president's Commission on Critical Infrastructure Protection was created on July 15, 1996, by Executive Order 13010 to bring the public and private sectors together to assess and develop strategies to address infrastructure vulnerabilities. The banking and finance sector was identified as one of the eight critical infrastructures requiring review and assurance strategies, and in 1999, the banking and finance sector established the FS-ISAC.
35. FDIC, *Putting an End to Account-Hijacking Identity Theft*; http://www.fdic.gov/consumers/consumer/idtheftstudy/industry.html (alt URL: http://cipbook.infracritical.com/book5/chapter9/ch9ref32.pdf).
36. Ibid.
37. http://www.fsisac.com.
38. http://www.saic.com.

39. http://www.nerc.com.
40. U.S. Department of Homeland Security integrated legacy operations of the NIPC, CIAO, NCS, and Energy Assurance Office, and developed the functional organizational components of the Infrastructure Assurance (IA) and Infrastructure Protectorate (IP) directorates. Office of Management and Budget, *FY 2003 Report to Congress on Federal Government Information Security Management*, White House, March 1, 2004; http://georgewbush-whitehouse.archives.gov/omb/inforeg/fy03_fisma_report.pdf (alt URL://cipbook.infracritical.com/chapter9/ch9ref33.pdf).
41. The CIPAG brings together the generation and transmission providers, public and investor-owned utilities, power marketers, regional transmission organizations and independent system operators, electric power associations, and government agencies. Both Canadian and U.S. entities participate.
42. U.S. Department of Homeland Security integrated legacy operations of the NIPC, CIAO, NCS, and Energy Assurance Office, and developed the functional organizational components of the Infrastructure Assurance (IA) and Infrastructure Protectorate (IP) directorates. Office of Management and Budget, *FY 2003 Report to Congress on Federal Government Information Security Management*, White House, March 1, 2004; http://georgewbush-whitehouse.archives.gov/omb/inforeg/fy03_fisma_report.pdf (alt URL://cipbook.infracritical.com/chapter9/ch9ref33.pdf).
43. Ibid.
44. http://www.ferc.gov.
45. Testimony of Michehl R. Gent, president and chief executive officer, North American Electric Reliability Council, hearing before the U.S. Senate Committee on Governmental Affairs, May 8, 2002, Securing Our Infrastructure: Private/Public Information Sharing.
46. Testimony to the U.S. House of Representatives Committee on Government Reform Subcommittee on Government Efficiency, Financial Management, and Intergovernmental Relations Discussing Activities Undertaken by the Electricity Sector to Address Physical and Cyber Security with Emphasis on the Electricity Sector—Information Sharing and Analysis Center (ES-ISAC), Louis G. Leffler, Manager—Projects North American Electric Reliability Council, July 24, 2002; http://www.esisac.com/public-docs/HouseCommitteeonGovtReform072402.pdf (alt URL: http://cipbook.infracritical.com/book5/chapter9/ch9ref34.pdf).
47. Ibid.
48. U.S. Department of Homeland Security integrated legacy operations of the NIPC, CIAO, NCS, and Energy Assurance Office, and developed the functional organizational components of the Infrastructure Assurance (IA) and Infrastructure Protectorate (IP) directorates. Office of Management and Budget, *FY 2003 Report to Congress on Federal Government Information Security Management*, White House, March 1, 2004; http://georgewbush-whitehouse.archives.gov/omb/inforeg/fy03_fisma_report.pdf (alt URL://cipbook.infracritical.com/chapter9/ch9ref33.pdf).
49. Testimony of Michehl R. Gent, president and chief executive officer, North American Electric Reliability Council, hearing before the U.S. Senate Committee on Governmental Affairs, May 8, 2002, Securing Our Infrastructure: Private/Public Information Sharing.
50. Testimony to the U.S. House of Representatives Committee on Government Reform Subcommittee on Government Efficiency, Financial Management and Intergovernmental Relations Discussing Activities Undertaken by the Electricity Sector to Address Physical and Cyber Security with Emphasis on the Electricity Sector—Information Sharing and Analysis Center (ES-ISAC), Louis G. Leffler, Manager—Projects North American Electric Reliability Council, July 24, 2002; http://www.esisac.com/public-docs/HouseCommitteeonGovtReform072402.pdf (alt URL: http://cipbook.infracritical.com/book5/chapter9/ch9ref34.pdf).

51. Ibid.
52. Ibid.
53. Ibid.
54. Ibid.
55. Ibid.
56. http://www.esisac.com.
57. Ibid.
58. Testimony to the U.S. House of Representatives Committee on Government Reform Subcommittee on Government Efficiency, Financial Management, and Intergovernmental Relations Discussing Activities Undertaken by the Electricity Sector to Address Physical and Cyber Security with Emphasis on the Electricity Sector—Information Sharing and Analysis Center (ES-ISAC), Louis G. Leffler, Manager—Projects North American Electric Reliability Council, July 24, 2002; http://www.esisac.com/public-docs/HouseCommitteeonGovtReform072402.pdf (alt URL: http://cipbook.infracritical. com/book5/chapter9/ch9ref34.pdf).
59. Ibid.
60. U.S. Fire Administration, Federal Emergency Management Agency, Critical Infrastructure Protection (EMR-ISAC); http://www.usfa.dhs.gov/fireservice/subjects/ emr-isac/index.shtm (alt URL: http://cipbook.infracritical.com/chapter9/ch9ref35.pdf).
61. Ibid.
62. Ibid.
63. Ibid.
64. Ibid.
65. U.S. Fire Administration, Federal Emergency Management Agency, CIP/EMR-ISAC Factsheet, March 2005; http://www.usfa.dhs.gov/fireservice/subjects/emr-isac/fact-sheet.shtm (alt URL: http://cipbook.infracritical.com/book5/chapter9/ch9ref36.pdf).
66. http://www.it-isac.com.
67. http://www.ncs.gov/faq.html (alt URL http://cipbook.infracritical.com/book5/chapter9/ ch9ref37.pdf).
68. http://www.ncs.gov/ncc (alt URL: http://cipbook.infracritical.com/book5/chapter9/ ch9ref38.pdf).
69. *Federal Register*, Vol. 49, No. 67, April 5, 1984; http://www.au.af.mil/au/awc/awcgate/ execordr/eo12472.htm (alt URL: http://cipbook.infracritical.com/book5/¬chapter9/ ch9ref39.pdf).
70. http://www.ncs.gov/library/issuances/NCSD%203-9.pdf and http://www.fas.org/nuke/ guide/usa/c3i/ncs.htm (alt URL: http://cipbook.infracritical.com/book5/chapter9/ ch9ref40.pdf, http://cipbook.infracritical.com/book5/chapter9/ch9ref41.pdf, and http:// cipbook.infracritical.com/book5/chapter9/ch9ref42.pdf).
71. Financial and Banking Information Infrastructure Committee, *Sponsorship of Priority Telecommunications Access for Private Sector Entities through the National Communications System Government Emergency Telecommunications Service (GETS) and Wireless Priority Service (WPS)*; http://www.fbiic.gov/gets/GETS_policy.htm (alt URL: http://cipbook.infracritical.com/book5/chapter9/ch9ref43.pdf).
72. The Financial and Banking Information Infrastructure Committee (FBIIC) is chartered under the president's Working Group on Financial Markets, and is charged with improving coordination and communication among financial regulators, enhancing the resiliency of the financial sector, and promoting the public-private partnership. The Treasury's Assistant Secretary for Financial Institutions chairs the committee. Members of the FBIIC include representatives of the Commodity Futures Trading Commission, the Conference of State Bank Supervisors, the Farm Credit Administration, the Federal Deposit Insurance Corporation, the Federal Housing Finance Board, the Federal Reserve Bank of New York, the Federal Reserve

Board, the Homeland Security Council, the National Association of Insurance Commissioners, the National Credit Union Administration, the North American Securities Administrators Association, the Office of the Comptroller of the Currency, the Office of Federal Housing Enterprise Oversight, the Office of Thrift Supervision, the Securities and Exchange Commission, and the Securities Investor Protection Corporation. http://www.fbiic.gov (alt URL: http://cipbook.infracritical.com/book5/chapter9/ch9ref44.pdf).

73. Ibid.

74. Ibid.

75. Refer to Section 9.28 of the *Telecommunications Service Priority (TSP)*; http://www.ncs.gov/library/issuances/NCSD%203-1.pdf (URL: http://cipbook.infracritical.com/book5/chapter9/ch9ref45.pdf).

76. Financial and Banking Information Infrastructure Committee, *Sponsorship of Priority Telecommunications Access for Private Sector Entities through the National Communications System Government Emergency Telecommunications Service (GETS) and Wireless Priority Service (WPS)*; http://www.fbiic.gov/gets/GETS_policy.htm (alt URL: http://cipbook.infracritical.com/book5/chapter9/ch9ref43.pdf).

77. http://www.fbiic.gov/gets/GETS_policy.htm (alt URL: http://cipbook.infracritical.com/book5/chapter9/ch9ref43.pdf).

78. http://gets.ncs.gov (alt URL: http://cipbook.infracritical.com/book5/chapter9/ch9ref46.pdf).

79. Ibid.

80. Financial and Banking Information Infrastructure Committee, *Sponsorship of Priority Telecommunications Access for Private Sector Entities through the National Communications System Government Emergency Telecommunications Service (GETS) and Wireless Priority Service (WPS)*; http://www.fbiic.gov/gets/GETS_policy.htm (alt URL: http://cipbook.infracritical.com/book5/chapter9/ch9ref43.pdf).

81. http://www.fbiic.gov/gets/GETS_policy.htm (alt URL: http://cipbook.infracritical.com/book5/chapter9/ch9ref43.pdf).

82. http://www.fbiic.gov/gets/GETS_policy.htm (alt URL: http://cipbook.infracritical.com/book5/chapter9/ch9ref43.pdf).

83. http://www.fbiic.gov/gets/GETS_policy.htm (alt URL: http://cipbook.infracritical.com/book5/chapter9/ch9ref43.pdf).

84. Financial and Banking Information Infrastructure Committee, *Sponsorship of Priority Telecommunications Access for Private Sector Entities through the National Communications System Government Emergency Telecommunications Service (GETS) and Wireless Priority Service (WPS)*; http://www.fbiic.gov/gets/GETS_policy.htm (alt URL: http://cipbook.infracritical.com/book5/chapter9/ch9ref43.pdf).

85. In its role as a payments system operator, the Federal Reserve has traditionally sponsored significant participants in the payments system for NCS services. The Federal Reserve therefore intends to contact those organizations that clearly qualify under the criteria and ask them to provide the names of individuals who should receive GETS cards. The Federal Reserve will notify the other FBIIC agencies of institutions they have contacted.

86. http://tsp.ncs.gov (alt URL: http://cipbook.infracritical.com/book5/chapter9/ch9ref47.pdf) and http://www.ncs.gov/library/fact_sheets/FS-TSP%20(DHS).pdf (alt URL: http://cipbook.infracritical.com/book5/chapter9/ch9ref57.pdf).

87. http://www.its.bldrdoc.gov/projects/devglossary/_telecommunications_service_priority_system.html (alt URL: http://cipbook.infracritical.com/book5/chapter9/ch9ref48.pdf).

88. *Federal Register*, Vol. 49, No. 67, April 5, 1984. http://www.au.af.mil/au/awc/awcgate/execordr/eo12472.htm (alt URL: http://cipbook.infracritical.com/book5/chapter9/ch9ref39.pdf).

89. http://www.ncs.gov/shares/ (alt URL: http://cipbook.infracritical.com/book5/chapter9/ch9ref49.pdf), http://www.ncs.gov/library/SHARES/SHARES%20Bulletin%202012.pdf (alt URL: http://cipbook.infracritical.com/book5/chapter9/ch9ref50.pdf), and http://www.ncs.gov/library/fact_sheets/FS-SHARES%20(DHS).pdf (alt URL: http://cipbook.infracritical.com/book5/chapter9/ch9ref58.pdf).

90. http://www.ncs.gov/shares/ (alt URL: http://cipbook.infracritical.com/book5/chapter9/ch9ref49.pdf), http://www.ncs.gov/library/SHARES/SHARES%20Bulletin%202012.pdf (alt URL: http://cipbook.infracritical.com/book5/chapter9/ch9ref50.pdf), and http://www.ncs.gov/library/fact_sheets/FS-SHARES%20(DHS).pdf (alt URL: http://cipbook.infracritical.com/book5/chapter9/ch9ref58.pdf).

91. *NRIC Network Interoperability: The Key to Competition*, July 15, 1997.

92. http://www.ncs.gov/nstac/nstac_publications.html (alt URL: http://cipbook.infracritical.com/book5/chapter9/ch9ref51.pdf).

93. http://www.ncs.gov/nstac/nstac.html (alt URL: http://cipbook.infracritical.com/book5/chapter9/ch9ref52.pdf).

94. Ibid.

95. Ibid.

96. Ibid.

97. Ibid.

98. Ibid.

99. Ibid.

100. Ibid.

101. Ibid.

102. Ibid.

103. Ibid.

104. Ibid.

105. Ibid.

106. Ibid.

107. The Priority Access Service (PAS) program was developed by the Federal Communications Commission (FCC), and is managed by the OMNCS. OMNCS is a federal government organization established to perform NS/EP telecommunications functions among its 23 member organizations. OMNCS's primary mission is to develop a responsive, survivable, and enduring national telecommunication infrastructure to support the NS/EP telecommunication needs of the federal government. As a first step in satisfying the mission requirements, OMNCS developed and deployed GETS. GETS is designed and maintained in a state of readiness that makes use of available PSTN resources, should outages occur during an emergency or crisis. In general, PAS is intended to provide authorized personnel priority access to telecommunications (both wireless and wireline). For the purposes of this chapter, PAS will be used to refer to all priority access, particularly the wireless component of PAS.

108. U.S. Department of Homeland Security SAFECOM, *Emerging Wireless Technologies Priority Access Services in the Mobile Environment*; http://www.safecomprogram.gov/NR/rdonlyres/CBF883D7-39FB-4B14-A9AD-D3E0793840C6/0/emerging_wireless_technologies_priority_access.pdf (alt URL: http://cipbook.infracritical.com/book5/chapter9/ch9ref53.pdf).

109. http://gets.ncs.gov (alt URL: http://cipbook.infracritical.com/book5/chapter9/ch9ref46.pdf) and http://www.ncs.gov/library/fact_sheets/FS-GETS%20(DHS).pdf (alt URL: http://cipbook.infracritical.com/book5/chapter9/ch9ref54.pdf).

110. http://wps.ncs.gov (alt URL: http://cipbook.infracritical.com/book5/chapter9/ch9ref55.pdf) and http://www.ncs.gov/library/fact_sheets/FS-WPS%20(DHS).pdf (alt URL: http://cipbook.infracritical.com/book5/chapter9/ch9ref56.pdf).

111. Ibid.

112. Ibid.
113. http://www.safecomprogram.gov (alt URL: http://cipbook.infracritical.com/book5/chapter9/ch9ref59.pdf).
114. Ibid.
115. Ibid.
116. http://www.ncs.gov/library/ACN/ACN%20Report%20Vol.%20IV,%20No.%201%20-%20Spring%202005.pdf (alt URL: http://cipbook.infracritical.com/book5/chapter9/ch9ref60.pdf).
117. Ibid.
118. http://www.energyisac.com/index.cfm. (Note: This domain no longer exists.)
119. http://www.energysec.org.
120. Taken from ENERGYSEC's press release, Industry Group Expands Energy Security Initiatives, February 3, 2009; http://www.energysec.org/EnergySec/Welcome_files/energysec-press-release-3-Feb.pdf (alt URL: http://cipbook.infracritical.com/book5/chapter9/ch9ref11.pdf).
121. http://www.dhs.gov/xnews/releases/press_release_0671.shtm (alt URL: http://cipbook.infracritical.com/book5/chapter9/ch9ref61.pdf).
122. Ibid.
123. http://www.chemtrec.com.
124. http://www.hcisac.org. (Note: This Internet domain name has succumbed to domain squatting.)
125. http://cipbook.infracritical.com/book5/chapter9/ch9ref12.pdf.
126. http://www.highwayisac.com.
127. Ibid.
128. http://www.cargotips.org.
129. http://www.truckline.com.
130. http://www.highwatch.com.
131. The Food and Agriculture Sector abandoned its information sharing model sometime early in 2008. The Food and Agriculture Sector was the first infrastructure sector to form an ISAC, and was established before DHS came into existence. However, the Food Marketing Institute, the former owner and sponsor for the ISAC, suspended, and eventually disbanded, all ISAC activities because it had not received any terrorism-based threat information; essentially, either no one had any information to share or no one wanted to share. Nonetheless, FMI disconnected service for the ISAC sometime in 2008. Former URL: http://www.fmi.org/isac; output from current URL: http://cipbook.infracritical.com/book5/chapter9/ch9ref13.pdf.
132. http://cipbook.infracritical.com/book5/chapter9/ch9ref13.pdf.
133. Joseph Straw, Food Sector Abandons Its ISAC, *Security Management Magazine*, September 2008; http://www.securitymanagement.com/article/food-sector-abandons-its-isac-004590 (alt URL: http://cipbook.infracritical.com/book5/chapter9/ch9ref14.pdf).
134. http://www.foodshield.org (alt URL: http://cipbook.infracritical.com/book5/chapter9/ch9ref15.pdf).
135. http://www.foodshield.org (alt URL: http://cipbook.infracritical.com/book5/chapter9/ch9ref15.pdf).
136. National Food Safety System (NFSS); http://www.foodsafety.gov/~dms/fs-toc.html (alt URL: http://cipbook.infracritical.com/book5/chapter9/ch9ref17.pdf).
137. FDA is leading an effort to improve coordination and communication among public health and food regulatory officials at all levels of government, particularly around foodborne illness outbreaks. Known as the NFSS, this project will contribute significantly toward more effective implementation of existing food safety programs.
138. http://www.foodshield.org/about/history.cfm (alt URL: http://cipbook.infracritical.com/book5/chapter9/ch9ref16.pdf).

139. The NCFPD, a Homeland Security Center of Excellence led by the University of Minnesota, is a multidisciplinary and action-oriented research consortium that addresses the vulnerability of the nation's food system to attack through intentional contamination with biological or chemical agents. It seeks to defend the safety of the food system—from prefarm inputs through consumption—by establishing best practices, developing new tools, and attracting new researchers to prevent, manage, and respond to food contamination events.

140. http://www.ncfpd.umn.edu/ (alt URL: http://cipbook.infracritical.com/book5/chapter9/ch9ref20.pdf).

141. http://www.foodprotectioneducation.org/ (alt URL: http://cipbook.infracritical.com/book5/chapter9/ch9ref21.pdf).

142. CSREES is an agency within the USDA, part of the executive branch of the federal government. Congress created CSREES through the 1994 Department Reorganization Act, by combining the USDA's Cooperative State Research Service (CSRS) and Extension Service (ES) into a single agency; http://www.csrees.usda.gov/about/about.html (alt URL: http://cipbook.infracritical.com/book5/chapter9/ch9ref22.pdf).

143. http://www.csrees.usda.gov/fo/agriculturalandfoodresearchinitiativeafri.cfm (alt URL: http://cipbook.infracritical.com/book5/chapter9/ch9ref23.pdf).

144. http://www.csrees.usda.gov/newsroom/news/2008news/12171_afri.html (alt URL: http://cipbook.infracritical.com/book5/chapter9/ch9ref24.pdf).

145. http://www.csrees.usda.gov/funding/afri/pdfs/program_announcement.pdf (alt URL: http://cipbook.infracritical.com/book5/chapter9/ch9ref25.pdf).

146. The USDA's CSREES announced the addition of the Agriculture and Food Research Initiative (AFRI) to its funding opportunities available in 2009.

147. http://www.fmi.org.

148. http://www.msisac.org/ (alt URL: http://cipbook.infracritical.com/book5/chapter9/ch9ref62.pdf).

149. http://www.isaccouncil.org (alt URL: http://cipbook.infracritical.com/book5/chapter9/ch9ref63.pdf).

150. http://www.wwisac.com (alt URL: http://cipbook.infracritical.com/book5/chapter9/ch9ref64.pdf).

151. http://www.reisac.org.

152. http://www.reisac.org/about.html.

153. http://www.rer.org.

154. http://ren-isac.net.

155. http://www.biotech-isac.org. (Note: This domain no longer exists.)

156. http://www.rxpop.com/scam_alert.asp (alt URL: http://cipbook.infracritical.com/book5/chapter9/ch9ref27.pdf).

157. http://www.siteadvisor.com/sites/biopharma-isac.com/postid?p = 1116038 (alt URL: http://cipbook.infracritical.com/book5/chapter9/ch9ref28.pdf).

158. http://72.14.207.104/search?q = cache:7w03gjeHQiYJW; www.seasecure.com/m-isac.htm&hl-en&gl-us&ct-clnk&cd-1.

159. http://www.wagner.nyu.edu/transportation/files/summer04.pdf (alt URL: http://cipbook.infracritical.com/book5/chapter9/ch9ref65.pdf).

160. Ibid.

161. Ibid. Marine Transportation System National Advisory Council; http://www.mtsnac.org. Maritime Security Council; http://www.maritimesecurity.org.

162. http://www.maritimesecurity.org/background_info.htm (alt URL: http://cipbook.infracritical.com/book5/chapter9/ch9ref66.pdf).

163. Marine Transportation System National Advisory Council; http://www.mtsnac.org (alt URL: http://cipbook.infracritical.com/book5/chapter9/ch9ref67.pdf).

164. Marine Transportation System National Advisory Council; http://www.mtsnac.org/member.htm. American Association of Port Authorities; http://www.aapa-ports.org. American Maritime Congress; http://www.usflag.org. American Trucking Associations; http://www.truckline.com. Association of Metropolitan Planning Organization; http://www.ampo.org. Boat Owners Association of the United States; http://www.boatus.com. Gulf of Mexico States Partnership, Inc.; http://www.gomsa.org. I-95 Corridor Coalition; http://www.i95.org. Intermodal Association of North America; http://www.intermodal.org. International Longshore and Warehouse Union; http://www.ilwu.org. International Longshoreman's Association; http://www.ilaunion.org. Lake Carriers' Association; http://www.lcaships.com. Maritime Information Services of North America; http://www.misnadata.org. Maritime Security Council; http://www.maritimesecurity.org. National Association of Counties; http://www.naco.org. National Governor's Association; http://www.nga.org. National Industrial Transportation League; http://www.nitl.org. National Waterways Conference; http://www.waterways.org. Pacific Maritime Association; http://www.pmanet.org. Propeller Club of the United States; http://www.propellerclubhq.com. Shipbuilders Council of America; http://www.shipbuilders.org. Society of Naval Architects and Marine Engineers; http://www.sname.org. Waterfront Coalition; http://www.portmod.org. U.S. Chamber of Commerce; http://www.chamber.org. U.S. Maritime Alliance, Ltd.; http://www.usmx.com. World Shipping Council; http://www.worldshipping.org.

165. http://www.us-nesco.org.

10 Supervisory Control and Data Acquisition

10.1 INTRODUCTION

This chapter introduces terms and concepts that are associated with automated control systems, of which supervisory control and data acquisition (SCADA) is a part. Some of the terms introduced involve information technology (IT)-related security methodologies and what methods would be used to breach security controls and their mechanisms.

10.2 WHAT ARE CONTROL SYSTEMS?

Generally speaking, most control systems are computer based. These control systems are used by many infrastructures and industries to monitor and control sensitive processes and physical functions. Typically, control systems collect sensor measurements and operational data from the field, process and display this information, and relay control commands to local or remote equipment. In the electric power industry, they can manage and control the transmission and delivery of electric power, for example, by opening and closing circuit breakers and setting thresholds for preventive shutdowns. Using integrated control systems, the oil and gas industry can control the refining operations on a plant site as well as remotely monitor the pressure and flow of gas pipelines and control the flow and pathways of gas transmission. In water utilities, control systems can remotely monitor well levels; control the wells' pumps; monitor water flows, tank levels, or water pressure in storage tanks; monitor water quality characteristics such as pH, turbidity, and chlorine residual; and control the addition of chemicals. Control system functions vary from simple to complex; they may be used to simply monitor processes running—for example, environmental conditions within a small office building (the simplest form of site monitoring) to managing most (or, in most cases, all) activities for a municipal water system, or even a nuclear power plant. Within certain industries, such as chemical and power generation, safety systems are typically implemented to mitigate a disastrous event if control and other systems fail.

Control systems were not always computer based. In fact, there are still many pneumatic control systems. Some are analog systems, based on operational amplifier circuits. Some are mechanical feedback systems, and others are hydraulic—for example, the set point for many pressure-reducing valves is made by setting the position of a hydraulic pilot valve configuration.

In addition to guarding against both physical attack and system failure, organizations may establish backup control centers that include uninterruptible power supplies and backup generators.[1]

10.3   TYPES OF CONTROL SYSTEMS

The two primary types of control systems are:

1. Distributed control systems (DCS); these are typically used within a single process or generating plant or used over a smaller geographic area or even a single site location.
2. SCADA systems; these are typically used for larger-scale environments that may be geographically dispersed in an enterprise-wide distribution operation.

A utility company may use a DCS to generate power, and use a SCADA system to distribute it.[2]

Control loops in a SCADA system tend to be open, whereas control loops in DCS systems tend to be closed. The SCADA system communications infrastructure tends to be slower, and less reliable, and so the remote terminal unit (RTU) in a SCADA system has local control schemes to handle that eventuality. In a DCS, networks tend to be highly reliable, high-bandwidth campus local area networks (LANs). The remote sites in a DCS can afford to send more data and centralize the processing of that data.

10.4   COMPONENTS OF CONTROL SYSTEMS

A control system typically consists of a master control system or central supervisory control and monitoring station, consisting of one or more human-machine interfaces in which an operator may view displayed information about the remote sites or issue commands directly to the system. Typically, this is a device or station that is located at a site in which application servers and production control workstations are used to configure and troubleshoot other control system components. The central supervisory control and monitoring station is generally connected to local controller stations through a hardwired network or to remote controller stations through a communications network that may be communicated through the Internet, a public switched telephone network (PSTN), or a cable or wireless (such as radio, microwave, or WiFi) network.

Each controller station has an RTU, a programmable logic controller (PLC), a DCS controller, and other controllers that communicate with the supervisory control and monitoring station. The controller stations include sensors and control equipment that connect directly with the working components of the infrastructure (e.g., pipelines, water towers, and power lines). Sensors take readings from infrastructure equipment such as water or pressure levels, electrical voltage, etc., sending messages to the controller. The controller may be programmed to determine a course of action, sending a message to the control equipment instructing it what to do (e.g., to turn off a valve or dispense a chemical). If the controller is not programmed to determine a course of action, the controller communicates with the supervisory control and monitoring station before sending a command back to the control equipment. The control system may also be programmed to issue alarms back to the control operator when certain conditions are detected. Handheld devices such as personal digital assistants (PDAs) may be used to locally monitor controller stations. Controller station technologies are becoming more intelligent and automated and can communicate with the supervisory central monitoring and control station less frequently, requiring less human intervention. Historically, security concerns about control stations have been less frequent, requiring less human intervention.

10.5 VULNERABILITY CONCERNS ABOUT CONTROL SYSTEMS

Security concerns about control systems have been historically related primarily to protecting against physical attacks or the misuse of refining and processing sites or distribution and holding facilities. However, more recently there has been a growing recognition that control systems are vulnerable to cyber attacks from numerous sources, including hostile governments, terrorist groups, disgruntled employees, and other malicious intruders.

In October 1997, President Clinton's Commission on Critical Infrastructure Protection specifically discussed the potential damaging effects on the electric power and oil and gas industries of successful attacks on control systems.[3] Sometime in 2002, the National Research Council identified "the potential for attack on control systems" as requiring "urgent attention."[4] And, in February 2003, President Bush outlined his concerns over "the threat of organized cyber attacks capable of causing debilitating disruption to our nation's critical infrastructures, economy, or national security," noting that "disruption of these systems can have significant consequences for public health and safety," and emphasizing that the protection of control systems has become "a national priority."[5]

Several factors have contributed to the escalation of risk of these control systems, which include the following concerns:

- The adoption of standardized technologies with known vulnerabilities
- The connectivity of many control systems via, through, within, or exposed to unsecured networks, networked portals, or mechanisms connected to unsecured networks
- Implementation constraints of existing security technologies and practices within the existing control systems infrastructure (and its architectures)
- The connectivity of insecure remote devices in their connections to control systems
- The widespread availability of technical information about control systems, most notably via publicly available or shared networked resources such as the Internet

10.6 ADOPTION OF STANDARDIZED TECHNOLOGIES WITH KNOWN VULNERABILITIES

Historically, proprietary hardware, software, and network protocols made it rather difficult to understand how control systems operated, as information was not commonly or publicly known, was considered proprietary in nature, and was therefore not susceptible to hacker attacks. Today, however, to reduce costs and improve performance, organizations have begun transitioning from proprietary systems to less expensive, standardized technologies that use and operate under platforms that run operating systems such as Microsoft Windows, UNIX, and LINUX systems, along with the common networking protocols used by the Internet. These widely used standardized technologies have commonly known vulnerabilities such that more sophisticated and effective exploitation tools are widely available and relatively easy to use. As a consequence, both the number of people with the knowledge to wage attacks and the number of systems subject to attack have increased.

10.7 CONNECTIVITY OF CONTROL SYSTEMS TO UNSECURED NETWORKS

Corporate enterprises often integrate their control systems within their enterprise networks. This increased connectivity has significant advantages, including providing decision makers with access to real-time information allowing site engineers and production control managers to monitor and control the process flow and its control of the entire system from within different points of the enterprise network. Enterprise networks are often connected to networks of strategic partners as well as to the Internet. Control systems are increasingly using wide-area networks and the Internet to transmit data to their remote or local stations and individual devices. This convergence of control networks with public and enterprise networks potentially exposes the control systems to additional security vulnerabilities. Unless appropriate security controls are deployed within and throughout the enterprise and control system network, breaches in enterprise security may affect operations.

10.8 IMPLEMENTATION CONSTRAINTS OF EXISTING SECURITY TECHNOLOGIES

The uses of existing security technologies, as well as use of strong user authentication and patch management practices, are typically not implemented in control systems, as control systems operate in real time; control systems are typically not designed with security in mind and usually have limited processing capabilities to accommodate or handle security measures or countermeasures.

Existing security technologies such as authorization, authentication, encryption, intrusion detection, and filtering of network traffic and communications require significantly increased bandwidth, processing power, and memory—much more than control system components typically have or are capable of sustaining. The entire concept behind control systems was integrated systems technologies, which were small, compact, and relatively easy to use and configure. Because controller stations are generally designed to perform specific tasks, they use low-cost, resource-constrained microprocessors. In fact, some devices within the electrical industry still use the Intel 8088 processor, which was introduced in 1978. Consequently, it is difficult to install existing security technologies without seriously degrading the performance of the control systems, thus requiring the need for a complete overhaul of the entire control system infrastructure and its environment.

Furthermore, complex password-controlling mechanisms may not always be used to prevent unauthorized access to control systems, partly because this could hinder a rapid response to safety procedures during an emergency, or could affect the performance of the overall environment. As a result, according to experts, weak passwords that are easy to guess, shared, and infrequently changed are reportedly common in control systems, including the use of default passwords or even no password at all.

Current control systems are based on standard operating systems as they are typically customized to support control system applications. Consequently, vendor-provided software patches are generally either incompatible or cannot be implemented without compromising service by shutting down "always on" systems or affecting interdependent operations.

10.9   INSECURE CONNECTIVITY TO CONTROL SYSTEMS

Potential vulnerabilities in control systems are exacerbated by insecure connections, either within the corporate enterprise network or external to the enterprise or controlling station. Organizations often leave access links (such as dial-up modems to equipment and control information) open for remote diagnostics, maintenance, and examination of system status. Such links may not be protected with authentication or encryption, which increases the risk that an attempted external penetration could use these insecure connections to break into remotely controlled systems. Some control systems use wireless communications systems, which are especially vulnerable to attack, or leased lines that pass through commercial telecommunications facilities; in either situation, neither method of communication performs any security methodologies whatsoever, and if there are any security measures implemented, they are capable of being easily compromised. Without encryption to protect data as they flow through these insecure connections or authentication mechanisms to limit access, there is limited protection for the integrity of the information being transmitted, and the process may be subjected to interception, monitoring of data from interception, and eventually penetration.

10.10   PUBLICLY AVAILABLE INFORMATION ABOUT CONTROL SYSTEMS

Public information about critical infrastructures and control systems is available through widely available networks such as the Internet. The risks associated with the availability of critical infrastructure information poses a serious threat to those critical infrastructures being served, as demonstrated by a George Mason University graduate student whose dissertation reportedly mapped every industrial sector connected via computer networks using tools and materials that were publicly available on the Internet, and none of the data, site maps, or tools used were classified or sanitized. A prime example of publicly available information is with regard to the electric power industry, in which open sources of information such as product data, educational materials, and maps (even though outdated) are still available, showing line locations and interconnections that are currently being used; additional information includes filings of the Federal Energy Regulatory Commission, industrial publications on various subject matters pertaining to the electric power industry, and other materials—all of which are publicly available via the Internet.

10.11   CONTROL SYSTEMS MAY BE VULNERABLE TO ATTACK

Entities or individuals with intent to disrupt service may take one or more of the following methods, which may be successful in their attack(s) of control systems.[6]

- Disrupt the operations of control systems by delaying or blocking the flow of information through the networks supporting the control systems, thereby denying availability of the networks to control systems operators and production control managers.
- Attempt, or succeed at making unauthorized changes to programmed instructions within PLC, RTU, or DCS controllers, change alarm thresholds, or issue unauthorized commands to control station equipment, which could potentially result in damage to equipment (if tolerances have been exceeded), premature shutdown of processes (shutting down transmission lines or causing cascading termination of service to the electrical grid), or rendering disablement of control station equipment.
- Send falsified information to control system operators either to disguise unauthorized changes or to initiate inappropriate actions to be taken by systems operators—that is, falsified information is sent or displayed back to systems operators who may think that an alarmed condition has been triggered, resulting in system operators acting on this falsified information, thus potentially causing the actual event.
- Modify or alter control system software or firmware such that the net effect produces unpredictable results (such as introducing a computer "time bomb" to go off at midnight every night, thus partially shutting down some of the control systems, causing a temporary brownout condition; a time bomb is a forcibly introduced piece of computer logic or source code that causes certain courses of action to be taken when either an event or triggered state has been activated).
- Interfere with the operation and processing of safety systems (e.g., tampering with or denial of service of control systems that regulate processing control rods within a nuclear power generation facility).
- Many remote locations containing control systems (as part of an enterprise DCS environment) are often unstaffed and may not be physically monitored through surveillance; the risk of threat remains and may be higher

if the remote facility is physically penetrated at its perimeter and intrusion attempts are then made to the control systems networks from within.

- Many control systems are vulnerable to attacks of varying degrees. These attack attempts range from telephone line sweeps (wardialing), to wireless network sniffing (wardriving), to physical network port scanning, to physical monitoring and intrusion.

10.12 CONSEQUENCES RESULTING FROM CONTROL SYSTEM COMPROMISES

Some consequences resulting from control system compromises are as follows:

- Although computer network security is undeniably important, unlike enterprise network security, a compromised control system can have significant impacts within real-world life. These impacts can have far-reaching consequences not previously thought, or in areas that could affect other industrial sectors and their infrastructures.
- Enterprise network security breaches can have financial consequences: Customer privacy becomes compromised, computer systems need to be rebuilt, etc.
- A breach of security of a control system can have a cascade effect on other systems, either directly or indirectly connected to those control systems that have been compromised; however, not only can property be destroyed, but people can be hurt, or even worse, people can get killed.[7]

10.13 WARDIALING

Before there was AOL or AT&T Yahoo digital subscriber line (DSL), or any popular Internet service provider (ISP) of today, many people directly connected with remote computer systems via modems. Instead of dialing up the ISP and surfing a Web site or downloading e-mail, users would access bulletin board systems (BBS) to do their personal business; in many cases, these BBS would have features specific to those sites and locations. Some of these features included interactive chat rooms (similar to many of the instant messaging services provided by AOL, Yahoo, and MSN), e-mail, file up/download areas, etc. Many national corporate enterprises made use of BBS services for internal employees of the company. Companies would grant a specific number of employees (while on the road) access to corporate servers for e-mail or private phone lines to make telephone calls billed back to the sponsoring company. Phone companies would (and still do) use special numbers to perform diagnostics, troubleshoot, and configure their networks remotely. Special tones, or the sequencing of these tones, could be sent through telephone lines to activate or deactivate specific services.

Shortly after these services became available, individuals with less than honorable intentions or motives (often stating that they were merely "curious") began seeking out these special or private telephone numbers, or the tones associated with the diagnostic functions of the various telephone companies. Thus the method of "phreaking" was born. A phreaker is an individual who specializes in unauthorized penetration and access of telephone systems. One of the easiest methods of determining the existence of these special or private telephone numbers is by calling each telephone number within a range or block of suffixed numbers within a given prefix or area code. Each telephone number dialed is checked for a modem carrier tone that uniquely identifies that the telephone number may be associated with a computer or network-connected device. Many of the dial-up blocks were performed manually, and it was not long before those individuals found faster, more efficient methods of dialing the telephone numbered blocks through custom-written software. The software applications would dial up every telephone number that was included within a list of telephone numbers to dial, going through the list number by number, dialing and recording its findings until something interesting would show up. This method of sequential dialing with the intent of exploiting the service connected to, and associated with, the telephone number found is called *wardialing*.

10.13.1   Goals of Wardialing

The main goal of wardialing is simple: access. This includes access to a specific company's system; access to free long-distance service; access to an anonymous connection to anonymously access another computer system or entire network; access to a place to hide illegal or contraband software, data, or information; or access with intent to steal data, information, or software. Whatever the case may be, those who are wardialing a remote location, or attempting to find a remote location, are attempting to find access into the remote telephone system, computers, and its network.

10.13.2   Threats Resulting from Wardialing

The combination of loosely controlled telephone infrastructures (compared to a typical Internet perimeter location) and the ubiquity of modems means that it is prudent to understand and manage telephone-based vulnerabilities. Some of the information or outcomes of information obtained from wardialing includes the following;

Carrier detection. Determining (through several methods) whether the carrier is a modem or a facsimile; may be capable of determining the manufacturer of the device that is answering.
Banner logging and identification. Many systems identify not only the name of the organization that is using or sponsoring the carrier answering device, but also the basic functionalities of the device that answered based on its name or a brief description.
System identification. Once connected, individuals may determine the type of system through a series of scanning attempts that would identify the computer manufacturer type, model, and operating system running on the computer system.

Network identification. It may be possible to scan other computing devices if the device has been compromised and may be capable of traversing within and throughout the enterprise network.

10.14   WARDRIVING

Similar to wardialing efforts, the principle and primary goal of wardriving remains the same: access via wireless connectivity. This method of scanning is a form of wireless network sniffing from a stationary, sometimes remote, location to the target point.[8] Many control systems are implementing, or have implemented, wireless connectivity at remote locations. This may be for several reasons, but some of the more obvious reasons stand out: (1) access at a remote facility without having to enter the facility or site location, (2) use of PDA devices to access critical control stations within and throughout the remote facility without being tethered to a cable, or (3) remote distribution of telemetry data and information back to a centralized monitoring facility.

10.15   WARWALKING

Similar to wardriving, the warwalking method of wireless network sniffing is performed at or near the target point and is performed by a pedestrian, meaning that instead of a person being in an automotive vehicle, the potential intruder may be sniffing the network for weaknesses or vulnerabilities on foot, posing as a person walking, but may have a handheld PDA device or laptop computer.[9]

10.16   THREATS RESULTING FROM CONTROL SYSTEM ATTACKS

There have been a number of reported exploitations of several control systems throughout the country. Resulting from the penetration attempts, intruders were successful at several locations.

Sometime in 1998, during a two-week military exercise code named "Eligible Receiver," staff from the National Security Agency (NSA) used widely available tools and software to simulate how sections of the U.S. electrical power grid's control systems networks could be disabled through computer-based attacks. Their attempts were successful, demonstrating how within several days, portions or all of the country's national power grid could have been rendered useless. The attacks also demonstrated the impotency capabilities of command-and-control elements within the U.S. Pacific.[10]

In spring of 2000, a former employee of an Australian company that develops manufacturing software applied for a job in the local government but was rejected. The disgruntled former employee reportedly used a radio transmitter device on numerous occasions to remotely access control systems of a sewage treatment system, releasing an estimated 264,000 gallons of untreated raw sewage into nearby waterways.[11]

10.17   ISSUES IN SECURING CONTROL SYSTEMS

A significant challenge in effectively securing control systems is based on several criteria that may or may not prevent capabilities of properly securing control systems environments and their networks. Some of the issues surmounting from securification efforts include the following:

- Lack or unavailability of specialized security technologies and their implementation.
- Computing resources within control systems that are needed to perform some security functions may be limiting in their capabilities, and thus may be ineffective against attack.
- Control systems architectures may prevent any security implementation such that (1) configuration and layout of implementation may prohibit any such implementation; (2) performance considerations (again, possibly due to configuration or the layout of implementation) may be prohibitive such that redesign, or reimplementation, may be cost-prohibitive or time-prohibitive; and (3) additional security mechanisms may be completely ineffective, and would require a redesign, or reimplementation, of the entire control systems architecture.
- Criticality of specific control systems may not allow for outages without significant cost to the enterprise or customers resulting from lack of service.
- Many organizations are reluctant to spend more money to secure a control system. Hardening security of control systems would require industries to expend more resources, including acquiring more personnel to safeguard the secured control systems, providing additional training for personnel, and potentially prematurely replacing control systems that typically have an average life span of about 20 years.
- Political and legal entanglements insofar as to who controls and maintains the control systems infrastructure and who has responsibility for securing those environments. Conflicting priorities, lack of concern, and lack of interest due to an expansive financial burden to harden those environments perpetuate the lack of IT strategies that could be deployed to mitigate any potentially exposed vulnerability of control systems without affecting performance or the significant cost involved.
- Industrial plants and the instrumentation they include tend to be long-life-cycle projects that have upwards to 20-year project cycles and are by no means uncommon. As a result, the devices that were deployed as part of that construction may be virtual antiques by the time the facility is finally decommissioned, and there is no provision for refreshing those devices in any manner similar to that of computer workstation upgrades.
- Similarly, if security upgrades were probable and capable, the life cycles of the projects for implementation would be considerably longer than standard, conventional computer system implementations. One of the caveats might be that by the time the security upgrade was completed, there would be a vulnerability or exploit available that could jeopardize continued upgrade

implementations, and thus cause disruptions in the life cycle process of the upgrade project.

- Many antiviral software packages have little or no effect on the control systems architectures, as these architectures often predate initial computer-based viruses.
- Remote devices (RTU and PLC) may be difficult to upgrade. These devices might utilize a hardware-based operating system that was burned into a read-only memory (ROM) chip. ROM chips are not rewritable, and some of the chips may no longer be manufactured.
- Remote devices may be physically sealed and not be upgraded or may be located in a difficult-to-reach location, or have no removable media.
- The worst-case scenario might be that the manufacturer of the remote devices may no longer be in business, may not be producing upgrades, or may not be allowing (or be allowed for legal reasons) the upgrades.
- If the remote devices are capable of being upgraded and have some security capabilities added, the sheer number of devices (may be in the thousands or even tens of thousands of devices) poses serious issues with password aging and retention.
- Because of the sheer volume of devices, many control systems operators may have a unitary password for all remote devices or find common methods of maintaining passwords remotely (which bears the possibility of being compromised).

Antivirus software often must be customized to handle a control system to avoid certain files for scanning, such as the log files, the human-machine interface (HMI), trend history files, etc. This limits their utility in the field. Having an antivirus utility scanning these files runs the risk of either (1) having them automatically removed by the antivirus software (thinking that they are infected) or (2) causing performance issues (slowness of the HMI application) within the HMI environment.

10.18 METHODS OF SECURING CONTROL SYSTEMS

Several steps may be taken to address potential threats to control systems:

- Research and develop new security techniques to protect or enhance control systems. There are currently some open systems development efforts.
- Develop security policies, standards, and procedures that are implemented on, for, or with control systems security in mind. Use of consensus standardization would have encouragement within the industry for investing in stronger securification methods of control systems.
- If developing independent security policies, standards, and procedures is not applicable, then implement similar security policies, standards, and procedures taken from the plethora of widely available IT security practices. A good example might be the segmentation of control systems networks with firewall and possibly network-based intrusion detection systems technologies, along with strong authentication practices.

- Define and implement a security awareness program to employees, contractors, and especially customers.
- Define and implement information sharing capabilities that promote and encourage the further development of more secure architectures and security technology capabilities and enhancements. Organizations can benefit from the education and distribution of corporate-wide information about security and the risks related to control systems, best practices, and methods.[13]
- Define and implement effective security management programs and practices that include or take into consideration the control systems security and its management.
- Conduct periodic audits that test and ensure security technologies' integrity is at expected levels of security. Review information with all necessary parties involved, mitigating potential risk issues. Audits should be based on standard risk assessment practices for mission-critical business units and their functional subunits.[14]
- Define and implement logging mechanisms for forensics purposes.
- Define and implement mission-critical business continuity strategies and continuity plans within organizations and industries, which ensure safe and continued operation in the event of an unexpected interruption or attack. Elements of continuity planning typically include: (1) assessments performed against the target mission-critical business unit for criticality of operations and identifying supporting resources to mitigate (if any), (2) developing methods that will prevent and minimize potential damage and interruption of service, (3) developing and documenting comprehensive continuity plans, and (4) periodic testing and evaluation of the continuity plans (similar to performing security audits, but specialized against disaster recovery and business continuity efforts of the control systems environments), making adjustments where necessary or as needed.[15]

10.19   TECHNOLOGY RESEARCH INITIATIVES OF CONTROL SYSTEMS

Research and development of newer technologies is a constant process, providing additional security options in efforts of protecting control systems. Several federally funded entities have ongoing efforts to research, develop, and test new technologies. Those entities are as follows:

Sandia National Laboratories. Current development of improved SCADA technologies at the Sandia SCADA Development Laboratory, in which industry representatives can test, improve, and enhance security of its SCADA architectures, systems, and components.

Idaho National Engineering and Environmental Laboratory. Current development of the National SCADA Test Bed, which is a full-scale infrastructure testing facility that will allow for large-scale testing of SCADA systems before exposing those architectures and technologies to production networks, and for testing newer standards and protocols before implementation.

Los Alamos National Laboratory. Conjointly working together, both Sandia and Los Alamos are cooperatively developing critical infrastructure modeling, simulation, and analysis centers known as the National Infrastructure Simulation and Analysis Center. The center provides modeling and simulation capabilities for the analysis of all critical infrastructures, particularly the electricity, oil, and gas industrial sectors.

10.20 SECURITY AWARENESS AND INFORMATION SHARING INITIATIVES

Several efforts to develop and disseminate security awareness about control systems vulnerabilities and take proactive measures/countermeasures are being coordinated mostly between government agencies, with some industrial sector participation. Some of those initiatives are as follows:

Department of Homeland Security (DHS). The DHS created a National Cyber Security Division (NCSD) to identify, analyze, and reduce cyber threats and vulnerabilities, disseminate threat warning information, coordinate incident response, and provide technical assistance in continuity of operations and recovery planning. The Critical Infrastructure Assurance Office (now part of the DHS) within the department coordinates the federal government's initiatives on critical infrastructure assurance and promotes national outreach and awareness campaigns about critical infrastructure protection.

Sandia National Laboratories, Environmental Protection Agency, and industrial groups. Sandia National Laboratories has collaborated with the Environmental Protection Agency and industry groups to develop a risk assessment methodology for assessing the vulnerability of water systems in major U.S. cities. Sandia has also conducted vulnerability assessments of control systems within the electric power, oil and gas, transportation, and manufacturing industries. Sandia is involved with various activities to address the security of our critical infrastructures, including developing best practices, providing security training, demonstrating threat scenarios, and furthering standards efforts.

North American Electric Reliability Council (NERC). Designated by the Department of Energy as the electricity sector's Information Sharing and Analysis Center coordinator for critical infrastructure protection, the NERC facilitates communication between the electricity sector, the federal government, and other critical infrastructure sectors. The council has formed the Critical Infrastructure Protection Advisory Group, which guides computer security activities and conducts security workshops to raise awareness of cyber and physical security in the electricity sector. The council also formed a Process Controls Subcommittee within the Critical Infrastructure Protection Advisory Group to specifically address control systems.

Federal Energy Regulatory Commission. The Federal Energy Regulatory Commission regulates interstate commerce in oil, natural gas, and electricity. The commission has published a rule to promote the capturing of critical energy infrastructure information, which may lead to increased information sharing capabilities between industry and the federal government.

Process Control Systems Cyber Security Forum (PCSF). The PCSF is a joint effort between Kema Consulting and LogOn Consulting, Inc. The forum studies the computer security issues surrounding the effective operation of control systems and focuses on issues, challenges, threats, vulnerabilities, best practices/lessons learned, solutions, and related topical areas for control systems. It currently holds workshops on control system computer security. At the end of 2008, the PCSF contract with the contracting companies was not renewed, and the site was immediately shut down. Management within the DHS have indicated that the former PCSF Web site will be integrated within the DHS's Control Systems Security Program (CSSP) Web site.

Chemical Sector Cyber Security Program. The Chemical Sector Cyber Security Program is a forum of 13 trade associations and serves as the Information Sharing and Analysis Center for the chemical sector. The Chemical Industry Data Exchange is part of the Chemical Sector Cyber Security Program and is working to establish a common security vulnerability assessment methodology and to align the chemical industry with the ongoing initiatives at the Instrumentation Systems and Automation Society, the National Institute of Standards and Technology (NIST), and the American Chemistry Council.

The President's Critical Infrastructure Protection Board and Department of Energy. The President's Critical Infrastructure Protection Board and the Department of Energy developed "21 Steps to Improve the Cyber Security of SCADA Networks." These steps provide guidance for improving implementation and establishing underlying management processes and policies to help organizations improve the security of their control networks.

Joint Program Office for Special Technology Countermeasures. The Joint Program Office has performed vulnerability assessments on control systems, including the areas of awareness, integration, physical testing, analytic testing, and analysis.

10.21   PROCESS AND SECURITY CONTROL INITIATIVES

Several efforts to develop policies, standards, and procedures that will assist in the securification of control systems are being coordinated between the government and industry to identify and prevent potential threats, assess infrastructure vulnerabilities, and develop guidelines and standards for mitigating risks through protective measures. Some of those initiatives have already begun, whereas others are still being considered and developed.

The President's Critical Infrastructure Protection Board. In February 2003, the board released the National Strategy to Secure Cyberspace.[16] The protection board document provides a general strategic picture, specific recommendations and policies, and the rationale for these initiatives. The strategy ranks control network security as a national priority and designates the DHS to be responsible for developing best practices and new technologies to increase control system security.[17]

Instrumentation, Systems, and Automation Society. The Instrumentation, Systems, and Automation Society is composed of users, vendors, government, and academic participants representing the electric utilities, water, chemical, petrochemical, oil and gas, food and beverage, and pharmaceutical industries. It has been working on a proposed standard since October 2002. The new standard addresses the security of manufacturing and control systems. It is to provide users with the tools necessary to integrate a comprehensive security process. One report, ISA-TR99.00.01, *Security Technologies for Manufacturing and Control Systems*, describes electronic security technologies and discusses specific types of applications within each category, the vulnerabilities addressed by each type, suggestions for deployment, and known strengths and weaknesses. The other report, ISA-TR99.00.02, *Integrating Electronic Security into the Manufacturing and Control Systems Environment*, provides a framework for developing an electronic security program for manufacturing and control systems, as well as a recommended organization and structure for the security plan.[18]

Gas Technology Institute and Technical Support Working Group. Sponsored by the federal government's Technical Support Working Group, the Gas Support Working Group Technology Institute has researched a number of potential encryption methods to prevent hackers from accessing natural gas company control systems. This research has led to the development of an industry standard for encryption. The standard would incorporate encryption algorithms to be added to both new and existing control systems to control a wide variety of operations. This standard is outlined in the American Gas Association's report, numbered 12-1.

NIST and the NSA. The NIST and NSA have organized the Process Controls Security Requirements Forum to establish security specifications that can be used in procurement, development, and retrofitting of industrial control systems. NIST and NSA have both developed a set of security standards and certification processes.

NERC. The NERC has established a computer security standard for the electricity industry. The council requires members of the electricity industry to self-certify that they are meeting computer security standards. It should be noted, however, that at the time of writing, the standard does not apply to control systems.

Electric Power Research Institute. The Electric Power Research Institute has developed the Utility Communications Architecture, a set of standardized guidelines providing interconnectivity and interoperability for utility data communication systems for real-time information exchange.

10.22   SECURING CONTROL SYSTEMS

As part of methodologies for securing critical infrastructure control systems, here are some suggested recommendations insofar as implementation of a more secured environment involving control systems is concerned:

- Implement auditing controls over process systems; systems are periodically audited.
- Develop policies, standards, and procedures that are managed and periodically updated.
- Assist in the development of secured architectures that can integrate with computer technologies today and 10 years from now.
- Implement segments networks that are protected with firewalls and intrusion detection technology; periodically test intrusion attempts to ensure that security countermeasures operate correctly.
- Develop a method for exception tracking.
- Develop and implement company-wide incident response plans (IRPs); IRP documentation should work with existing disaster recovery planning and business continuity planning documentation, in case of an outage.

10.23   IMPLEMENT AUDITING CONTROLS

- Develop methodologies of understanding with levels of awareness for corporate management such that stateful computer-based security mechanisms are implemented for process control systems.
- Control systems auditing does not have the same focus as computer-based security auditing. Audits conducted have a far-reaching impact on all aspects involved; thus control systems utilized must take into consideration real-life scenarios involving loss of life, loss of financial or capital gain or monetary loss, and loss of property.
- Testing and evaluation of control systems during an auditing routine is not without risk. Although the audits may be similar in nature to their counterparts from other industrial sectors, it is important to note that technical audits must be performed following a carefully outlined guideline or plan, by certified or licensed technical professionals who are knowledgeable in the areas of control systems operation.

10.24   DEVELOP POLICY MANAGEMENT AND
CONTROL MECHANISMS

Develop security policies, standards, and procedures for the control systems to:

- Set and define a statement of goals and objectives for the control system device, responsibilities broken down based on department, group, and individual for supporting and responding to emergency or disaster conditions or situations, and acceptable responses, as part of the incident response planning team, which will be an overseeing group or committee in its implementation.

- Define within the policies, standards, and procedures sections that all documentation is subject to change at any time, and should be periodically revisited for validity, content, and functionality.
- Define within the policies, standards, and procedures verbiage that the documentation is representative of goals and objectives in terms of achievement, not specifically as to how, or the method of performing any security task. Essentially, security policies should be at a strategic, possibly tactical, level.

10.25 CONTROL SYSTEMS ARCHITECTURE DEVELOPMENT

- Develop and implement a multiple-level network infrastructure, segmenting the control systems architecture from that of the remainder of the corporate enterprise network; use firewalls and intrusion detection technologies to provide this level of protection.
- Simpler architectures could be divided within a facility into two distinctive levels: (1) All internetworking and interlayer network traffic flows through firewall and intrusion detection systems areas, and (2) provide a single point of control to oversee, manage, and maintain control of all network traffic in and out of areas involving control systems.

10.26 SEGMENT NETWORKS BETWEEN CONTROL SYSTEMS AND CORPORATE ENTERPRISE

Implementing the use of firewall and intrusion detection technologies is not required; however, implementing these two very important technologies would reduce risk but not completely remove the risk (if any).

- Essentially, the firewall is the lock on the door; the firewall is not the "burglar alarm." This is where an intrusion detection system would be useful.
- Require network intrusion detection systems to monitor any and all network traffic, and identify any unintended or malicious activity on, within, or through the network.
- Control systems network traffic patterns tend to be very repetitive and consistent based on their simplicity, such that the definition of network traffic matrices may be enough to determine what is accessing the control systems networks.

10.27 DEVELOP METHODOLOGIES FOR EXCEPTION TRACKING

This area essentially identifies any exceptions for any rule so that if the device or environment were to be secured tightly, it would be unable to operate properly; therefore defining an exception listing makes good sense.[19]

- A layered security model is very strong (if implemented properly) as designed without exception; however, as with any system, there may be circumstances in which exceptions might have to be made. If one or more exceptions are to be made, identify those exceptions within a list and keep it with the rest of the security documentation as part of the auditing process (e.g., support vendor may require the use of dial-in capabilities utilizing computer modems for technical support-related issues).
- Require that any recordkeeping of exceptions listed is kept safe, and that, by any other means, any other method of access or communications remains secured.

10.28   DEFINE AN INCIDENT RESPONSE PLAN

With any critical infrastructure environment, the continued operation of the business unit is crucial to the success of the business; therefore a "what if" scenario is highly recommended. This document or suite of documents should coincide with any business continuity planning documentation or disaster recovery planning documentation. Develop an incident response plan for security incidents, in that there is definition of a process to (1) deal with incidents in advance (if applicable) and (2) establish a security response team (SRT). The SRT is a central resource that provides testing, guidance, and solutions in the event that an incident of a serious nature is reported.

10.29   SIMILARITIES BETWEEN SECTORS

Not all industrial sectors have specialized or proprietary policies, standards, or procedures related to their specific industrial sector; however, it should be noted that best security practices should generally be coordinated between the various sectors, thus reinforcing their availability, capabilities, and enhancements, and encouraging the dissemination of useful and worthwhile information that would be of great significance to possibly more than one industrial sector.

10.30   U.S. COMPUTER EMERGENCY READINESS TEAM CSSP

The U.S. DHS NCSD CSSP was created to reduce control system risks within and across all critical infrastructure sectors by coordinating efforts among federal, state, local, and tribal governments, as well as control systems owners, operators, and vendors. The CSSP coordinates activities to reduce the likelihood of success and severity of impact of a cyber attack against critical infrastructure control systems through risk mitigation activities. These risk mitigation activities have resulted in the following tools:[21]

- *Catalog of Control Systems Security: Recommendations for Standards Developers*
- Control System Cyber Security Self-Assessment Tool (CS²SAT)
- CSSP documents
- Critical Infrastructure and Control Systems Security Curriculum
- Cyber Security Procurement Language for Control Systems

- Recommended practices
- Training

The DHS NCSD established the CSSP to guide a cohesive effort between the government and industry to improve the security posture of control systems within the nation's critical infrastructure. The CSSP assists control systems vendors and asset owners/operators in identifying security vulnerabilities and developing measures to strengthen their security posture and reduce risk through sound mitigation strategies.[22]

The CSSP has established the Industrial Control Systems Joint Working Group (ICSJWG) for federal stakeholders to provide a forum by which the federal government can communicate and coordinate its efforts to increase the cyber security of control systems in critical infrastructures. These efforts facilitate the interaction and collaboration between and among federal departments and agencies regarding control systems cyber security initiatives.[23]

The ICSJWG is a team of individuals from various federal departments and agencies who have roles and responsibilities in securing industrial control systems within the critical infrastructure of the United States. Since there are similar cyber security challenges from sector to sector, this collaboration effort benefits the nation by promoting and leveraging existing work and maximizing the efficient use of resources.[24]

The ICSJWG is a collaborative and coordinating body operating under the Critical Infrastructure Partnership Advisory Council (CIPAC) requirements. The ICSJWG will provide a vehicle to facilitate communications and partnerships across the critical infrastructure and key resources (CIKR) sector between federal agencies and departments, as well as private asset owner/operators of industrial control systems. The goal of the ICSJWG is to continue and enhance the facilitation and collaboration within the industrial control systems stakeholder community in securing CIKR by accelerating the design, development, and deployment of secure industrial control systems.[25]

As a collaboration body, the ICSJWG is connected with various stakeholders involved in industrial control systems, including participants from the international community, government, academia, the vendor community, owner/operators, and systems integrators. The ICSJWG shall serve as a sector-sponsored joint cross-sector working group operating under the auspices and in full compliance with the requirements of the CIPAC. Stakeholders participating in the ICSJWG will have the opportunity to address efforts of mutual interest within various stakeholder communities, build on existing efforts, reduce redundancies, and contribute to national and international CIKR security efforts.[26,27]

The CSSP is working in tandem with the members of the control community to help develop and vet recommended practices, provide guidance in supporting the CSSP's incident response capability, and participate in leadership working groups to ensure that the community's (cyber security working groups, as part of President Obama's cyber security initiative) cyber security concerns are considered in our products and deliverables.[28]

The CSSP is also working to facilitate discussions between the federal government and the control systems vendor community, establishing relationships that are intended to foster an environment of collaboration to address common control systems cyber security issues. The CSSP is also developing a suite of tools, which, when complete, will provide asset owners and operators with the ability to measure the security posture of their control systems environments and to identify the appropriate cyber security mitigation measures they should implement.[29]

To obtain additional information or request involvement or assistance, contact cssp@hq.dhs.gov; to join the ICSJWG, contact ICSJWG@dhs.gov.

10.31   CONTROL SYSTEMS CYBER SECURITY EVALUATION TOOL (CSET)

The Cyber Security Evaluation Tool (CSET®) is a self-contained software tool that runs on a desktop or laptop computer. It evaluates the cybersecurity of an automated, industrial control, or business system using a hybrid risk and standards-based approach, providing relevant recommendations for improvement. The United States Department of Homeland Security's (DHS) Control Systems Security Program (CSSP) developed the CSET application and offers it to all through the United States Computer Emergency Readiness Team's (US-CERT) Web site.[30]

The CSET software tool guides users through a step-by-step process to assess their control system and information technology network security practices against recognized industry standards. The output from CSET is a prioritized list of recommendations for improving the cybersecurity posture of the organization's enterprise and industrial control cyber systems environments. The tool derives these recommendations from a database containing several cybersecurity standards, guidelines, and practices. Each recommendation is linked to a set of actions that can be applied to enhance cybersecurity controls.[31]

CSET has been designed for easy installation and use on a stand-alone laptop or workstation. It incorporates a variety of available standards from organizations such as National Institute of Standards and Technology (NIST), North American Electric Reliability Corporation (NERC), International Organization for Standardization (ISO), United States Department of Defense (DoD), and others. While using the tool, when the user selects one or more of the standards, CSET will open a set of questions to be answered. The answers to these questions will be compared against a selected security assurance level, and a detailed report will be generated to show areas for potential improvement. CSET provides an excellent means of performing a self-assessment of the security posture of a given control systems environment.[32]

CSET utilizes the following standards and guidelines for its assessments:

- CFATS Risk Based Performance Standard (RBPS) 8: Chemical Facilities Anti-Terrorism Standard, Risk-Based Performance Standards Guidance 8 – Cyber, 6 CFR Part 27
- DHS Catalog of Control Systems Security: Recommendations for Standards Developers, Revisions 6 and 7
- DoD Instruction 8500.2 Information Assurance Implementation, February 2, 2003

- ISO/IEC 15408 revision 3.1: Common Criteria for Information Technology Security Evaluation, Revision 3.1
- NERC Reliability Standards CIP-002-009 Revisions 2 and 3
- NIST Special Publication 800-82 Guide to Industrial Control Systems Security, June 2011
- NIST Special Publication 800-53, Recommended Security Controls for Federal Information Systems Rev 3 and with Appendix I, ICS Controls
- NRC Regulatory Guide 5.71 Cyber Security Programs for Nuclear Facilities, January 201033

Some of the key benefits include:

- Contributing to an organization's risk management and decision-making process;
- Raising awareness and facility discussions specific to cybersecurity within the organization;
- Highlighting vulnerabilities within the organization's systems while providing recommendations in ways that may address any discovered vulnerability or threats;
- Identifying areas of strengths and best practices that are currently being followed within the organization;
- Providing a method to systematically compare and monitor any improvements in the assessed cyber systems; and
- Providing a common industry-wide tool for assessing cyber systems.[34]

The CSET software tool may be downloaded free of charge from this Web site: https://www.us-cert.gov/control_systems/csetdownload.html. Alternatively, the CSET software is available on DVD from the DHS, National Cyber Security Division (NCSD). To request a copy, please send an email to: CSET@dhs.gov. Please insert "CSET" within the title block of the email and include your name, organization name, complete street address (no P.O. boxes), and phone number in your email request.[35]

10.32   SCADA COMMUNITY CHALLENGES

One of the more interesting challenges is how to address security-related issues within the SCADA/control systems community, and the sectors it supports, as SCADA/control systems enterprises do not operate in a context similar to that of their traditional IT counterparts. It is probable that one of the more significant aspects to SCADA is the scope by which it dictates how issues are to be addressed.

Many technologies within the IT realm, such as Structured Query Language (SQL) database transaction speeds, have traditionally been viewed by SCADA/control systems engineers as having inadequate speed for control system data storage purposes. Although the technology has made this operation outmoded (Moore's law), most opinions are difficult to shake, and thus many process control engineers continue having difficulties accepting IT solutions within their environments. Based on some of the challenges mentioned in this paragraph, the problem is not so much a matter of data management as it is about trend and statistical analysis.

Of the larger problems is that forensics and evidentiary discovery practices are often associated with security management practices. Within control systems, these priorities are a little bit different than normalized systems, which are usually listed in the following order:

1. Safety
2. Availability
3. Security

IT-based architectures may be completely inverted from the priorities listed above, and thus there appears to be a conflict between what/how SCADA/control systems operate, and more importantly, how the corporation's enterprise defines its priorities. Several industries are currently attempting to either reach a compromise or figure out how both environments—IT and SCADA—can work together. Observationally, in some industries, such as nuclear power generation, these environments may never coexist together—ever.

Some of the larger issues associated with control systems involve legacy architectures no longer supported, utilize equipment that cannot be taken offline immediately or easily, and pose serious operational and financial risks to the companies using them. Unless these systems are interconnected with newer systems or are upgraded, there would be no easy method of determining a plausible cause for any given event or incident. Outside of what may be found at the company's control center, there are little forensic data to be found as control center computers do not lend themselves to traditional forensics analysis unless taken offline or removed off-site. Given the nature of most control systems, if it is an ongoing operational need, it may be very difficult to remove the servers in question for an extended analysis.

10.33   THE FUTURE OF SCADA

In the future, control systems will have to be segmented and configured so that high-risk sections of the control system will be carefully protected. First, ensure that logging takes place in more than one part of a control system. When the gates of a dam are opened, there should be not only a digital signature of the operator who initiates the command at the master station from which it was sent, but also the signature of the operator at the RTU where the command was executed.

Protocols such as IEC-60870 and DNP3 have recently added secure authentication features to make this possible. The new specification can be found in IEC-62351.

The future holds much promise with protocols such as IEC-61850. However, it is an extremely complex undertaking that mixes many features into one layer. The maintenance management system is a nice feature to integrate the SCADA data with, but it may not be the best thing to place on the SCADA communications infrastructure. One of these operational elements is tactically significant, and the other is strategically significant.

We may want to consider ways of segmenting and separating traffic for security reasons. This could entail reexamining the lower layers of the communications infrastructure.

SCADA infrastructure needs to use a variety of ways to connect to remote stations. The goal is to avoid having common carrier problems disable a control system that it might depend on. Multihead RTU devices may be in the future of many SCADA systems.

Note the convergence of DCS and SCADA technologies. The SCADA concept originally grew from dealing with the constraints of high latency, low reliability, and expensive bandwidth. DCS concepts originally grew from the need to network everything to one central computer where everything could be processed all at once. DCS systems are also getting smarter about how they distribute the functional pieces, and SCADA systems are handling closed loops more often, as the communications infrastructure gets faster and more reliable.

These two system paradigms may converge into what is known as the programmable automation controller.

The languages of control systems in IEC-601131 are not well defined. There is an opportunity to add certain features that might also include security. This could assist considerably in auditing and protecting control systems processes.

10.34 SCADA RESOURCES

Many of the available resources at the time of writing are accessible online through the Internet, via blogs, online discussion forums, and mailing lists. Shown in the following sections are a few of the online resources that are available through the Internet. The list is broken down based on public vs. private sector resources.

Note that some of these resources require a registration form filled out, along with a small fee (usually annual).

10.34.1 BLOGS

Within the past several years, blogs have taken the main stage, allowing both private individuals and organizations to express their opinions about what is right and wrong with SCADA and control systems, along with technical discussions about how to fix, repair, or remediate security vulnerabilities found throughout the Internet.[36]

10.34.2 SCADASEC MAILING LIST

A group of enthusiastic technicians, security developers, risk managers, homeland security researchers, engineers, asset and infrastructure managers, and security professionals have started a new discussion forum at http://scadasec.infracritical.com[38] to bring together academics and industry people interested in the subject of SCADA and control systems security, related technologies such as agents, distributed architectures, and nontechnical methodologies, and varied discussions relating to impacts from risk to its representative nations' infrastructures (United States and Canada), etc.

The goal is to create a place in which anyone who works for a critical infrastructure sector, industry, or organization can ask questions, publish articles, and read about what others are doing, specifically pertaining to SCADA and control systems security activities. Many active members are IT, control systems engineers, and technical personnel, as well as asset/owners from the energy, water, and transportation sectors.

The mailing list may be accessed free of charge, is publicly available, and stores all discussions within an Internet-accessible archive (which is also available free of charge).[37] Additionally, an online search engine of all archived postings from the mailing list may be obtained free of charge and is publicly available.[38]

10.34.3 ONLINE SCADA AND SCADA SECURITY RESOURCES

As Web sites come and go, these links will also grow and shrink dynamically. For this book, we give "snapshots" of Web sites containing relevant information pertaining to SCADA and control systems security. To access these static Web site links, visit http://scadalinks.infracritical.com.[39] Also note that control systems vendors, integrators, and consultants may offer similar services. There is a significant Wiki entry (http://www.controlglobal.com/articles/2005/487.html) to help track the whereabouts of product support companies as they are bought and sold in the marketplace.

10.35 AUTHORS' NOTES

Although SCADA and control systems security has been a continuous, evolutionary process since about the mid-1990s, the events of September 11, 2001, increased awareness and attention toward these devices and architectures. Without their continuous operations, much of a nation's security structures would fail. We depend on these devices; our livelihoods are dependent on them. Otherwise, life as we know it would be drastically altered, and we would either revert back to pretechnological times or shift to something entirely different. Thus concerns by industry subject matter experts of this issue should not be taken lightly.

NOTES

1. Library of Congress, *Critical Infrastructure: Control Systems and the Terrorist Threat*, CRS Report for Congress, CRS-RL31534, February 21, 2003; www.fas.org/irp/crs/RL31534.pdf; updated version (January 20, 2004): http://www.fas.org/sgp/crs/homesec/RL31534.pdf (alt URL: http://cipbook.infracritical.com/book5/chapter10/ch10ref1.pdf and http://cipbook.infracritical.com/book5/chapter10/ch10ref1a.pdf).
2. Ibid.
3. President's Commission on Critical Infrastructure Protection, *Critical Foundations: Protecting America's Infrastructures*, Washington, DC, October 1997; http://www.fas.org/sgp/library/pccip.pdf (alt URL: http://cipbook.infracritical.com/book5/chapter10/ch10ref2.pdf).
4. National Research Council, *Making the Nation Safer: The Role of Science and Technology in Countering Terrorism*, Washington, DC, December 2002.

5. White House, *The National Strategy to Secure Cyberspace*, Washington, DC, February 2003; http://georgewbush-whitehouse.archives.gov/pcipb/ and http://georgewbush-whitehouse.archives.gov/pcipb/cyberspace_strategy.pdf (alt URL: http://cipbook. infracritical.com/book5/chapter10/ch10ref3.pdf and http://cipbook.infracritical.com/ book5/chapter10/ch10ref3a.pdf).

6. U.S. General Accounting Office, *Critical Infrastructure Protection: Challenges and Efforts to Secure Control Systems*, GAO-04-354, Washington, DC, March 15, 2004; GAO-04-354 (alt URL: http://cipbook.infracritical.com/book5/chapter10/ch10ref4.pdf).

7. Joe St. Sauver, SCADA Security, NLANR/Internet2 Joint Techs Meeting, University of Oregon, Columbus, OH, July 21, 2004.

8. http://www.wardriving.com.

9. http://wiki.personaltelco.net/index.cgi/WarDriving.

10. http://www.fas.org/irp/news/1998/08/98082502_ppo.html (alt URL: http://cipbook. infracritical.com/book5/chapter10/ch10ref5.pdf).

11. Ibid.

12. http://www.ncbi.nlm.nih.gov/entrez/query.fcgi?cmd = Retrieve&db = PubMed&list_ uids = 11005165&dopt = Abstract (alt URL: http://cipbook.infracritical.com/book5/ chapter10/ch10ref6.pdf).

13. U.S. General Accounting Office, *Homeland Security: Information Sharing Responsibilities, Challenges, and Key Management Issues*, GAO-03-1165T, Washington, DC, September 17, 2003; http://www.gao.gov/new.items/d031165t.pdf (alt URL: http://cipbook.infracritical.com/book5/chapter10/ch10ref7.pdf).

14. U.S. General Accounting Office, *Federal Information System Controls Audit Manual*, GAO/AIMD-12.19.6, Washington, DC, January 1999; http://www.gao.gov/special.pubs/ ai12.19.6.pdf, along with the summary, which may be found here: http://www.gao.gov/ special.pubs/ai12196.97.html (alt URL: http://cipbook.infracritical.com/book5/chapter10/ch10ref8.pdf and http://cipbook.infracritical.com/book5/chapter10/ch10ref8a.pdf).

15. U.S. General Accounting Office, *Critical Infrastructure Protection: Challenges for Selected Agencies and Industry Sectors*, GAO-03-233, Washington, DC, February 28, 2003, and U.S. General Accounting Office, *Critical Infrastructure Protection: Efforts of the Financial Services Sector to Address Cyber Threats*, GAO-03-173, Washington, DC, January 30, 2003; http://www.gao.gov/new.items/d03233.pdf, along with the summary, which may be found here: http://www.gao.gov/high-lights/d03233high.pdf (alt URL: http://cipbook.infracritical.com/book5/chapter10/ ch10ref9.pdf and http://cipbook.infracritical.com/book5/chapter10/ch10ref9a.pdf).

16. White House, *The National Strategy to Secure Cyberspace*, Washington, DC, February 2003; http://georgewbush-whitehouse.archives.gov/pcipb/and http://georgewbush-whitehouse.archives.gov/pcipb/cyberspace_strategy.pdf (alt URL: http://cipbook.infra-critical.com/book5/chapter10/ch10ref3.pdf and http://cipbook.infracritical.com/book5/ chapter10/ch10ref3a.pdf).

17. U.S. General Accounting Office, *Critical Infrastructure Protection: Significant Challenges Need to Be Addressed*, GAO-02-961T, Washington, DC, July 24, 2002; http://www.gao.gov/new.items/d02961t.pdf (alt URL: http://cipbook.infracritical.com/ book5/chapter10/ch10ref10.pdf).

18. U.S. General Accounting Office, *Critical Infrastructure Protection: Challenges in Securing Control Systems*, GAO-04-140T, Washington, DC, October 1, 2003; http:// www.gao.gov/new.items/d04140t.pdf (alt URL: http://cipbook.infracritical.com/book5/ chapter10/ch10ref11.pdf).

19. BCIT, *Myths and Facts behind Cyber Security of Industrial Control*, April 2003.

20. http://www.wardriving.com.

21. http://www.us-cert.gov/control_systems/ (alt URL: http://cipbook.infracritical.com/ book5/chapter10/ch10ref12.pdf).

22. http://www.us-cert.gov/control_systems/csfaq.html (alt URL: http://cipbook.infracritical.com/book5/chapter10/ch10ref13.pdf) and http://www.us-cert.gov/control_systems/pdf/CSSP_FactSheet_sml.pdf (alt URL: http://cipbook.infracritical.com/book5/chapter10/ch10ref14.pdf).

23. Ibid.

24. http://www.us-cert.gov/control_systems/csfaq.html (alt URL: http://cipbook.infracritical.com/book5/chapter10/ch10ref13.pdf and http://cipbook.infracritical.com/book5/chapter10/ch10ref14.pdf).

25. http://www.us-cert.gov/control_systems/icsjwg/ (alt URL: http://cipbook.infracritical.com/book5/chapter10/ch10ref16.pdf).

26. http://www.us-cert.gov/control_systems/icsjwg/ (alt URL: http://cipbook.infracritical.com/book5/chapter10/ch10ref16.pdf).

27. http://www.dhs.gov/xprevprot/committees/editorial_0843.shtm (alt URL: http://cipbook.infracritical.com/book5/chapter10/ch10ref17.pdf).

28. http://www.us-cert.gov/control_systems/csfaq.html (alt URL: http://cipbook.infracritical.com/book5/chapter10/ch10ref13.pdf) and http://www.us-cert.gov/control_systems/pdf/CSSP_FactSheet_sml.pdf (alt URL: http://cipbook.infracritical.com/book5/chapter10/ch10ref14.pdf).

29. Ibid.

30. http://www.us-cert.gov/control_systems/pdf/DHS_CyberSecurity_CSSP-CSET-v4.pdf (alt URL: http://cipbook.infracritical.com/book5/chapter10/ch10ref15.pdf).

31. https://www.us-cert.gov/control_systems/satool.html (alt URL: http://cipbook.infracritical.com/book5/chapter10/ch10ref16.pdf).

32. https://www.us-cert.gov/control_systems/satool.html (alt URL: http://cipbook.infracritical.com/book5/chapter10/ch10ref16.pdf).

33. http://www.us-cert.gov/control_systems/pdf/DHS_CyberSecurity_CSSP-CSET-v4.pdf (alt URL: http://cipbook.infracritical.com/book5/chapter10/ch10ref15.pdf).

34. https://www.us-cert.gov/control_systems/satool.html (alt URL: http://cipbook.infracritical.com/book5/chapter10/ch10ref16.pdf).

35. https://www.us-cert.gov/control_systems/satool.html (alt URL: http://cipbook.infracritical.com/book5/chapter10/ch10ref16.pdf).

36. http://scadalinks.infracritical.com.

37. http://scadasec.infracritical.com.

38. http://mlsearch.infracritical.com.

39. http://scadalinks.infracritical.com.

11 Critical Infrastructure Information

11.1 INTRODUCTION

This chapter introduces concepts surrounding the reclassification of information and provides some introspective views as to how both industry and government are altering how information is perceived. There is much publicly available information about our infrastructures that describes demographic, financial, and security-related details. Those who are familiar with these environments are often able to locate public information as it pertains to the operation, description, geographic/geospatial mapping data, system, or access information about a specific critical infrastructure or its sectors. This level of accessibility is currently being reviewed by both private and public sectors, and represents a continuous process that is undergoing some serious reconsideration in terms of information classification.

11.2 WHAT IS CRITICAL INFRASTRUCTURE INFORMATION?

Critical infrastructure information[1] (CII)[2] is defined a type of designation of data or information that is representative of a critical infrastructure, or its sector, and is considered sensitive in nature but remains unclassified (this implies the federal government's "sensitive but unclassified" designation, as discussed later in this chapter). In some regard, CII is information[3] that is a form of metadata[4]—that is, it is data[5] about data, or more appropriately, data containing additional data. CII has also been called another definition of the term *information*. As defined by more than one credible source, the term *information* is defined as data that have been transformed through analysis and interpretation into a form useful for drawing conclusions and making decisions. Thus CII is clearly *not* the same as information.

Therefore CII is specifically defined as consisting of any of five criteria such that it:

1. Represents information directly relating to specific data, tasks, or information relating to any given critical infrastructure or its sector
2. Represents information generated by, produced by, or indirectly related to such information that results from or is resulting from daily operations of any given critical infrastructure or its sector
3. Represents geographical or geospatial information pertaining to locations, access points, methods of access to or from a site, facility, or area that is representative of a critical infrastructure or its sector
4. Represents any other information that may be indirectly related to or from any given critical infrastructure that is deemed, labeled, or marked

as "protected critical infrastructure information" (as defined within the Critical Infrastructure Information Act of 2002), or as accepted by the U.S. Department of Homeland Security (DHS)

5. Represents any recently defined or newly found or discovered information that could be utilized to destroy, dismantle, render useless or inoperative, incapacitate, or lessen the usefulness of any given critical infrastructure, or any impacts resulting from said methods against, to, from, or within any given critical infrastructure or its sector

To sum up, *critical infrastructure information*[6] is loosely defined as consisting of any of the five criteria such that it:

- Relates to information about critical infrastructures or its sectors
- Relates to information produced from the operations of those critical infrastructures, such as patient information, financial records, and transaction logs
- Relates to mapping information about locations or directions to any critical infrastructure site, facility, or work area
- Relates to information that the government considers protected critical infrastructure information
- Relates to any newly found or discovered information about a critical infrastructure, such as exploit information and "how-to FAQs" that would explain how to disable, dismantle, or destroy, say, a high-energy electrical transmission tower

A few additional criteria may hold true to the refined definition of CII, which might include the following alternative criteria:

- Relates to information about future developments of critical infrastructures, such as maps or architectural drawings or designs of power generation facilities.
- Relates to information about discontinued or dismantled critical infrastructures that are no longer in use, such as dismantled nuclear power generation facilities, or long-term nuclear material storage facilities.
- Relates to geological information about locations to any critical infrastructure, such as earthquake-prone sites, facilities, or areas of critical infrastructures that would show possible weaknesses of that location.
- Relates to any meteorological information about locations to any critical infrastructure.

CII was implemented, through regulation, via the Critical Infrastructure Information Act of 2002 in February 2004. As of March 2, 2004, a U.S. Department of Justice report stated that the CII designation would apply only to documents that were or are in the possession of the U.S. DHS.

11.3 HOW DOES THE GOVERNMENT INTERPRET CII?

Exemption 1 of the Freedom of Information Act (FOIA) protects data owners from disclosure of national security information concerning national defense or foreign policy, provided that it has been properly classified in accordance with the substantive and procedural requirements of an executive order.[7] As of October 14, 1995, the executive order in effect was Executive Order (E.O.) 12958 issued by President Clinton and amended in 1999 by E.O. 13142.[8,9]

Section 1.5 of the order specifies the types of information that may be considered for classification: military plans, weapons systems, or operations; foreign government information; intelligence activities, sources or methods, or cryptology; foreign relations or foreign activities, including confidential sources; scientific, technological, or economic matters relating to national security; federal government programs for safeguarding nuclear materials and facilities; or vulnerabilities or capabilities of systems, installations, projects, or plans relating to national security.[10] The categories of information that may be classified appear broad enough to include homeland security information concerning critical infrastructures. Under E.O. 12958, information may not be classified unless "its disclosure reasonably could be expected to cause damage to the national security."[11]

On March 19, 2002, the White House Chief of Staff issued a directive to the heads of all federal agencies addressing the need to protect information concerning weapons of mass destruction as well as other sensitive homeland security-related information.[12]

The implementing guidance for the directive concerned sensitive homeland security information that was currently classified, as well as previously unclassified or declassified information.[13] The guidance stipulated that if information was currently classified, then its classified status should be maintained in compliance with E.O. 12958. This included extending the duration of classification as well as exempting such information from automatic declassification as appropriate.

For previously unclassified or declassified information concerning weapons of mass destruction and other sensitive homeland security-related information, the implementing guidelines stipulated that if it has never been publicly disclosed under proper authority, it may be classified or reclassified as outlined within E.O. 12958.

If the information was subject to a previous request for access, such as an FOIA request, classification, or reclassification, then it is subject to the special requirements of that executive order.[14]

11.4 EXEMPTION 3 OF THE FOIA

As outlined under Exemption 3 of the FOIA, information protected from disclosure under other statutes is also exempt from public disclosure.[15]

Exemption 3 allows the withholding of information prohibited from disclosure by another statute if and only if the other statute meets one of three criteria:

1. Requires that records are to be withheld (with no agency discretion)
2. Grants discretion on whether to withhold information, but provides specific criteria outlining the exercise of that discretion
3. Describes the types of records to be withheld

To support an Exemption 3 claim, the requested information must fit within a category of information that the statute authorizes to be withheld. As circular as this may sound, essentially, if the information does not fit the criteria established, it cannot be acted upon.[16] As with all FOIA exemptions, the government bears the burden of proving that requested records are properly withheld.[17] Numerous statutes have been held to qualify as Exemption 3 statutes under the exemption's first subpart, in which those statutes that require information to be withheld leave the agency with no discretion.[18]

Several statutes have failed to qualify under Exemption 3 because too much discretion was vested in the agency or because the statute lacked specificity regarding the records to be withheld.[19] Unlike other FOIA exemptions, if the information requested under FOIA meets the withholding criteria of Exemption 3, the information must be withheld.[20]

Congress has considered a number of proposals that address the disclosure under FOIA of cyber security information, of information maintained by the DHS, and of CII voluntarily submitted to the DHS.[21] Generally, legislation has specifically exempted the covered information from disclosure under FOIA, in effect creating an Exemption 3 statute for purposes of FOIA.[22]

11.5   EXEMPTION 4 OF THE FOIA

Exemption 4 of the FOIA exempts from disclosure "trade secrets and commercial or financial information obtained from a person and privileged or confidential."[23] The latter category of information (commercial information that is privileged or confidential) is relevant to the issue of the federal government's protection of private sector CII.[24]

To fall within this second category of Exemption 4, the information must satisfy three criteria. It must be:[25]

1. Considered commercial or financial
2. Obtained from an individual
3. Labeled or classified as confidential or privileged

The Washington, D.C., circuit court held that the terms *commercial* or *financial* should be given their ordinary meaning, and that records are commercial if the submitter has a "commercial interest" in them.[26] The second criterion, "obtained from a person," refers to a wide range of entities.[27] However, information generated by the federal government is not "obtained from a person," and as a result is excluded from Exemption 4's coverage.[28] Most Exemption 4 cases involved in a dispute are generally over whether the information was considered confidential.[29]

11.6   SECTION 214 OF THE HOMELAND SECURITY ACT

After extensive deliberation, which still appears to be continuing today, and no small amount of controversy involved, the U.S. DHS has regulations defining the Protected Critical Infrastructure Program within the implementation of Section 214 of the Homeland Security Act of 2002, 6 U.S.C.A. §133 (West Supp. 2003).[30] Section 214 of the Homeland Security Act, enacted in November 2002, contains a series of provisions aimed at promoting the flow of sensitive information specifically relating to the national critical infrastructures, of which approximately 85% are located within private sectors, to the federal government for homeland security purposes.[31]

This section established a new category defined as critical infrastructure information. Section 214 of the Homeland Security Act of 2002 (P.L. 107-269) exempted from disclosure under FOIA for Exemption 3[32] protection such that "critical infrastructure information (including the identity of the submitting person or entity) that is voluntarily submitted to a covered agency for use by that agency regarding the security of critical infrastructure (as defined within the USA PATRIOT Act) ...,[33] when accompanied by an express statement."[34] The new Exemption 3 statute for CII, which now applies to information held by DHS only, is one of "a growing trend [of] statutes enacted in recent years [that] contain disclosure prohibitions that are not general in nature but rather are specifically directed toward disclosure under the FOIA in particular."[35]

The Homeland Security Act defines "critical infrastructure information" to be representative of "information not customarily in the public domain and related to the security of critical infrastructure or protected systems":

A. Actual, potential, or threatened interference with, attack on, compromise of, or incapacitation of critical infrastructure or protected systems by either physical or computer-based attack or other similar conduct (including misuse of or unauthorized access to all types of communications and data transmission systems) that violates federal, state, or local law, harms interstate commerce of the United States, or threatens public health and safety.

B. The ability of critical infrastructures or protected systems to resist such interference, compromise, or incapacitation, including any planned or past assessment, projection or estimate of the vulnerability of critical infrastructure or a protected system, including security testing, risk evaluation thereto, risk management planning, or risk audit.

C. Any planned or past operational problem or solution regarding critical infrastructure ... including repair, recovery, reconstruction, insurance, or continuity to the extent it relates to such interference, compromise, or incapacitation.[36]

A "covered agency" is defined as the U.S. DHS.[37] The submission of CII is considered voluntary if done in the absence of the DHS exercising its legal authority to compel access to or submission of such information.[38] Information submitted to the Securities and Exchange Commission pursuant to Section 12(i) of the Securities and Exchange Act of 1934 is explicitly not protected by this provision.[39]

Besides exempting from FOIA CII that has been submitted voluntarily with the appropriate express statement to the DHS, the Homeland Security Act also states that the information shall not be subject to any agency rules or judicial doctrine regarding ex parte communications with decision-making officials.[40]

The act also prohibits such information, without the written consent of the person or entity submitting such information in good faith, from being used directly by the DHS, any other federal, state, or local authority, or any third party, in any civil action.[41]

Nor may the information, without the written consent of the person or entity submitting such information, be used or disclosed by any officer or employee of the United States for any purpose other than the purposes of the subtitle except in the furtherance of a criminal investigation or prosecution, or when disclosed to either House of Congress, or to the Comptroller General or other authorized General Accounting Office official, in the conduct of official business.[42]

11.7 ENFORCEMENT OF SECTION 214 OF THE HOMELAND SECURITY ACT

Any federal official or employee who knowingly publishes, divulges, discloses, or makes known in any manner or to any extent not authorized by law, any protected information, is subject to removal, imprisonment up to one year, and fines.[43] If the information is disclosed to state or local officials, it may not be used for any purpose other than the protection of critical infrastructures, and it may not be disclosed under state disclosure laws.[44]

The protections afforded protected information do not result in waiver of any privileges or protections provided elsewhere in law.[45] Finally, no communication of CII to the DHS shall be considered an action subject to the requirements of the Federal Advisory Committee Act.[46]

For information to be considered protected, it must be accompanied with a written statement to the effect that "this information is voluntarily submitted to the federal government in expectation of protection from disclosure as provided by the Critical Infrastructure Information Act of 2002 (the name given to Subtitle B)." The Secretary of the DHS is to establish procedures for handling the information once it is received. Only those agency components or bureaus designated by the president or the Secretary of Homeland Security as having a critical infrastructure program may receive CII from the department.

The above protections for information voluntarily submitted by a person or entity to the DHS do not limit or otherwise affect the ability of a state, local, or federal government entity, agency, or authority, or any third party, under applicable law, to obtain CII (including any information lawfully and properly disclosed generally and broadly to the public) and to use that information in any manner permitted by law.[47]

Submittal to the government of information or records that are protected from disclosure is not to be construed as compliance with any requirement to submit such information to a federal agency under any other provision of law.[48] Finally, the act does not expressly create a private right of action for enforcement of any provision of the act.[49]

11.8 WHAT DOES "SENSITIVE BUT UNCLASSIFIED" MEAN?

In recent years, more reports and information contained on Web sites have introduced a new data classification referred to as "sensitive but unclassified," especially when dealing with information pertaining to a critical infrastructure such as the national power grid. The term *sensitive but unclassified* (SBU)[50] is an informal designation applicable to all types and forms of information that, by law or regulation, require some form of protection, but are outside the formal system for classifying national security information.[51]

As a general rule, information may be exempt from release to the public under the FOIA.[52,53] This section reviews the most common types of sensitive unclassified information.[54]

The U.S. Department of Defense (DOD) also uses the term *controlled unclassified information* (CUI)[55] to refer to certain types of sensitive information within DOD that require controls and protective measures.[56] CUI includes "for official use only" (FOUO) and information with comparable designations that is received from other agencies, DOD Unclassified Controlled Nuclear Information (UCNI), "sensitive information" as defined in the Computer Security Act of 1987, and DOD technical data.[57]

Some information that is not formally designated as sensitive is nonetheless inappropriate for putting on a public, *unsecured* Web site.[58] Federal law defines most categories of sensitive unclassified information, whereas others, such as the FOUO classification, are defined by organization policy, and several government organizations use different names for this category of information.[59]

Most legislative authorities are very specific in identifying the protected category of information, whereas others are general and leave much discretion to the agency or company.[60] Procedures for safeguarding sensitive unclassified information depend on the category of information and, in some cases, vary from one agency or company to another.[61]

Generally speaking, the law provides protection for established categories of protected information only when the owners of the information have taken reasonable or required steps to protect it.[62] These steps are sometimes stated in the law or regulation; however, they are often left up to the information owner to develop internally.[63] Legal history shows that the following elements are the key to successful enforcement of an information protection program.

The organization must have:[64]

- An established information security policy
- A system or mechanism to identify specific information that is to be protected (this includes periodic reviews of the need for continued protection)
- Procedures for safeguarding and controlling protected information such that any risk of exposure is only to those who have specific need for knowledge of the information, as well as a duty to protect its safety
- Duty to protect and safeguard information may be imposed or regulated by law (for some categories), or established by a confidential agreement
- A system or mechanism of warnings and markings advising of the sensitivity or handling requirements of the information

11.9 INFORMATION HANDLING PROCEDURES

Procedures for handling the various categories of sensitive unclassified information vary from one agency or company to another.[65] This is due to different legal and regulatory requirements for each category and the agency or organization's implementation of those requirements.[66] Factors affecting the implementation are the degree of sensitivity of the information, nature of the threat to the information, vulnerability of the information, options that are available for protecting the information, and organizational facilities/capabilities for secure handling, storage, and transmission.[67]

11.10 FREEDOM OF INFORMATION ACT

The public has a right to information concerning the activities of its government. The FOIA requires all government organizations (mostly federally related) to conduct their activities in an open manner and to have a system for providing the public with the maximum amount of accurate and timely information allowed by law.[68] Agencies commonly have an FOIA office for processing public requests for information.[69]

The FOIA allows nine exemptions from this mandatory release policy.[70] The purpose of the exemptions is to preclude the unauthorized disclosure of information that requires protection.

These exemption categories reflect laws, executive orders, regulations, or court decisions that either require or permit protection of certain classes of information.[71] The exemption categories, in turn, also help define information that may be protected.[72] For example, U.S. DOD Regulation 5200.1-R defines FOUO information as "unclassified information that may be exempt from mandatory release to the public under the Freedom of Information Act (FOIA)."[73]

DOD Regulation 5200.1-R, Appendix C, describes the nine FOIA exemptions as written below.[74] The wording reflects the history of court decisions interpreting the FOIA, and therefore differs from the language of the act itself.[75]

To be exempt from mandatory release, information must fit into one of the following categories, and there must be a legitimate government purpose served by withholding it.[76]

- Exemption 1: Information that is currently and properly classified.
- Exemption 2: Information that pertains solely to the internal rules and practices of the agency. This exemption has two profiles: high and low. The high profile permits withholding of a document that, if released, would allow circumvention of an agency rule, policy, or statute, thereby impeding the agency in the conduct of its mission. The low profile permits withholding if there is no public interest in the document, and it would be an administrative burden to process the request.
- Exemption 3: Information specifically exempted by statute establishing particular criteria for withholding. The language of the statute must clearly state that the information will not be disclosed.
- Exemption 4: Information such as trade secrets and commercial or financial information obtained from a company on a privileged or confidential basis

that, if released, would result in competitive harm to the company, or impair the government's ability to obtain like information in the future, or to protect the government's interest in compliance with program effectiveness.

- Exemption 5: Interagency memoranda that are deliberative in nature. This exemption is appropriate for internal documents that are part of the decision-making process and contain subjective evaluations, opinions, and recommendations.
- Exemption 6: Information the release of which could reasonably be expected to constitute a clearly unwarranted invasion of the personal privacy of individuals.
- Exemption 7: Records or information compiled for law enforcement purposes that (1) could reasonably be expected to interfere with law enforcement proceedings, (2) would deprive a person of a right to a fair trial or impartial adjudication, (3) could reasonably be expected to constitute an unwarranted invasion of the personal privacy of others, (4) disclose the identity of a confidential source, (5) disclose investigative techniques or procedures, or (6) could reasonably be expected to endanger the life or physical safety of any individual.
- Exemption 8: Certain records of agencies responsible for supervision of financial institutions.
- Exemption 9: Geological and geophysical information concerning wells.

FOIA requires agencies to promulgate policies to implement the requirements of the act and to publish these policies in the *Federal Register*.[77] Each agency is responsible for establishing an appropriate administrative system to manage the FOIA.[78]

The act has no requirements for protection of information. It only permits withholding information from disclosure, when appropriate.[79]

When an FOIA request seeks public release of information held under Exemption 4 (commercial information provided to the government on a confidential basis), the responsible government agency must determine whether the public's right to know outweighs the companies' right to protection of proprietary information.[80] If the agency determines that the information should be released under FOIA, E.O. 12600 requires that the company be advised and be given an opportunity to present its arguments for continued protection before the information is released.[81]

11.11   NEED TO KNOW

Not all CII is defined as "protected critical infrastructure information" and may be defined or categorized as something other than CII; one of those designations may be "need to know." Need to know is one of the most fundamental security principles.[82] The practice of need to know limits the damage that can be done by a trusted insider who might betray one's trust. Failures in implementing a need-to-know principle may cause serious damage to an organization.[83]

Need to know imposes multiple responsibilities on whoever as well as all other authorized holders of protected information:[84]

- When certain individuals perform their job, one is expected to limit their requests for information to that which is a need to know. Under some circumstances, an individual may be expected to explain and justify his or her need to know when asking others for information.
- Ensure that anyone to whom protected information is given has a legitimate need to know that information. In some cases, one may need to ask the other person for sufficient information to enable that person to make an informed decision about his or her need-to-know status.
- Refrain from discussing protected information in hallways, cafeterias, elevators, rest rooms, or smoking areas where persons who do not have a need to know the subject of conversation may overhear the discussion.

A caveat of the need-to-know classification is that need to know is difficult to implement as it conflicts with our natural desire to be friendly and helpful.[85] It also requires a level of personal responsibility that many of us find difficult to accept. The importance of limiting sensitive information to those who have a need to know is underscored, however, every time a trusted insider is found to have betrayed that trust.[86] Although every individual with access to a particular computer network is approved for that system, that person may not have a need to know all of the information coming across the system.[87]

11.12 "FOR OFFICIAL USE ONLY"

"For official use only" (FOUO) is a document designation, not a classification.[88] This designation is used by the U.S. DOD and a number of other federal agencies to identify information or material that, although unclassified, may not be appropriate for public release.[89]

There is no national policy governing use of the FOUO designation.[90] DOD Directive 5400.7 defines FOUO information as "unclassified information that may be exempt from mandatory release to the public under the Freedom of Information Act (FOIA)."[91,92] The policy is implemented by DOD Regulations 5400.7-R and 5200.1-R.[93]

Note: The FOUO designation is also used by the CIA as well as a number of other federal agencies, but each agency is responsible for determining how it shall be used. The categories of protected information may be quite different from one agency to another, although in every case the protected information must be covered by one of the nine categories of information that are exempt from public release under FOIA.[94]

Some agencies use different terminology for the same types of information. For example, the U.S. Department of Energy uses "official use only" (OUO).[95] The U.S. Department of State uses "sensitive but unclassified" (SBU) (formerly called "limited official use" (LOU)).[96] The U.S. Drug Enforcement Administration uses "DEA sensitive." In all cases, the designations refer to unclassified, potentially sensitive information that is or may be exempt from public release under the FOIA.[97]

The fact that information is marked FOUO does not mean it is automatically exempt from public release under FOIA.[98] If a request for the information is received, it must be reviewed to see if it meets the FOIA dual test:[99]

1. If it fits into one of the nine FOIA exemption categories
2. If there is a legitimate government purpose served by withholding the data

Consequently, on the other hand, the absence of the FOUO or other markings does not automatically mean the information must be released in response to an FOIA request.[100]

11.13   ENFORCEMENT OF FOUO INFORMATION

Administrative penalties may be imposed for misuse of FOUO information.[101] Criminal penalties may be imposed depending on the actual content of the information (privacy, export control, etc.).[102,103]

11.14   REVIEWING WEB SITE CONTENT

With its many benefits, the Internet can also do a great deal of harm if not used properly.[104] Information on the Internet that may be intended for a limited audience is often available to a worldwide audience.[105] The World Wide Web was not designed with security in mind, and unencrypted information is at high risk of compromise to any interested adversary or competitor.[106] It is very easy to search the Web and put together related pieces of information from different sites. For example, the search engine SearchMil.com (www.searchmil.com) specializes in indexing sites with a .mil domain name. It claims (as of August 2001) to have indexed more than 1 million pages of military sites, with the number of pages still growing rapidly.[107]

The DOD has been among the first government departments to take the lead in spelling out rules for what should and should not go on online and how information should be reviewed before it is posted on a Web site.[108] The DOD policy should be reviewed before posting DOD or DOD-controlled information to a Web site.[109]

The DOD policy applies to all unclassified DOD Web sites, requiring a review and approval process of requests received from DOD contractors and subcontractors as well as other government agencies to post DOD information on their Web sites.[110]

DOD guidelines take into account what security access controls, if any, are in effect for the site, the sensitivity of the information, and the target audience for which the information is intended.[111] Briefly, most types of sensitive unclassified information discussed are usually not permitted for public viewing, and thus should not be displayed on a Web site unless that site is protected by encryption.[112]

In other words, DOD technical information, FOUO information, export-controlled information, unclassified nuclear information, and Privacy Act information may not be posted on an unencrypted Web site.[113] Decisions on the handling of proprietary or trade secret information in the private sector are made by the owners of that information.[114]

DOD guidelines also require that judgments about the sensitivity of information take into account the potential consequences of "aggregation." The term *sensitive by*

TABLE 11.1

DOD Guidance on Reviewing Web Sites

Access Control	Level of Vulnerability	Information Can Be
Open—no access limitations, plain text, unencrypted.	Extremely high. Subject to worldwide dissemination and access by everyone on the Internet.	Nonsensitive, of general interest to the public, cleared and authorized for public release. Worldwide dissemination must pose limited risk even if information is combined with other information reasonably expected to be in the public domain.
Limited by Internet domain (e.g., military, government) or IP address. Plain text, unencrypted.	Very high. This limitation is not difficult to circumvent.	Nonsensitive, not of general interest to the public although approved and authorized for public release. Intended for DOD or other specifically targeted audiences.
Limited by requirement for user ID and password. Plain text, unencrypted.	High. Still vulnerable to hackers, as user IDs and passwords can be compromised if encryption is not used.	Nonsensitive information that is appropriate only for a specifically targeted audience.
User certificate based (software). Requires public key infrastructure (PKI) encryption through use of Secure Sockets Layer.	Moderate. This provides a moderate level of secure access control.	Sensitive unclassified information, and information that is "sensitive by aggregation."
User certificate based (hardware). Requires PKI encryption.	Very low vulnerability.	Sensitive unclassified information and information that is "sensitive by aggregation," where extra security is required.

aggregation refers to the fact that information on one site may seem unimportant, but when combined with information from other sites it may form a much larger and more complete picture that was neither intended nor desired.[115] In other words, the combination of information from multiple Web sites may amount to more than the sum of its parts. Similarly, the compilation of large amounts of information together from one Web site may increase the sensitivity of that information and make it more likely that that Web site will be accessed by those seeking information that might be used against the United States.[116]

Table 11.1 from the DOD guidance on reviewing Web sites[117] has been modified to fit into a smaller space. It is a guide to determining an acceptable level of risk, but the listed types of access controls are not necessarily the only options available for protecting information.

There are several common mistakes that people make when deciding what to put on a Web site. One is to ignore the danger associated with personal data on the Internet. Another is to assume that information is not sensitive just because it is not marked with any sensitivity indicator. A third is that people underestimate the ease and potential significance of "point-and-click aggregation" of information.

FOUO information and other sensitive information are normally marked with a sensitivity indicator at the time of creation. However, the absence of any sensitivity marking is not a valid basis for assuming that information is nonsensitive. Before putting unmarked information on a Web site, it must be examined for the presence of information that requires protection and qualifies as exempt from public release.

People who have not developed strong skills at searching the Internet may underestimate the amount and nature of the information that can be found there and the ease with which it can be located. The vast quantity of information on the Internet, combined with powerful computer search engines, has spawned sophisticated data mining techniques for the rapid collection and combination of information from many different sites. Very little knowhow is needed, as the tools of the Internet have been designed to do this. A single user sitting at a computer in a foreign country can now identify, aggregate, and interpret information available on the Internet in ways that sometimes provide insights into classified or sensitive unclassified programs or activities.

Information relevant to operations security (OPSEC) is a particular concern. Commanders and program managers responsible for OPSEC need to identify what needs to be protected and then take a "red team" approach to how outsiders might obtain unauthorized knowledge. As a double check, military reserve units have been tasked to conduct ongoing OPSEC and threat assessments of DOD Web sites.

One useful tool is to conduct keyword searches on the Internet to learn what related information may already be out there that others might use to deduce information about any sensitive activities. As sites are visited or newsgroup messages are read, personnel should determine if information could be used in conjunction with the information in question, or with information from some other site, to deduce if it is considered sensitive information.

11.15   EXPORT-CONTROLLED INFORMATION

There may be some CII that is related to a device or information that may be shared outside of the United States. If the device contains cryptographic information or is a protected cryptographic mechanism, it may be protected as an export-controlled device, as well as its information.

Export-controlled information[118] or material is any information or material that cannot be released to foreign nationals or representatives of a foreign entity without first obtaining approval or license from the Department of State for items controlled by the International Traffic in Arms Regulations (ITAR) or the Department of Commerce for items controlled by the Export Administration Regulations (EAR).[119] Export-controlled information is controlled as sensitive information and marked accordingly.[120]

One objective of ITAR and EAR is to prevent foreign citizens, industry, or governments or their representatives, from obtaining information that is contrary to the national security interests of the United States.[121]

Different laws and regulations use different definitions of a U.S. person, U.S. national, and foreign national. This is a source of considerable confusion when implementing international security programs.[122]

The rules are especially confusing when dealing with an immigrant alien who possesses a green card for permanent residence in the United States.[123] For the purpose of export control regulations, such an individual is a "U.S. person" and may be allowed access to export-controlled information without an export license.[124] If the export-controlled information is classified, however, the regulations for release of classified information apply. According to the *National Industrial Security Program Operating Manual*, a permanent resident with a green card is still a foreign national and not a "U.S. person." Therefore such an individual cannot have access to classified export-controlled information.[125]

11.16   ENFORCEMENT OF EXPORT-CONTROLLED INFORMATION

The penalty for unlawful export of items or information controlled under the ITAR is up to two years imprisonment or a fine of $100,000, or both.[126] The penalty for unlawful export of items or information controlled under the EAR is a fine of up to $1,000,000 or five times the value of the exports, whichever is greater; or for an individual, imprisonment of up to 10 years or a fine of up to $250,000, or both.[127]

11.17   SOURCE SELECTION DATA

Source selection data[128] are information related to the decision-making process (including the decision itself) for an award of a contract to industry.[129] Information in this category is generally only sensitive until after a formal award of the contract. Such information must be protected from disclosure outside the government and limited within the government to individuals with a need to know that information.[130]

Federal Acquisition Regulations[131] (FAR)[132] specify procedures to be followed to protect source selection data.[133] Bids may not be disclosed except on a need-to-know basis and only to government employees (FAR Part 14.401[134]—Receipt and Safeguarding of Bids (48 C.F.R.)).[135]

Proprietary and source selection information may only be disclosed to individuals authorized by the head of an agency (FAR Part 3.104-5[136]—Disclosure, Protection, and Marking of Proprietary and Source Selection Information). For contracts over $100,000, the names of individuals having access to the file shall be listed with the contract file.[137]

11.18   ENFORCEMENT OF SOURCE SELECTION DATA

For knowing disclosure of nongovernment information to which a government agency has gained access in connection with a procurement action, Title 41 U.S.C. 423—

Procurement Integrity provides both civil and criminal penalties.[138] The criminal penalty is up to five years imprisonment. The civil penalty is a fine of up to $100,000.[139]

This applies mainly to government employees who receive nongovernment information, but it also applies to nongovernment personnel who receive sensitive procurement information from government (e.g., if government gives industry a bid package containing information from a potential subcontractor).[140] This procurement integrity law applies only before the awarding of a contract. Once a contract has been awarded, other laws with lesser penalties may apply.[141]

Title 18 U.S.C. 1905 applies to disclosure by a government employee of any information provided to the government by a company or other nongovernment organization, if the provider of the information identified it as proprietary or as being provided to the government in confidence.[142] The penalty is mandatory removal from office (termination of employment), and the offender may be fined not more than $1,000 and imprisoned for not more than one year.[143]

11.19   PRIVACY INFORMATION

Privacy information is information about an individual including, but not limited to, personal identifying information, social security number, payroll number, and information on education, financial transactions, medical history, including results of drug testing, and criminal or employment history.[144]

The Privacy Act addresses information contained in a "federal system of records."[145] A system of records is a collection of information on individuals in which the information is retrievable by the individual's name, identifying number, symbol, or other identifying particular.[146] An "individual" is defined in the act as "a citizen of the U.S. or an alien lawfully admitted for permanent residence."[147]

The Privacy Act requires that privacy information in the custody of the federal government be protected from unauthorized disclosure and provides for both civil and criminal penalties for violation of the act.[148]

Privacy information in the custody of government contractors is not covered by the Privacy Act unless the contractor is performing on a contract under which the contractor is provided access to or custody of such information by the federal government.[149] Under this condition, the law would apply to contractor personnel the same way as it applies to government personnel.[150]

11.20   ENFORCEMENT OF PRIVACY INFORMATION

Title 5 U.S.C. 552a allows civil remedies against the United States for noncompliance, criminal penalties for individual acts of noncompliance, and criminal penalties for maintaining a system of records without meeting the reporting requirements of the Privacy Act.[151]

Title 12 U.S.C. 3417 of the Right to Financial Privacy Act allows civil penalties to agencies and requires an investigation by the Office of Personnel Management and appropriate disciplinary action for federal employees disclosing financial information.[152]

Title 18 U.S.C. 1905 applies to disclosure by a government employee of any information provided to the government by a company or other nongovernment organization, if the provider of the information identified it as proprietary or as being provided to the government in confidence.[153]

The penalty is mandatory removal from office (termination of employment), and the offender may be fined not more than $1,000 and imprisoned for not more than one year.[154]

Additionally, several recent acts of legislation have been implemented that protect and safeguard private information of the general public, specifically in the financial and healthcare sectors. Those pieces of legislation include:

1. The Gramm-Leach-Bliley Act, which includes provisions to protect consumers' personal financial information held by financial institutions. There are three principal parts to the privacy requirements: the Financial Privacy Rule, Safeguards Rule, and pretexting provisions.[155]
2. The Health Insurance Portability and Accountability Act, which regulates and protects the confidentiality, integrity, and availability of personal health information.[156]

11.21   UNCLASSIFIED CONTROLLED NUCLEAR INFORMATION

UCNI,[157] which is regulated and governed under the jurisdiction of the U.S. Department of Energy, includes unclassified facility design information, operational information concerning the production, processing, or utilization of nuclear material for atomic energy defense programs, safeguards and security information, nuclear material, and declassified or controlled nuclear weapon information once classified as restricted data.[158]

Conversely, DOD UCNI is unclassified information on security measures (including security plans, procedures, and equipment) for the physical protection of DOD special nuclear material, equipment, or its facilities.[159]

Information is designated UCNI only when it is determined that its unauthorized disclosure could reasonably be expected to have a significant adverse effect on the health and safety of the public or the common defense and security by significantly increasing the likelihood of the illegal production of nuclear weapons or the theft, diversion, or sabotage of special nuclear material, equipment, or facilities.[160]

11.22   ENFORCEMENT OF UCNI

Violation of Section 148 of the Atomic Energy Act[161] carries a civil fine not exceeding $110,000. In addition, the individual may be subject to a criminal penalty under Section 223 of the act.

11.23   CRITICAL ENERGY INFRASTRUCTURE INFORMATION

Critical energy infrastructure information (CEII) was defined by the Federal Energy Regulatory Commission (FERC) as information concerning proposed or existing critical infrastructure (physical or virtual) that:[162]

- Relates to the production, generation, transmission, and distribution of energy
- Is potentially useful for planning an attack on a critical infrastructure from the energy sector
- Is exempt from mandatory disclosure under the FOIA
- Provides strategic information beyond specific locations of energy sector critical infrastructures

FERC established procedures for gaining access to CEII that would otherwise not be available under the FOIA.[163]

- CEII is defined as infrastructure explicitly covering proposed facilities, and does not distinguish among projects or portions of projects.
- Procedures detailing geospatial or geographical location information are excluded from the definition of CEII.
- CEII rules address some issues that are specific to state agencies, and clarify that energy market consultants should be able to gain access to CEII when they need it.
- CEII rules modify the proposed CEII process and delegate the responsibility to the CEII coordinator to process requests for CEII and to determine what information qualifies as CEII.

11.24   ENFORCEMENT OF CEII

Non-Internet public documents (documents that are not for disclosure to the general public and are subject to CEII restrictions) are the direct result of FERC Order 630, which was issued on February 21, 2003. FERC's Order 630 established CEII regulations.[164] Any member of the public may file a CEII request under 18 C.F.R. §388.113 or an FOIA request under 18 C.F.R. §388.108.[165] Absent a waiver from the commission, natural gas pipelines and public utilities are still required to comply with commission regulations that may require that CEII be made available in county public reading rooms or from companies upon request, as appropriate.[166]

11.25   CONTROLLED UNCLASSIFIED INFORMATION

As part of an effort by the federal government to streamline unclassified but sensitive information and documentation, President Bush issued a Memorandum for the Heads of Executive Departments and Agencies entitled "Designation and Sharing of Controlled Unclassified Information (CUI)" on May 9, 2008, outlining the intentions of consolidating the hundreds of unique markings and labels (which include FOUO and "sensitive but unclassified") under three designations. These designations dictate the sensitivity of information, and how it should be handled and distributed.[167]

"Controlled unclassified information" is a categorical designation that refers to unclassified information that does not meet the standards for National Security Classification under E.O. 12958, as amended, but is (1) pertinent to the national interests of the United States or to the important interests of entities outside the federal government, and (2) under law or policy requires protection from unauthorized disclosure, special handling safeguards, or prescribed limits on exchange or dissemination. Henceforth, the designation CUI replaces "sensitive but unclassified."[168] This new designation would be used throughout the federal government, as well as the military.[169]

All CUI shall be (1) categorized into one of three combinations of safeguarding procedures and dissemination controls, and (2) so indicated through the use of the following corresponding markings:

1. "Controlled with standard dissemination." The information requires standard safeguarding measures that reduce the risks of unauthorized or inadvertent disclosure. Dissemination is permitted to the extent that it is reasonably believed that it would further the execution of a lawful or official purpose.[170]
2. "Controlled with specified dissemination." The information requires safeguarding measures that reduce the risks of unauthorized or inadvertent disclosure. Material contains additional instructions on what dissemination is permitted.[171]
3. "Controlled enhanced with specified dissemination." The information requires safeguarding measures more stringent than those normally required since the inadvertent or unauthorized disclosure would create risk of substantial harm. Material contains additional instructions on what dissemination is permitted.[172]

The National Archives and Records Administration (NARA) will define "enforcement mechanisms and penalties for improper handling of CUI."[173] The "controlled" document designation would inform, but not determine, that such information could be made public in response to an FOIA request.[174]

All CUI documentation produced either by or for the federal government is to be marked with the "controlled" designation regardless of how it is presented. President Bush's memorandum defines that "oral communications should be prefaced with a statement describing the controls when necessary to ensure that recipients are aware of the information's status."[175]

11.26   LESSONS LEARNED PROGRAMS

The Lessons Learned programs are part of the national network of lessons learned and best practices for whatever subject matter that the department, agency, or organization is responsible for. The Lessons Learned programs are general, unclassified information that is shared in order to improve operational safety by benefiting from the experience of others.

Information is prepared and distributed whenever there is an opportunity to share a valuable new work practice or warn others of an adverse practice, experience, or product. Information also constitutes archived information provided or contributed by its membership base, which may include white papers written by member constituents or articles taken from third-party news or reference sources.[176]

11.27   INFRAGARD

InfraGard is a Federal Bureau of Investigation (FBI) program that began at its Cleveland field office in 1996.[177] It was a local effort to gain support from the information technology industry and academia for the FBI's investigative efforts in the cyber arena.[178] The program expanded to other FBI field offices, and in 1998 the FBI assigned national program responsibility for InfraGard to the former National Infrastructure Protection Center (NIPC) and to the FBI Cyber Division in 2003.[179] InfraGard and the FBI have developed a relationship of trust and credibility in the exchange of information concerning various terrorism, intelligence, criminal, and security matters.[180]

InfraGard is an information sharing and analysis effort serving the interests and combining the knowledge base of a wide range of members.[181] At its most basic level, InfraGard is a partnership between the FBI and the private sector, and is an association of businesses, academic institutions, state and local law enforcement agencies, and other participants dedicated to sharing information and intelligence to prevent hostile acts against the United States.[182] Its local chapters are geographically linked with FBI field office territories, and each chapter has an FBI special agent coordinator assigned to it; the FBI coordinator works closely with supervisory special agent program managers in the Cyber Division at FBI Headquarters in Washington, D.C.[183]

While under the direction of NIPC, the focus of InfraGard was originally cyber infrastructure protection.[184] After September 11, 2001, however, NIPC expanded its efforts to include physical and cyber threats to critical infrastructures; consequently, InfraGard's mission expanded accordingly.[185]

In March 2003, NIPC was transferred to the DHS, which has responsibility for critical infrastructure protection (CIP) matters.[186] The FBI retained InfraGard as an FBI-sponsored program and works with DHS in support of its CIP mission, and facilitates InfraGard's continuing role in CIP activities and the further development of InfraGard's ability to support the FBI's investigative mission, especially as it pertains to counterterrorism and cyber crimes.[187]

11.28   SENSITIVE UNCLASSIFIED NONSAFEGUARDS INFORMATION (SUNSI)

The U.S. Nuclear Regulatory Commission (NRC) must protect classified and sensitive unclassified nonsafeguards information (SUNSI) related to U.S. government programs for the physical protection and safeguarding of nuclear materials or facilities to ensure that such information is protected against unauthorized disclosure.[188]

Sensitive unclassified nonsafeguards information (SUNSI) is information that is generally not publicly available and encompasses a wide variety of categories (e.g., personnel privacy, attorney-client privilege, confidential source, etc.).

Information about a licensee's or applicant's physical protection or material control and accounting program for special nuclear material not otherwise designated as safeguards information or classified as national security information or restricted data is required by 10 C.F.R. 2.390[189] to be protected in the same manner as commercial or financial information (i.e., they are exempt from public disclosure).[190]

11.29   SAFEGUARDS INFORMATION (SGI)

Safeguards information (SGI) is a special category of sensitive unclassified information authorized by Section 147 of the Atomic Energy Act to be protected. Safeguards information concerns the physical protection of operating power reactors, spent fuel shipments, strategic special nuclear material, or other radioactive material.

While SGI is considered to be sensitive unclassified information, its handling and protection more closely resemble the handling of classified confidential information than other sensitive unclassified information. The categories of individuals who are permitted access to SGI are listed in 10 C.F.R. 73.21.[191,192]

11.30   AUTHORS' NOTES

We expect to see more compartmentalization of unclassified but sensitive information within and throughout the U.S. government, military, and private sectors. As people begin to identify information as important and sensitive, disparaged groups will then attempt to classify said information as "sensitive"; all information is relative to its private sector organization and its functionalities. Therefore not all information of one nature is categorically the same or similar to that from another infrastructure sector.

NOTES

1. Although there appear to be several references, both government and industry, that give regard to the definition of the term *critical infrastructure information*, there do not appear to be any contextual data provided that demonstrate a defined term. All in all, all interested parties involved appear to be more concerned about what to do with the information rather than defining it; if it is defined, it consumes numerous volumes of text outlining an overtly detailed explanation, which, simply put, might be explained with but a few bulleted items. Therefore this definition is by no means perfect; however, it is an attempt at defining what it means and signifies.
2. This definition represents a consensus of observed statements, as well as online and printed materials that were reviewed from both government and industry viewpoints. It is an attempted abbreviated version of what was observed. The shortest/smallest definition of the term *critical infrastructure information* consumed approximately 34 pages of material.
3. *Information*—Data that have been transformed through analysis and interpretation into a form useful for drawing conclusions and making decisions.
4. *Metadata*—It is either: (1) Information about a data set that is provided by the data supplier or the generating algorithm and which provides a description of the content, format, and utility of the data set; metadata provide criteria that may be used to select data for a particular scientific investigation. (2) Information describing a data set, including data user guide, descriptions of the data set in directories, and inventories, and any additional information required to define the relationships among these. Source: ESADS, EPO, IWGDMGC.

5. *Data*—The collection of material or facts on which a discussion or an inference is based. Data are the product of measurement. The word *data* is the plural of datum. Compare information (referred to as a lexicon definition).

6. Critical Infrastructure Information Act of 2002, Section 212(3), page 17; URL: http://www.dhs.gov/xlibrary/assets/CII_Act.pdf.

7. 5 U.S.C. §552(b)(1).

8. 3 C.F.R. 333 (1996), reprinted in 50 U.S.C. §435 note.

9. Congressional Research Service—The Library of Congress, *Critical Infrastructure Information: Disclosure and Homeland Security*, Report for Congress, RL31547, January 29, 2003; http://www.fas.org/sgp/crs/RL31547.pdf (alt URL: http://cipbook.infracritical.com/book5/chapter11/ch11ref4.pdf).

10. http://www.fas.org/sgp/crs/RL31547.pdf (alt URL: http://cipbook.infracritical.com/book5/chapter11/ch11ref4.pdf).

11. E.O. No. 12958, §1.2(a)(4); E.O. 12958: Classified National Security Information; signed: April 17, 1995; *Federal Register* page and date: 60 F.R. 19825; April 20, 1995; revoked: E.O. 12356, April 6, 1982; amended by: E.O. 12972, September 18, 1995; E.O. 13142, November 19, 1999; E.O. 13292, March 25, 2003; see: Order of October 13, 1995; Order of February 27, 1996; Order of February 26, 1997; Final Rule of July 1, 1997 (62 F.R. 36984); E.O. 13231, October 16, 2001; Military Order of November 13, 2001 (66 F.R. 57833); Order of December 10, 2001 (66 F.R. 64347); E.O. 13284, January 23, 2003; E.O. 13311, July 29, 2003; Order of September 17, 2003 (68 F.R. 55257); E.O. 13329, February 24, 2004; E.O. 13354, August 27, 2004; E.O. 13356, August 27, 2004; Order of April 21, 2005; E.O. 13387, October 14, 2005; E.O. 13388, October 25, 2005; E.O. 13462, February 29, 2008; E.O. 13467, June 30, 2008; E.O. 13470, July 30, 2008; URL: http://www.archives.gov/federal-register/executive-orders/1995.html (alt URL: http://cipbook.infracritical.com/book5/chapter11/ch11ref25.pdf and http://cipbook.infracritical.com/book5/chapter11/ch11ref25a.pdf).

12. See White House Memorandum for Heads of Executive Departments and Agencies Concerning Safeguarding Information Regarding Weapons of Mass Destruction and Other Sensitive Documents Related to Homeland Security, March 19, 2002; reprinted in FOIA Post, posted March 21, 2002; http://www.usdoj.gov/oip/foia_guide07/exemption9.pdf (alt URL: http://cipbook.infracritical.com/book5/chapter11/ch11ref24.pdf).

13. See Memorandum from Acting Director of Information Security Oversight Office and Co-Directors of Office of Information and Privacy to Departments and Agencies, March 31, 2002; reprinted in FOIA Post, posted March 21, 2002; http://www.usdoj.gov/oip/foia_guide07/basic_foia_ref.pdf and http://www.usdoj.gov/oip/basicreferences.htm (alt URL: http://cipbook.infracritical.com/book5/chapter11/ch11ref26.pdf and http://cipbook.infracritical.com/book5/chapter11/ch11ref26a.pdf).

14. Congressional Research Service—The Library of Congress, *Critical Infrastructure Information: Disclosure and Homeland Security*, Report for Congress, RL31547, January 29, 2003; http://www.fas.org/sgp/crs/RL31547.pdf (alt URL: http://cipbook.infracritical.com/book5/chapter11/ch1ref4.pdf).

15. Ibid.

16. Ibid.

17. Ibid.

18. Ibid.

19. See CRS Congressional Distribution Memorandum, American Law Division, Freedom of Information Act: Statutes Invoked under Exemption 3 by Gina Stevens, July 11, 2002; updated reference; http://www.fas.org/irp/crs/RL31547.pdf (alt URL: http://cipbook.infracritical.com/book5/chapter11/ch11ref27.pdf).

20. Congressional Research Service—The Library of Congress, *Critical Infrastructure Information: Disclosure and Homeland Security*, Report for Congress, RL31547, January 29, 2003; http://www.fas.org/sgp/crs/RL31547.pdf (alt URL: http://cipbook.infracritical.com/book5/chapter11/ch1ref4.pdf).

21. Congressional Research Service—The Library of Congress, *Critical Infrastructure Information: Disclosure and Homeland Security*, Report for Congress, RL31547, January 29, 2003; http://www.fas.org/sgp/crs/RL31547.pdf (alt URL: http://cipbook.infracritical.com/book5/chapter11/ch1ref4.pdf).

22. Ibid.

23. 5 U.S.C. §552(b)(4).

24. Congressional Research Service—The Library of Congress, *Critical Infrastructure Information: Disclosure and Homeland Security*, Report for Congress, RL31547, January 29, 2003; http://www.fas.org/sgp/crs/RL31547.pdf (alt URL: http://cipbook.infracritical.com/book5/chapter11/ch1ref4.pdf).

25. Ibid.

26. *Public Citizen Health Research Group v. FDA*, 704 F.2d 1280, 1290 (D.C. Cir. 1983).

27. See *Nadler v. FDIC*, 92 F.3d 93, 95 (2d Cir. 1996) (term *person* includes "individual, partnership, corporation, association, or public or private organization other than an agency," quoting definition found in Administrative Procedure Act, 5 U.S.C. §551(2)).

28. See *Allnet Communications Servs. v. FCC*, 800 F. Supp. 984, 988 (D.D.C. 1992).

29. Congressional Research Service—The Library of Congress, *Critical Infrastructure Information: Disclosure and Homeland Security*, Report for Congress, RL31547, January 29, 2003; http://www.fas.org/sgp/crs/RL31547.pdf (alt URL: http://cipbook.infracritical.com/book5/chapter11/ch1ref4.pdf).

30. FOIA Post, Critical Infrastructure Information Regulations Issued by DHS, February 27, 2004; http://www.usdoj.gov/oip/foiapost/2004foiapost6.htm (alt URL: http://cipbook.infracritical.com/book5/chapter11/ch11ref28.pdf).

31. Ibid.

32. Exemption 3 of the Freedom of Information Act, 5 U.S.C. §552(b)(3) (2000).

33. "Systems or assets, whether physical or virtual, so vital to the United States that the incapacity or destruction of such systems and assets would have a debilitating impact on security, national economic security, national public health or safety, or any combination of those matters." P.L. 107-56, Section 1016.

34. Congressional Research Service—The Library of Congress, *Critical Infrastructure Information: Disclosure and Homeland Security*, Report for Congress, RL31547, January 29, 2003; http://www.fas.org/sgp/crs/RL31547.pdf (alt URL: http://cipbook.infracritical.com/book5/chapter11/ch1ref4.pdf).

35. FOIA Post, Agencies Rely on Wide Range of Exemption 3 Statutes, February 16, 2003; http://www.usdoj.gov/oip/foiapost/2003foiapost4.htm (alt URL: http://cipbook.infracritical.com/book5/chapter11/ch11ref29.pdf).

36. P.L. 107-296, §212(3).

37. Ibid.

38. Congressional Research Service—The Library of Congress, *Critical Infrastructure Information: Disclosure and Homeland Security*, Report for Congress, RL31547, January 29, 2003; http://www.fas.org/sgp/crs/RL31547.pdf (alt URL: http://cipbook.infracritical.com/book5/chapter11/ch1ref4.pdf).

39. Ibid.

40. Congressional Research Service—The Library of Congress, *Critical Infrastructure Information: Disclosure and Homeland Security*, Report for Congress, RL31547, January 29, 2003; http://www.fas.org/sgp/crs/RL31547.pdf (alt URL: http://cipbook.infracritical.com/book5/chapter11/ch1ref4.pdf).

41. Ibid.

42. Ibid.
43. Ibid.
44. Ibid.
45. Ibid.
46. The Federal Advisory Committee Act (FACA) requires that the meetings of all federal advisory committees serving executive branch entities be open to the public. The FACA specifies nine categories of information, similar to those in FOIA, which may be permissively relied on to close advisory committee deliberations. 5 U.S.C. App. 2.
47. Congressional Research Service—The Library of Congress, *Critical Infrastructure Information: Disclosure and Homeland Security*, Report for Congress, RL31547, January 29, 2003; http://www.fas.org/sgp/crs/RL31547.pdf (alt URL: http://cipbook.infracritical.com/book5/chapter11/ch1ref4.pdf).
48. Ibid.
49. Ibid.
50. http://www.wrc.noaa.gov/wrso/security_guide/intro-5.htm#Sensitive (alt URL: http://cipbook.infracritical.com/book5/chapter11/ch11ref5.pdf).
51. The U.S. Department of State uses "sensitive but unclassified" (SBU) as a document designation comparable to "for official use only."
52. The FOIA establishes a presumption that records in the possession of agencies and departments of the executive branch of the federal government are accessible to the people. This was not always the approach to federal information disclosure policy. Before the enactment of the FOIA in 1966, the burden was on the individual to establish a right to examine these government records. There were no statutory guidelines or procedures to help a person seeking information. There were no judicial remedies for those denied access. With the passage of the FOIA, the burden of proof shifted from the individual to the government. Those seeking information are no longer required to show a need for information. Instead, the need-to-know standard has been replaced by a right-to-know doctrine. The government now has to justify the need for secrecy. The FOIA sets standards for determining which records must be disclosed and which records may be withheld. The law also provides administrative and judicial remedies for those denied access to records. Above all, the statute requires government organizations to provide the fullest possible disclosure of information to the public.
53. http://frwebgate.access.gpo.gov/cgi-bin/getdoc.cgi?dbname = 106_cong_reports& docid = f:hr050.106.pdf (Web link no longer exists).
54. Information taken from the National Oceanic and Atmospheric Administration Web site, in which information posted on the various categories of sensitive unclassified information is based on a research report prepared for Personnel Security Research Center by John Tippit & Associates.
55. Assistant Secretary of Defense for Command, Control, Communications, and Intelligence, *DOD Guide to Marking Classified Documents*, DOD 5200.1-PH, April 1997: http://www.dtic.mil/dtic/pdf/customer/STINFOdata/DoD5200_1ph.pdf (alt URL: http://cipbook.infracritical.com/book5/chapter11/ch11ref30.pdf), along with http://www.wrc.noaa.gov/wrso/briefings/DOD%20Marking%20Guide.ppt (alt URL: http://cipbook.infracritical.com/book5/chapter11/ch11ref10.ppt).
56. http://www.wrc.noaa.gov/wrso/security_guide/intro-5.htm#Sensitive (alt URL: http://cipbook.infracritical.com/book5/chapter11/ch11ref5.pdf).
57. DOD Regulation 5200.1-R, Information Security Program.
58. http://www.wrc.noaa.gov/wrso/security_guide/intro-5.htm#Sensitive (alt URL: http://cipbook.infracritical.com/book5/chapter11/ch11ref5.pdf).
59. Ibid.
60. Ibid.

61. Ibid.
62. Ibid.
63. Ibid.
64. Ibid.
65. Ibid.
66. Ibid.
67. Ibid.
68. http://www.wrc.noaa.gov/wrso/security_guide/foia.htm (alt URL: http://cipbook.infra-critical.com/book5/chapter11/ch11ref6.pdf).
69. Ibid.
70. Ibid.
71. Ibid.
72. Ibid.
73. DOD Regulation 5200.1-R, Information Security Program.
74. http://www.wrc.noaa.gov/wrso/security_guide/foia.htm (alt URL: http://cipbook.infra-critical.com/book5/chapter11/ch11ref6.pdf).
75. Ibid.
76. Ibid.
77. Ibid.
78. Ibid.
79. Ibid.
80. Ibid.
81. Ibid.
82. http://www.wrc.noaa.gov/wrso/security_guide/need-2.htm#Need-to-Know   (alt URL: http://cipbook.infracritical.com/book5/chapter11/ch11ref7.pdf).
83. Ibid.
84. Ibid.
85. Ibid.
86. Ibid.
87. Ibid.
88. http://www.wrc.noaa.gov/wrso/security_guide/fouo.htm#For Official (alt URL: http://cipbook.infracritical.com/book5/chapter11/ch11ref8.pdf).
89. Ibid.
90. Ibid.
91. Ibid.
92. DOD Regulation 5200.1-R, Information Security Program.
93. http://www.wrc.noaa.gov/wrso/security_guide/fouo.htm#For Official (alt URL: http://cipbook.infracritical.com/book5/chapter11/ch11ref8.pdf).
94. Ibid.
95. Ibid.
96. Ibid.
97. Ibid.
98. Ibid.
99. Ibid.
100. Ibid.
101. Ibid.
102. Ibid.
103. 5 U.S.C. 301—Departmental Regulations: DOD Regulation 5200.1-R—The Information Security Program; DOD Directive 5400.7—The Freedom of Information Act (FOIA) Program; DOD Regulation 5400.7-R—The DOD Freedom of Information Act Program; DOD Regulation 5400.11-R—Department of Defense Privacy Program.

104. http://www.wasc.noaa.gov/wrso/security_guide/website.htm#Pre-Publication   (alt
     URL: http://cipbook.infracritical.com/book5/chapter11/ch11ref9.pdf).
105. Ibid.
106. Ibid.
107. Ibid.
108. Ibid.
109. Ibid.
110. Ibid.
111. Ibid.
112. Ibid.
113. Ibid.
114. Ibid.
115. Ibid.
116. Ibid.
117. Office of the Assistant Secretary of Defense (C31), *Web Site Administration Policies
     and Procedures*, November 25, 1998, approved by the Deputy Secretary of Defense,
     December 7, 1998. The full document is available on the Internet. Revised http://
     permanent.access.gpo.gov/lps48254/www.foia.af.mil/afcio_web_site_policy-
     19sep01.doc (alt URL: http://cipbook.infracritical.com./chapter11/ch11ref12.doc
     and http://cipbook.infracritical.com/book5/chapter11/ch11ref12a.pdf).
118. E.O. 12923: Continuation of Export Control Regulations, 30 June 1994: Title 22
     U.S.C. 2778 et seq.—Arms Export Control Act; Title 50 U.S.C. 2401 et seq.—Export
     Administration Act of 1979 (as amended); Title 50 U.S.C., Appendix, Section 10—
     Trading with the Enemy Act of 1917; Title 15 C.F.R. Part 770, Export Administration
     Regulations; Title 15 C.F.R. Part 779, Technical Data; Title 22 C.F.R. (Department of
     State) Subchapter M, The International Traffic in Arms Regulation (ITAR), Part 121-
     130. Additional information includes: E.O. 12923: Continuation of Export Control
     Regulations; signed: June 30, 1994, *Federal Register* page and date: 59 F.R. 34551; July
     5, 1994; revoked by: E.O. 12924, August 19, 1994; see: E.O. 12002, July 7, 1977; E.O.
     12214, May 2, 1980; E.O. 12735, November 16, 1990; E.O. 12755, March 12, 1991;
     E.O. 12851, June 11, 1993; http://www.archives.gov/federal-register/executive-orders/
     pdf/12923.pdf (alt URL: http://cipbook.infracritical.com/book5/chapter11/ch11ref31.
     pdf).
119. http://www.wrc.noaa.gov/wrso/security_guide/export.htm#Export-Control   (alt
     URL: http://cipbook.infracritical.com/book5/chapter11/ch11ref13.pdf).
120. Ibid.
121. Ibid.
122. Ibid.
123. Ibid.
124. Ibid.
125. Ibid.
126. Ibid.
127. Ibid.
128. Title 41 U.S.C. 421—Federal Acquisition Regulatory Council; Title 41 U.S.C. 423—
     Procurement Integrity; FAR Part 3.104-1—Procurement Integrity, General (48 C.F.R.);
     FAR Part 3.104.3—Statutory Prohibitions and Restrictions (48 C.F.R.); FAR Part
     3.104-5—Disclosure, Protection, and Marking of Proprietary and Source Selection
     Information; FAR Part 14.401—Receipt and Safeguarding of Bids (48 C.F.R.); FAR
     Part 15.407—Solicitation Provisions (48 C.F.R.); FAR Part 27.4—Rights in Data and
     Copyrights; FAR Part 52.215-12—Restriction on Disclosure and Use of Data (48 C.F.R.).
129. http://www.wrc.noaa.gov/wrso/security_guide/source.htm#Source_Selection   (alt
     URL: http://cipbook.infracritical.com/book5/chapter11/ch11ref14.pdf).

130. http://www.wrc.noaa.gov/wrso/security_guide/source.htm#Source_Selection (alt URL: http://cipbook.infracritical.com/book5/chapter11/ch11ref14.pdf).
131. http://www.arnet.gov/far (alt URL: http://cipbook.infracritical.com/book5/chapter11/ch11ref32.pdf), with current FAR regulation found here: http://www.arnet.gov/far/current/pdf/FAR.pdf (alt URL: http://cipbook.infracritical.com/book5/chapter11/ch11ref32a.pdf).
132. http://www.arnet.gov/far/facsframe.html, redirects to this URL: http://acquisition.gov/far/facs/2004-033%20Cmte%20Rpt%20(F)%20Matrix%20Mar%2020%2006.pdf (alt URL: http://cipbook.infracritical.com/book5/chapter11/ch11ref33.pdf).
133. http://www.wrc.noaa.gov/wrso/security_guide/source.htm#Source_Selection (alt URL: http://cipbook.infracritical.com/book5/chapter11/ch11ref14.pdf).
134. http://www.acqnet.gov/far/current/html/Subpart%2014_4.html#wp1090681.
135. http://www.wrc.noaa.gov/wrso/security_guide/source.htm#Source_Selection (alt URL: http://cipbook.infracritical.com/book5/chapter11/ch11ref14.pdf).
136. http://www.acqnet.gov/far/current/html/Subpart%203_1.html#wp1139379.
137. Ibid.
138. Ibid.
139. Ibid.
140. Ibid.
141. Ibid.
142. Ibid.
143. Ibid.
144. http://www.wrc.noaa.gov/wrso/security_guide/privacy.htm#Privacy Information (alt URL: http://cipbook.infracritical.com/book5/chapter11/ch11ref15.pdf).
145. Ibid.
146. Ibid.
147. Title 5 U.S.C. 552a—Records Maintained on Individuals (Privacy Act); Title 12 U.S.C. 3417—Civil Penalties; Title 18 U.S.C. 1905—Disclosure of Confidential Information Generally; Title 41 C.F.R. 201-6.1—Federal Information Resources Management Regulation; E.O. 12564—Drug Free Federal Workplace; OMB Circular No. A-130—Management of Federal Information Resources, Appendix 1, Federal Agency Responsibilities for Maintaining Records about Individuals; P.L. 100-71—The Supplemental Appropriations Act of 1987, Section 503; P.L. 104-13—Paperwork Reduction Act of 1955.
148. http://www.wrc.noaa.gov/wrso/security_guide/privacy.htm#Privacy Information (alt URL: http://cipbook.infracritical.com/book5/chapter11/ch11ref15.pdf).
149. Ibid.
150. Ibid.
151. Ibid.
152. Ibid.
153. Ibid.
154. Ibid.
155. http://www.ftc.gov/privacy/privacyinitiatives/glbact.html (alt URL: http://cipbook.infracritical.com/book5/chapter11/ch11ref16.pdf).
156. http://www.hhs.gov/ocr/hipaa (alt URL: http://cipbook.infracritical.com/book5/chapter11/ch11ref17.pdf).
157. 42 U.S.C. 2168—Atomic Energy Act of 1954; 10 C.F.R. Part 1017—Identification and Protection of Unclassified Controlled Nuclear Information; DOD Regulation 5200.1-R—Information Security Program; additional information may be found here: http://afsf.lackland.af.mil/Organization/AFXOF/Identification%20and%20Handling%20of%20DoD%20UCNI.doc (alt URL: http://cipbook.infracritical.com/book5/chapter11/ch11ref34.doc).
158. http://www.wrc.noaa.gov/wrso/security_guide/ucni.htm#Unclassified Controlled (alt URL: http://cipbook.infracritical.com/book5/chapter11/ch11ref18.pdf).

159. Ibid.
160. Ibid.
161. 42 U.S.C. 2168—Atomic Energy Act of 1954; 10 C.F.R. Part 1017—Identification and Protection of Unclassified Controlled Nuclear Information; DOD Regulation 5200.1-R—Information Security Program; additional information may be found here: http://afsf.lackland.af.mil/Organization/AFXOF/Identification%20and%20Handling%20of%20DoD%20UCNI.doc (alt URL: http://cipbook.infracritical.com/book5/chapter11/ch11ref34.doc).
162. http://www.ferc.gov/legal/ceii-foia/ceii.asp (alt URL: http://cipbook.infracritical.com/book5/chapter11/ch11ref19.pdf).
163. http://www.ferc.gov/legal/maj-ord-reg/land-docs/ceii-rule.asp (alt URL: http://cipbook.infracritical.com/book5/chapter11/ch11ref20.pdf).
164. http://www.ferc.gov/help/filing-guide/file-ceii/ceii-guidelines/guidelines.pdf (alt URL: http://cipbook.infracritical.com/book5/chapter11/ch11ref21.pdf).
165. http://www.ferc.gov/legal/ceii-foia/ceii/classes.asp (alt URL: http://cipbook.infracritical.com/book5/chapter11/ch11ref22.pdf).
166. http://www.ferc.gov/legal/ceii-foia/ceii/classes.asp (alt URL: http://cipbook.infracritical.com/book5/chapter11/ch11ref22.pdf).
167. White House Memorandum for the Heads of Executive Departments and Agencies, Designation and Sharing of Controlled Unclassified Information (CUI), May 9, 2008; http://georgewbush-whitehouse.archives.gov/news/releases/2008/05/20080509-6.html (alt URL: http://cipbook.infracritical.com/book5/chapter11/ch11ref1.pdf).
168. Ibid.
169. Memorandum for Secretaries of the Military Departments, Transition to New Markings for Controlled Unclassified Information, December 28, 2007; http://www.fas.org/sgp/othergov/dod/cui122807.pdf (alt URL: http://cipbook.infracritical.com/book5/chapter11/ch11ref2.pdf).
170. Ibid.
171. Ibid.
172. Ibid.
173. http://www.archives.gov/press/press-releases/2008/nr08-107.html (alt URL: http://cipbook.infracritical.com/book5/chapter11/ch11ref3.pdf).
174. Walter Pincus, Keeping Secrets: In Presidential Memo, a New Designation for Classifying Information, *Washington Post*, May 19, 2008; http://www.washingtonpost.com/wp-dyn/content/article/2008/05/18/AR2008051801806.html?nav = rss_politics.
175. White House Memorandum for the Heads of Executive Departments and Agencies, Designation and Sharing of Controlled Unclassified Information (CUI), May 9, 2008; http://georgewbush-whitehouse.archives.gov/news/releases/2008/05/20080509-6.html (alt URL: http://cipbook.infracritical.com/book5/chapter11/ch11ref1.pdf).
176. U.S. Department of Energy, Environmental Safety and Health (http://www.eh.doe.gov/ll). U.S. Department of Transportation, Federal Transit Administration (http://www.fta.dot.gov/). National Aeronautics and Space Administration (http://llis.nasa.gov). U.S. Department of Homeland Security (http://www.llis.dhs.gov). U.S. Department of Health and Human Services (http://www.usability.gov/lessons). U.S. Department of Energy, Project Hanford (http://www.hanford.gov/lessons/sitell/sitehome.htm). Lawrence Livermore National Laboratory (http://www.llnl.gov/es_and_h/lessons/lessons.shtml). Library of Congress (http://memory.loc.gov/ammem/award/lessons/lessons.html). Federal Aviation Administration (http://www.asu.faa.gov/lesslrnd/).
177. U.S. Department of Justice Federal Bureau of Investigation, InfraGard Frequently Asked Questions (FAQ); http://www.infragard.net/about.php?mn = 1&sm = 1-0 (alt URL: cipbook.infracritical.com/book5/chapter11/ch11ref23.pdf).

178. U.S. Department of Justice Federal Bureau of Investigation, InfraGard Frequently Asked Questions (FAQ); http://www.infragard.net/about.php?mn = 1&sm = 1-0 (alt URL: cipbook.infracritical.com/book5/chapter11/ch11ref23.pdf).
179. Ibid.
180. Ibid.
181. Ibid.
182. Ibid.
183. Ibid.
184. Ibid.
185. Ibid.
186. Ibid.
187. Ibid.
188. http://www.nrc.gov/security/info-security.html (alt URL: http://cipbook.infracritical.com/book5/chapter11/ch11ref36.pdf).
189. http://www.nrc.gov/reading-rm/doc-collections/cfr/part002/part002-0390.html (alt URL: http://cipbook.infrarcritical.com/book5/chapter11/ch11ref37.pdf).
190. http://www.nrc.gov/security/info-security.html (alt URL: http://cipbook.infracritical.com/book5/chapter11/ch11ref36.pdf).
191. http://www.nrc.gov/reading-rm/doc-collections/cfr/part073/part073-0021.html (alt URL: http://cipbook.infracritical.com/book5/chapter11/ch11ref38.pdf).
192. http://www.nrc.gov/security/info-security.html (alt URL: http://cipbook.infracritical.com/book5/chapter11/ch11ref36.pdf).

Glossary

AAR: Association of American Railroads
AC: Area command
ACC: American Chemical Council
ACN: Alerting and Coordination Network
AES: Advanced Encryption Standard
AGA: American Gas Association
AMSA: Association of Metropolitan Sewage Agencies
AMWA: Association of Metropolitan Water Agencies
ANSI: American National Standards Institute
API: American Petroleum Institute
APTA: American Public Transportation Association
ASDWA: Association of State Drinking Water Administrators
ASME: American Society of Mechanical Engineers
ATA: American Trucking Associations
AWWA: American Water Works Association
AWWAR: American Water Works Association Research Foundation
BBS: Bulletin board system
BCP: Business continuity plan
BMF: Business master file
CANUTEC: Canadian Transport Emergency Centre of the Department of Transport
CC: Common Criteria
CC EAL: Common Criteria European Assurance Level
CDP: Center for Domestic Preparedness
CEII: Critical energy infrastructure information
CEM: Common evaluation methodology
CEO: Chief executive officer
CHEMTREC: Chemical Transportation Emergency Center
CIA: Critical infrastructure assurance
CIAO: Critical Infrastructure Assurance Office
CIDX: Chemical Industry Data Exchange
CII: Critical infrastructure information
CIKR: Critical infrastructure/key resource
CIO: Chief information officer
CIP: Critical infrastructure protection
CIPAC: Critical Infrastructure Partnership Advisory Council
CIPAG: Critical Infrastructure Protection Advisory Group
CN: Canadian National Railway
COBIT: Control Objectives for Information Technology
CRIS: Communications Resource Information Sharing
CRS: Congressional Report Summary
CS²SAT: Control System Cyber Security Self-Assessment Tool

CSF: Critical success factor
CSO: Chief security officer
CSSP: Control Systems Security Program
CUI: Controlled unclassified information
DCS: Distributed control systems
DES: Data Encryption Standard
DHS: U.S. Department of Homeland Security
DMAT: Disaster Medical Assistance Team
DOD: U.S. Department of Defense
DOE: U.S. Department of Energy
DOT: U.S. Department of Transportation
EAR: Export Administration Regulations
EMAC: Emergency Management Assistance Compact
E.O.: Executive order
EOC: Emergency operation center
EOP: Emergency operations plan
EPA: U.S. Environmental Protection Agency
ESF: Emergency support function
FASC: Finance/Administration Section Chief
FBI: Federal Bureau of Investigation
FBIIC: Financial and Banking Information Infrastructure Committee
FCC: Federal Communications Commission
FDA: U.S. Food and Drug Administration
FEMA: Federal Emergency Management Administration
FERN: Food Emergency Response Network
FIPS: Federal Information Processing Standards
FIRESCOPE: Firefighting Resources of Southern California Organized for
         Potential Emergencies
FISCAM: Federal Information System Controls Audit Manual
FISMA: Federal Information Security Management Act
FMI: Food Marketing Institute
FOIA: Freedom of Information Act
FOUO: For office use only
FRP: Federal Response Plan
GAO: General Accounting Office
GETS: Government Emergency Telecommunications System
GLBA: Gramm-Leach-Bliley Act
GTI: Gas Technology Institute
HAZMAT: Hazardous material
HAZWOPER: OSHA Hazardous Waste Operations and Emergency Response
HICS: Hospital Incident Command System
HIPAA: Health Insurance Portability and Accountability Act
HMI: Human-machine interface
HSOC: Homeland Security Operations Center
HSPD: Homeland Security President Directive
IAP: Incident action plan

IC: Incident commander
ICP: Incident command post
ICS: Incident command system
ICSJWG: Industrial Control Systems Joint Working Group
IEC: International Electrotechnical Commission
IEEE: Institute of Electrical and Electronics Engineers
IIMG: Interagency Incident Management Group
IRS: Internal Revenue Service
IS: Information systems
ISA: International Society of Automation
ISAC: Information Sharing and Analysis Center
ISO: International Organization for Standardization
IT: Information technology
ITAR: International Traffic in Arms Regulations
IXC: Interexchange carrier
JFO: Joint Field Office
JIC: Joint information center
JIS: Joint information system
LAN: Local area network
LEC: Local exchange carrier
LNO: Liaison officer
LSC: Logistics section chief
MACS: Multiagency coordination system
MCE: Mission-critical element
MCE: Multiagency coordination entity
MEI: Minimum essential infrastructure
MSC: Maritime Security Council
MTS: Maritime Transportation System
MTSNAC: Maritime Transportation System National Advisory Council
NAERG: *North American Emergency Response Guidebook*
NARA: National Archives and Records Administration
NAWC: National Association of Water Companies
NCC: National Coordination Council
NCS: National Communications System
NCSD: National Cyber Security Division
NERC: North American Energy Reliability Council
NEST: Nuclear Emergency Support Team
NFPA: National Fire Protection Association
NGO: Nongovernmental organization
NIC: NIMS Integration Center
NIIMS: National Interagency Incident Management System
NIMS: National Incident Management System
NIPC: National Infrastructure Protection Center
NIPP: National Infrastructure Protection Plan
NIST: National Institute of Standards and Technology
NRCC: National Response Coordination Center

NRF: National Response Framework
NRIC: Network Reliability and Interoperability Council
NRP: National Response Plan (deprecated)
NSA: National Security Agency
NSIE: Network Security Information Exchange
NSPD: National Security President Directive
NSTAC: National Security Telecommunications Advisory Committee
NWCG: National Wildfire Coordination Group
OAGi: Open Application Group, Inc.
ODP: Office of Domestic Preparedness
OMB: Office of Management and Budget
OPSEC: Operations security
OSC: Operations section chief
OSHA: Occupational Safety and Health Administration
PAS: Priority access service
PBX: Public branch exchange
PCS: Personal communications service
PCSRF: Process Control Security Requirements Forum
PDA: Personal digital assistant
PIN: Personal identification number
PIO: Public information officer
P.L.: Public law
PLC: Programmable logic controller
PPE: Personnel protective equipment
PSC: Planning section chief
PSO: Patient safety organization
PSQIA: Patient Safety and Quality Improvement Act
PSTN: Public switched telephone network
RRCC: Regional Response Coordination Center
RTU: Remote terminal unit
SAIC: Science Applications International Corporation
SBU: Sensitive, but unclassified (deprecated)
SCADA: Supervisory control and data acquisition
SCADASEC: SCADA security
SHARES HF: Shared Resources High Frequency (Radio Program)
SLGCP: U.S. Department of Homeland Security's Office of State and Local Government Coordination and Preparedness
SO: Safety officer
SOLAS: Safety of Life at Sea
SOX: Sarbanes-Oxley Act
SRT: Security response team
SVA: Security vulnerability assessment
TCSEC: Trusted Computer System Evaluation Criteria
TDEA: Triple DES
TSP: Telecommunications Service Priority
TTCI: Transportation Technology Center, Inc.

UC: Unified command
UCNI: Unclassified Controlled Nuclear Information
UCS: Unified command system
USACE: U.S. Army Corps of Engineers
U.S.C.: U.S. Code
USFA: U.S. Fire Administration
VAF: Vulnerability Assessment Framework
WAN: Wide area network
WERF: Water Environment Research Foundation
WMD: Weapons of mass destruction
WPS: Wireless Priority Services
WRF: Water Research Foundation
Y2K: Year 2000

Appendix

DESIGNATED SECTOR-SPECIFIC AGENCIES AND CRITICAL INFRASTRUCTURE SECTORS

Sector-Specific Agency	Sector	Description
Department of Agriculture Department of Health and Human Services Food and Drug Administration	Agriculture and food	Provides for the fundamental need for food. The infrastructure includes supply chains for feed and crop production. Carries out the postharvesting of the food supply, including processing and retail sales.
Department of Defense	Defense industrial base	Supplies the military with the means to protect the nation by producing weapons, aircraft, and ships, and providing essential services, including information technology and supply and maintenance.
Department of Energy	Energy	Provides the electric power used by all sectors and the refining, storage, and distribution of oil and gas. The sector is divided into electricity and oil and natural gas.
Department of Health and Human Services	Public health and health care	Mitigates the risk of disasters and attacks and also provides recovery assistance if an attack occurs. The sector consists of health departments, clinics, and hospitals.
Department of the Interior	National monuments and icons	Memorializes or represents monuments, physical structures, objects, or geographical sites that are widely recognized to represent the nation's heritage, traditions, or values, or widely recognized to represent important national cultural, religious, historical, or political significance.
Department of the Treasury	Banking and finance	Provides the financial infrastructure of the nation. This sector consists of commercial banks, insurance companies, mutual funds, government-sponsored enterprises, pension funds, and other financial institutions that carry out transactions.

Sector-Specific Agency	Sector	Description
Environmental Protection Agency	Drinking water and water treatment systems	Provides sources of safe drinking water from more than 53,000 community water systems and properly treated wastewater from more than 16,000 publicly owned treatment works.
Department of Homeland Security		
Office of Infrastructure Protection	Chemical	Transforms natural raw materials into commonly used products benefiting society's health, safety, and productivity. The chemical sector produces more than 70,000 products that are essential to automobiles, pharmaceuticals, food supply, electronics, water treatment, health, construction, and other necessities.
	Commercial facilities	Includes prominent commercial centers, office buildings, sports stadiums, theme parks, and other sites where large numbers of people congregate to pursue business activities, conduct personal commercial transactions, or enjoy recreational pastimes.
	Dams	Manages water retention structures, including levees, more than 77,000 conventional dams, navigation locks, canals (excluding channels), and similar structures, including larger and nationally symbolic dams that are major components of other critical infrastructures that provide electricity and water.
	Emergency services	Saves lives and property from accidents and disaster. This sector includes fire, rescue, emergency medical services, and law enforcement organizations.
	Nuclear reactors, materials, and waste	Provides nuclear power, which accounts for approximately 20% of the nation's electrical generating capacity. The sector includes commercial nuclear reactors and nonpower nuclear reactors used for research, testing, and training; nuclear materials used in medical, industrial, and academic settings; nuclear fuel fabrication facilities; the decommissioning of reactors; and the transportation, storage, and disposal of nuclear materials and waste.

Sector-Specific Agency	Sector	Description
	Critical manufacturing (announced March 3, 2008)	Provides crucial support to the economic prosperity and continuity of the United States. U.S. manufacturers design, produce, and distribute products that provide more than $1 of every $8 of the U.S. gross domestic product and employ more than 10% of the nation's workforce.
Office of Cyber Security and Communications	Information technology	Produces information technology and includes hardware manufacturers, software developers, and service providers, as well as the Internet as a key resource.
	Communications	Provides wired, wireless, and satellite communications to meet the needs of businesses and governments.
Transportation Security Administration	Postal and shipping	Delivers private and commercial letters, packages, and bulk assets. The U.S. Postal Service and other carriers provide the services of this sector.
Transportation Security Administration and U.S. Coast Guard	Transportation systems	Enables movement of people and assets that are vital to our economy, mobility, and security with the use of aviation, ships, rail, pipelines, highways, trucks, buses, and mass transit.
Immigration and Customs Enforcement, Federal Protective Service	Government facilities	Ensures continuity of functions for facilities owned and leased by the government, including all federal, state, territorial, local, and tribal government facilities located in the United States and abroad.

Index